Mel Gibson's Bible

Afterlives of the Bible
A series edited by Timothy K. Beal and Tod Linafelt

Mel Gibson's Bible: Religion, Popular Culture, and
The Passion of the Christ

Edited by Timothy K. Beal and Tod Linafelt

The University of Chicago Press :: Chicago and London

Timothy K. Beal is the Florence Harkness Professor of Religion and
director of the Baker-Nord Center for the Humanities at Case Western
Reserve University. His most recent book is *Roadside Religion: In Search
of the Sacred, the Strange, and the Substance of Faith*. Tod Linafelt is
associate professor of biblical literature at Georgetown University. He is
the author of *Surviving Lamentations: Catastrophe, Lament, and Protest
in the Afterlife of a Biblical Book*.

The University of Chicago Press, Chicago 60637
The University of Chicago Press, Ltd., London
© 2006 by The University of Chicago
Individual chapters © 2006 by their authors
All rights reserved. Published 2006
Printed in the United States of America

15 14 13 12 11 10 09 08 07 06   5 4 3 2 1

ISBN (cloth): 0-226-03975-7
ISBN (paper): 0-226-03976-5

Library of Congress Cataloging-in-Publication Data

Mel Gibson's Bible : religion, popular culture, and The Passion of the
    Christ / edited by Timothy K. Beal and Tod Linafelt.
        p.   cm. — (Afterlives of the Bible)
      ISBN 0-226-03975-7 (hardcover : alk. paper) — ISBN 0-226-03976-5
    (pbk. : alk. paper)
        1. Christianity and culture—United States.   2. Popular
    culture—Religious aspects—Christianity.   3. Mass media—Religious
    aspects—Christianity.   4. Christianity in mass media.   5. Gibson,
    Mel—Religion.   6. Passion of the Christ (Motion picture).   I. Beal,
    Timothy K. (Timothy Kandler), 1963–.   II. Linafelt, Tod, 1965–
    III. Series.
    BR115.C8M278   2006
    232.96—dc22   2005014261

For David M. Gunn,
Mentor, colleague, friend

Contents

Part Two: Ethical and Theological Responses

Part Three: Passion, Media, Audience

Illustrations

Acknowledgments

We are most grateful to Alan Thomas, editorial director at the University of Chicago Press, for his enthusiastic and ever thoughtful involvement in this book from its conception, a couple weeks after the opening of *The Passion*. We also thank Randy Petilos and Claudia Rex at Chicago for their invaluable help through the editing and production process.

Many thanks to the contributors to this volume for their outstanding work and for their patient cooperation. This is a truly stellar collection of scholars, and it has been an honor and privilege to work with them.

Versions of three chapters in this book were published previously. Chapter 1, "The Art of *The Passion*," by Jack Miles, is a revision of a review of *The Passion* that appeared under the title "Of Things Unseen" on www.beliefnet.com, the multi-faith Web site for religion, spirituality, inspiration, and more. It is used with permission. An earlier version of chapter 9, "No Pain, No Gain?," by Paula Fredriksen, was published online as "The Pain Principle" by *The New Republic* on 27 February 2004. It is used with permission of *The New Republic*. Finally, an earlier version of chapter 21, "They Know Not What They Watch," by Timothy K. Beal, was published in the "Review" magazine of *The Chronicle of Higher Education* on 19 March 2004 (volume 50, no. 28,

p. B14). Beal wishes to thank Liz McMillen, his editor at *The Chronicle,* for her interest in and work on that essay.

We gladly dedicate this book to our teacher and colleague, David M. Gunn, in gratitude for his continued support, inspiration, and friendship.

Introduction

As this volume began to take shape, in early summer 2004, the body of Ronald Reagan lay in state in the Capitol in Washington, D.C. More than 100,000 people filed past the flag-draped coffin and paid their respects to the fortieth president of the United States. Crowds of onlookers lined the streets as Reagan's coffin processed to the Capitol on a horse-drawn caisson, accompanied by a saddled steed, riderless but with a pair of the former president's boots standing in the stirrups. Earlier, a memorial service drew members of Congress and the Supreme Court, as well as diplomats and heads of state. The state funeral was marked by series of both twenty-one-gun and fifty-gun salutes at military bases across the country. A national day of mourning was declared by Congress. Media coverage was intense and tireless, with newspapers and television networks devoting many column inches of newsprint and many hours of airtime to the funeral events and to assessments of the significance of Reagan's life and presidency.

What a striking contrast all this high pageantry and mass-media attention offers to the death of Jesus of Nazareth around the thirtieth year of the Common Era in Roman-occupied Judea. By all accounts, it was an occasion of little fanfare. Roman records took no note of it. There were no throngs of mourners, no visits or messages

of consolation from heads of state or other dignitaries, no public assessments of his significance. In fact, the only accounts of Jesus's death
that come from the first century are the New Testament Gospels, and
the earliest of those were written nearly half a century after the event.
According to them, even Jesus's closest followers, with the exception of
a small group of women, had abandoned him by the time he died. The
passion of the one who came to be known as the Christ on that first
Good Friday received very little attention indeed.

But the passion of the Christ as played out in movie theaters around
the world during the Lenten and Easter seasons of 2004 was another
story altogether, a mass media event to rival even the death of a former
president of the most powerful nation on earth. Far from going virtually
unnoticed in a tiny political backwater, the death of Jesus in Mel Gibson's movie *The Passion of the Christ* took place in one of the most influential nations in the world, was witnessed by millions and millions, and
was the object of enormous media interest and critical analysis. Opening on Ash Wednesday (the beginning of the penitential season of Lent,
which leads into Easter), it had the highest-grossing opening weekend
in February, making nearly $84 million in over 3000 theaters. Within a
month it had reached $300 million in U.S. ticket sales alone. By mid-June
it had reached $370 million, close to the final numbers for *Lord of the
Rings: Return of the King* at $377 million. It is now the highest grossing
R-rated film of all time, having soundly beaten *The Matrix Reloaded*.
By March and April, the film was opening and breaking records in many
countries in Latin America, Asia, the Middle East, and Europe (in Italy,
it opened during Holy Week and grossed $25 million within a month's
time). By May it had become the highest-grossing film worldwide for
2004 (over $608 million). The heavily marketed and highly successful
DVD, released in late summer 2004, is sure to be popular for years to
come, not only among individual viewers but also among Protestant
and Catholic church communities and youth groups, which are using it
in their educational curricula and special worship services. (Icon sells a
Passion of the Christ church resource DVD for use during Holy Week
and Easter.) Gibson's spring 2005 release of *The Passion Uncut,* which
trims about six minutes of the goriest footage, is sure to increase the
movie's churchgoing audience.

But *The Passion of the Christ* is not simply a media phenomenon.
More important, it is also a religious phenomenon, especially in the
United States. Mel Gibson has said that he didn't want to create another
film experience; he wanted to create a religious experience. Judging from
audience responses, he has succeeded for many viewers, especially those

identified with evangelical Christianity. *The Passion* has been embraced by millions as a revelation of biblical proportions. For these viewers it has been elevated to the status of cinematic scripture, simultaneously creating and representing a shared religious experience and communion. Indeed, many Christians have embraced the film as a religious sacrament. Whole church congregations purchased large blocks of tickets in order to see the film together. So did Christian youth groups and college campus ministries. Affirming Gibson's claim that this is a religious experience, many Christian ministers and youth leaders recommended that viewers go to it not as a film but as a worship service. No popcorn, no sodas, no cell phones. Many groups were seen holding hands and praying in parking lots and ticket lines before and after screenings. Some organizations, such as Youth Specialties and Catholic.net, developed curricula for follow-up Bible studies and fellowship services. Indeed, for many, *The Passion of the Christ* is Gospel, a cinematic presentation of holy scripture, a twenty-first-century incarnation of the Word.

For many less sympathetic viewers, on the other hand, the film is a shocking revelation of the religious orientation of American mainstream culture, which is apparently closer to Gibson's than they had hoped. They are amazed by the popular devotional embrace of the film's seemingly gratuitous violence and its implication of the Jewish religious establishment as responsible for killing Jesus. Indeed, many are justifiably concerned that this film, like the pre–Vatican II Passion play tradition that inspired it, might even lead to an explosion of a very different sort of violence with a much stronger historical precedent: violence against Jews.

Whether one embraces it or despises it, no matter one's religious or nonreligious orientation, *The Passion* is impossible to ignore. It is an event within the cultural history of Christianity that reaches far beyond its immediate audience of sympathetic Christians. And if the equally controversial (though less financially successful) *Jesus Christ Superstar* of the 1970s is any indication, Gibson's film is sure to remain a prominent presence on the American religious landscape for decades to come.

The *Passion* phenomenon opens unique opportunities for conversation between scholars and the general public concerning religion and popular culture. Controversies surrounding the film have generated a tremendous demand for insight and information from scholars concerning the film's claims to historical accuracy, its use of violence, and its potentially anti-Jewish dimensions. Is the film historically accurate, as Mel Gibson declares it is? What biblical and nonbiblical sources does it use? How true is it to those sources? Is the Bible a historical document?

What is the difference between the Jesus of history and the Christ of faith? Why is the film accused of being anti-Semitic or anti-Jewish? Are the Gospels themselves anti-Jewish? Why is there so much violence in the film, and what is its theological meaning? What really happened at the Crucifixion? To scholars, some of these questions may appear simplistic and naive. To ignore them, however, is to miss an opportunity for serious public engagement with questions of broad relevance.

Indeed, *The Passion of the Christ* is not just a religious phenomenon. It is a biblical phenomenon. However you judge the artistic or theological merits of the film, it is a significant moment in the cultural afterlife of the biblical passion stories of Christian scripture. As such, it is an appropriate inaugural volume for the new University of Chicago Press book series, *Afterlives of the Bible,* which will publish books that explore the rich and complex cultural histories of Jewish and Christian biblical literature. This series will explore how biblical stories, themes, idioms, images, even the idea of "the Bible" itself are played out in various religious, literary, social, and political contexts. Too often biblical studies have focused exclusively on the meaning and historical significance of biblical texts in their earliest contexts—determining the most original text, identifying literary and oral sources, exploring their earliest historical contexts—and have neglected the afterlives of these texts, that is, the ways they have been appropriated and transformed in the context of particular cultural beliefs, practices, and institutions. We see attention to the afterlives of biblical literature as an opportunity for biblical studies to take its place at the center of larger ongoing conversations, within and without the academy, concerning religion and contemporary culture.

Gibson's movie is a striking example of what we mean by "afterlives of the Bible," in this case the Christian Bible. This film grows out of and is an interpretation of the ancient biblical Gospels, but at the same time it is thoroughly shaped—in terms of both its production and its reception by audiences—by its own cultural moment in the early years of the twenty-first century. It is a biblical-cultural-media phenomenon. Indeed, along with a few other filmic versions of the New Testament stories of Jesus, it represents the invention of a new media form for the Bible: cinematic scripture. Such a cinematic gospel text calls for new vocabularies and methods of analysis and interpretation that are very different from traditional biblical criticism but are nonetheless rigorous.

Ronald Reagan's funeral serves not only as a contrast with the little-noticed death of Jesus of Nazareth; it also demonstrates the potential for transformation in the cultural afterlife of a person, a text, an artwork, or an event. In the 1980s and 1990s, Reagan was a controversial and in many ways divisive figure. But in its (admittedly very early) cultural afterlife, Reagan's legacy has been whitewashed by the mainstream media, and he is now memorialized as an entirely uncontroversial president who enjoyed the support of an entire nation. Whether this version of Reagan will withstand more intense scrutiny in the coming years remains to be seen. But it is clear, no matter what verdicts historians, political scientists, and cultural critics may render, that the decade and a half between the time Reagan left office and the time of his death had a profound effect on his cultural legacy.

If such transformations can occur in less than a generation's time, how much richer and more complex is the cultural afterlife of Jesus of Nazareth, given the long stretch of history and the numerous and diverse cultures and media through which that afterlife has passed? And so the question of how Jesus has gone from a man who was largely deserted by his followers and executed as a criminal two thousand years ago to the hero of a blockbuster motion picture is both dauntingly complex and endlessly fascinating. Even though the question does not permit an exhaustive analysis, it must be addressed. Although Gibson firmly contends that the movie is simply a presentation of what actually happened to Jesus two millennia ago, clearly that is not the case. To understand the movie and its impact, it is necessary to understand something of the cultural afterlife that takes us from the historical event itself through the first narrative accounts of Jesus's death in the New Testament Gospels, through the church creeds formulated first at Nicaea and later at Chalcedon, through the medieval Passion plays, and through post-Enlightenment historical research, to twentieth-century evangelical Christianity (to mention only a handful of the many influences on the film).

The essays in this volume help us interpret Gibson's movie and understand its place in contemporary culture and society not simply as a movie, but as a cultural event. *The Passion* could only have happened as it did in this place at this time. Where else and when else than in turn-of-the-millennium America could a Hollywood star have amassed enough personal wealth to commit a reported $25 million of it to the making of a personal film project—and not just any project, but an intensely religious one? And where else and when else could there be such a huge audience for the finished product? Indeed, *The Passion of the Christ* is very much a product of its post-Reagan context, from the effects of particular economic policies to a political consolidation of religious conservatives that has trumped many of the older theological differences between evangelical Protestantism and Catholicism (and thus opened up the movie to a much larger audience).

The Passion, then, is an opportunity for scholarly dialogue with a broad public audience on the relationship between the Bible, media, and popular culture. It offers readily accessible interpretations of the film and its contexts by leading scholars, focusing on the most pressing questions and contentions within larger public engagements.

The scholars brought together here do not always agree with one another. That is by design. The scholarly community is no more unanimous in response to this film than is American society more generally. Some scholars are more sympathetic with those who have been so deeply moved by the film as a kind of religious experience. Others, far less sympathetic, nonetheless attempt to elaborate how the film works on people within a certain set of cultural conditions. Some argue strongly that the film fans the flames of anti-Judaism and anti-Semitism. Others reckon such allegations to be exaggerated. Some see the film as an outstanding piece of cinematography. Others pan it. Some argue that the liberties it takes with the gospel traditions of the New Testament are defensible as a cinematic form of biblical interpretation. Others see them as irresponsible and misleading. This book does not settle such matters. Rather, it provides solid, well-researched, intelligent information and interpretation from a variety of perspectives in order to give some additional traction to the public discussion, which has too often spun off track into sweeping generalizations, ungrounded accusations, and personal attacks.

This book is organized in three parts. The chapters in part 1 analyze and interpret The Passion primarily in relation to its religious sources, including the Gospels, other biblical texts (e.g., the serpent in Genesis 2–3), extrabiblical religious texts (e.g., Anne Catherine Emmerich's The Dolorous Passion of Our Lord Jesus Christ), and other traditions (e.g., the rosary). What are the film's primary literary sources, and how does it use them? What from these texts does it highlight and what does it ignore or elide? In what ways does the medium of film in fact require a radically different way of representing gospel narrative—that is, what can a cinematic religious narrative do that a literary one cannot?

Part 2 focuses on the ethical and theological implications of The Passion's particular presentation of the Christian Gospel. What do we make of its representations of women and female sexuality in the characters of the Virgin Mary, Mary Magdalene, and the figure of Satan, and of Jewish leaders and Jewish crowds in particular scenes? What about the film's extreme and sometimes gratuitous images of violence, which get far more attention here than in the Gospel narratives? What are the implications of focusing on the Passion of Jesus in terms of atoning for suffering rather than in terms of social justice?

Part 3 explores the film as a popular cultural-religious phenomenon. How do we understand the overwhelmingly positive response of so many viewers to this unusual mix of Hollywood, biblical narrative, and conservative Christian theology? How has the film worked to create a sense of "insider" identity for some and alienated so many others in a popular culture of ever-increasing religious diversity? What can we learn about religious dimensions—latent and otherwise—of contemporary mass culture from the reception of this film?

Representative of our desire to ground but not settle "the *Passion* controversy," this book speaks to two particular needs among students and general readers. First, it provides reliable information on the biblical and theological backgrounds and sources of the film. Many readers find it difficult to sort through the flood of newspaper, talk show, and Web site reviews for serious yet accessible information on how the film uses biblical literature and other sources, not to mention how to understand the Gospels themselves with respect to historical reconstruction on the one hand and faithful interpretation on the other. This book brings together some of the most well-respected and widely read scholars of biblical literature and the history of Christianity in order to examine the film's relationship to its various sources.

Second, this book frames specific topics for discussion concerning relationships between religion (especially the Christian Bible) and mass media in contemporary culture. Generally, the film has had a polarizing effect on its viewers and the general public. Most Christians (especially evangelicals and Catholics) are deeply moved by the film, and most others are powerfully repulsed. As a result, people are often at a loss for ways to converse about the theological and cultural issues it raises. Written by scholars who are known not only for their specific fields of academic research but also for their astute insights into contemporary culture more broadly, the essays address particular issues and questions prompted by *The Passion* in ways that will open opportunities for dialogue across religious divides.

Part One: *The Passion* **as Interpretation**

1

The Art of *The Passion*

Jack Miles

As a cinematic matter, the boldest innovation in Mel Gibson's *The Passion of the Christ* is its use of language and subtitles to create, in a religious film, the illusion of documentary. Dialogue in a number of recent English-language feature films has fostered this kind of illusion by shifting into a second language with accompanying subtitles for a few minutes at a time. *Dances with Wolves,* for example, shifted at several points into the Amerindian language Lakota. But it is almost unheard of for a film to unfold in its entirety in subtitles beneath a language other than that of its primary audience.

Aramaic and Latin, the two languages in which the dialogue of *The Passion* is spoken, are not just foreign but dead. Aramaic survives only in a few remote corners of the Middle East, in dialects different from the one heard in this film. Latin is no longer spoken anywhere. The documentary illusion created by modern subtitles under ancient languages thus simulates a voyage not so much to a distant land as to a distant era. To the extent that any work of art derived from a classic must make it new by making it strange, this is a brilliant stroke. Yet the brilliance has a deeply regrettable secondary effect.

Before speaking of the secondary effect, I should mention that I spent two years as a student in Rome at the Pontifical Gregorian University in an era when classes, textbooks, and oral examinations at that institution were still entirely in Latin. To that extent, I am a Latin speaker and, I might add, one particularly accustomed to hearing Latin as pronounced by native speakers of Italian. (Many of the actors in this film, including most of those who portray the Roman soldiers, are Italians.) Later, as a graduate student at Harvard University, I studied four different dialects of ancient Aramaic. In short, I belong to the overeducated sliver of the audience for *The Passion* that can hear both "original" languages with a measure of comprehension.

Before the film's release, Gibson and his collaborators were belittled in learned circles for filming in Latin. Did they not know, scholars sniffed, that Latin was a language Jews outside Italy did not speak? In general, the scholars were right: Greek, not Latin, was the English of the ancient world—every educated man's second language. Historical critics of the Gospels have had good reason to assume that if Pontius Pilate and Jesus of Nazareth—a Latin speaker and an Aramaic speaker—had the conversations that the Gospels report them having, they would have had them in Greek. And yet the truth is that no one knows for a fact that Pilate never troubled to learn Aramaic, the language of the common people of Galilee and Judea.

I call it a defensible artistic liberty, then, that Mel Gibson and his collaborator in the screenplay, Benedict Fitzgerald (the son of a distinguished translator of classical Greek), serve up a Pilate who speaks fluent Aramaic to the Jews who come before him. Just this, as it happens, creates the opportunity for a moment of linguistically concealed but rather stunning drama. When Pilate leads Jesus into his chambers for a private word, he addresses him condescendingly in Aramaic. Jesus answers the proud Roman serenely—and in flawless Latin. Did the historical Jesus speak Latin? Surely not, but Fitzgerald and Gibson are within their rights to choose, for artistic purposes, the Christ of faith over the Jesus of history. Their Jesus is God Incarnate. He can speak at will any human language he chooses.

There is an inevitable whiff of the schoolroom about William Fulco's translation of the Fitzgerald-Gibson script into the two ancient tongues, yet Fulco does his best to colloquialize the language where he can. Thus, the ignorant armored Romans who lash Jesus through the streets scream at him in Aramaic when he falls, "Qum!" (Get up!), but continue in Latin with mocking epithets such as *rex vermum* (king of worms). Adding a bit to the documentary effect, some of the shouted Aramaic never appears in the subtitles. An anonymous voice bellows "Mamzer!" from somewhere in the crowd, but the word "bastard" never appears at the bottom of the screen.

: : :

But I must turn now to the regrettable secondary effect of this otherwise brilliant stroke of linguistic illusion. Nowhere in the world is there a city of a million people who could hear the Aramaic that constitutes the bulk of the dialogue of this film as if it were their native language. One city, however, comes surprisingly close: Tel Aviv. Aramaic and Hebrew belong to the same northwest branch of the Semitic language family. A native speaker of Israeli Hebrew will hear the Aramaic of this film rather as a native speaker of Italian might hear Spanish. (I speak as a former student at the Hebrew University in Jerusalem who thirty-five years ago was semi-fluent in spoken Hebrew.) Nothing in this film will sound quite right in Tel Aviv, but much will sound vaguely familiar. And now and then will come a sentence of crystal clarity, coincidentally identical in the two languages.

So it happens at a critical moment in *The Passion of the Christ*. Reproducing the scene called in Western art "Ecce Homo" (Behold the Man), Pilate has just led Jesus—scourged, bloody, and crowned with thorns—before the Jewish high priests and a crowd of their followers, offering to release him with no further punishment. Rejecting the offer, a priest shouts a phrase in Aramaic that might or might not be intelligible in Tel Aviv. But then the Jewish crowd takes up the same cry in a slightly different grammatical form. They scream in unison a single, terrible word that happens to be identical in Israeli Hebrew and in Aramaic, and they scream it again and again as if it were a football cheer: "Yitstalev! Yitstalev! Yitstalev!" (Let him be crucified!). And the scene descends into chaos.

Given the agony of the twentieth century for world Jewry, given the complicity of Christianity in that agony, how can a Tel Aviv audience witness with anything less than utter horror this scene of a Jewish mob chanting for Christ's blood in what sounds like Hebrew? American Jews who know enough Israeli Hebrew—and a good many do—will hear the same words in the same deeply disturbing way. It is true that Matthew 27:25, "His blood be upon us and upon our children," the biblical line most notoriously used by Christian anti-Semites against Jews, is not shouted in unison in the film as it is in the Gospel, and that line does not appear in the subtitles. But what remains is nonetheless scandalous in contemporary context. Moreover, though few Americans know this, most Palestinians born under Israeli occupation speak Hebrew as well as Arabic. They, too, will understand "Yitstalev!" and they won't think only of Jesus.

No one can know from reading the Gospels how large a crowd of Jews gathered before Pilate or just how often or how loud they shouted, "Let him be crucified" (Matthew 27:22–23). In saying this, I speak not of what really happened, but only of what the writers intended their readers to imagine. In this scene, they cannot have intended us to imagine a crowd larger than could be accommodated in a throne room or a courtyard. Earlier in the gospel story, when Jesus enters Jerusalem in triumph, acclaimed as Messiah by the population, the gospel writers transparently intended us to imagine a crowd large enough to fill the streets of the city. Unfortunately, the larger crowd, cheering so differently, appears in the Gibson-Benedict script only as a few cryptic seconds of flashback. The result approaches a revision of the Apostles' Creed that every traditional Catholic (such as Mel Gibson) learns by heart as a child. The creed summarizes the earthly life of Christ as follows: "conceived by the Holy Spirit, born of the Virgin Mary, *suffered under Pontius Pilate,* was crucified, died, and was buried." Against the creed and beyond any of the Gospels, *The Passion of the Christ* seems determined to replace the Romans with the Jews and Pilate with Caiaphas. I find this substitution regrettable not only on religious or interreligious grounds, but also on artistic grounds, for this original and, in many ways, heartfelt film does not need the Jews as villains. It has another, cinematically stunning villain on hand in the person of Satan, and she (yes, she) is more than enough.

: : :

As the usual sort of he-devil, Satan has long since become an essentially comedic character. By contrast, Rosalinda Celentano's gray-faced, hollow-eyed terrorist, speaking in a weirdly masculine or masculinized voice, as if delivering a death threat in a disguised voice, is the most insinuatingly sinister Satan ever seen on screen (fig. 1). Hers is, in truth, one of the most memorable performances in the film. From the garden of Gethsemane to the bloody end, she smiles thinly on each scene from the shadows, quietly relishing each agonizing step as Jesus goes down to what seems to be his final defeat. Her omnipresence is matched only by that of Mary, Jesus's sorrowing mother (Maia Morgenstern), the ruthlessness of the one matched by the tenderness of the other. Madam Satan is deceived, of course; and after Jesus's death, we see her shrieking in impotent rage at the bottom of an abyss. The moment of Jesus's apparent defeat has proven to be her final downfall. Nothing remains but the understated denouement: Jesus's resurrection.

It has been suggested that by representing Satan as androgynous, Gibson intends to demonize homosexuals, but this strikes me as a gratuitous charge. Angels are androgynous and benevolent. What should devils be but androgynous and malevolent? I see Satan's presence in the film rather as its one substantial indication that Jesus himself is more than a mere man gratuitously abused.

There are, broadly, two ways to state the "success" of Jesus theologically, one without the Devil and one with him. One theology says that mankind deserved punishment for its sins, but Christ "took the rap," heroically and vicariously atoning for all the sins of history by his Passion and death. This theology has little need for Jesus's resurrection—his death accomplishes everything that needs accomplishing—and no real role for Satan to play, even as enemy. *The Passion of the Christ*—in this, like the Gospel story itself—offers few suggestions that Jesus is accepting punishment for mankind's sins. It is precisely because the Gospels say so little about vicarious punishment that J. S. Bach's Passion oratorios insert hymns that interrupt the gospel narrative to make this connection over and over again. The many viewers who have seen a theology of vicarious punishment in *The Passion of the Christ* have largely brought it with them into the theater, as non-Christian reviewers have been particularly effective in noting. In this, the filmgoers are heirs not just to Bach but also to centuries of later "washed in the blood of the Lamb" Protestant hymnody and preaching.

The second theology, dominant in early Christian art as well as in early Christian thought, tells Jesus's success as an epic tale requiring both Satan and the Resurrection. Back in the garden of Eden, it says, Satan led mankind through sin into death, but by the end of time Jesus will have led mankind from sin back into life: paradise lost will become paradise regained. Jesus will accomplish this by binding his followers to him in the endlessly repeated ritual of the Last Supper: just as he rose on the third day, so they will someday rise as well. It is in this way, as Augustine puts it, that "Christ's death kills death." In this story and in this theology of a new exodus—from mortality and estrangement from God (sinfulness rather than particular sins) to immortality and reconciliation with him—punishment for specific sins is not the central topic, and salvation does not consist of exoneration.

FIGURE 1 Satan speaking with Jesus in Gethsemane. Still from *The Passion of the Christ* (2004).

By including Satan so noticeably, *The Passion of the Christ* seems to me to tilt in this second theological direction, though Gibson and Fitzgerald weaken the sense of cosmic combat by failing to include any flashbacks to moments such as the Transfiguration, when Jesus's divinity was manifested to his disciples. Because Jesus's divinity is not asserted in cinematic terms through this or any other gospel incident, the film scarcely seems to have God Incarnate as its protagonist. The struggle seems to be between Satan and a helplessly human victim. All the same, because this Satan plays the role of villain to perfection, there is no artistic reason to draft any Jew into that role. And this makes all the more gratuitous and all the more regrettable the screenwriters' decision to go so far beyond the Gospels in demonizing Caiaphas and company.

: : :

Once the Jewish mob begins chanting "Yitstalev!" Jesus's trial quickly becomes a bloody melee, Jews and Romans attacking each other and battering Jesus at the same time. It is at this point that "His blood be upon us" is audible in the Aramaic, even though it does not appear below the screen. When Pilate finally washes his hands and turns Jesus over, he plainly means to say to both groups: Have at him, both of you, but leave me out of it. Already his soldiers have gone beyond his instructions (and beyond the Gospels) by brutally prolonging Jesus's scourging. Yet now, cynically, he allows them to do with the condemned man as they will. There is one noble Roman among the soldiers, as there were two brave Jewish dissenters at the court of the high priest. There is as well a decent Jewish bystander who, drafted by the soldiers into helping

Jesus carry his cross, becomes, almost against his will, Jesus's defender. But it is the Roman soldiers—loutish, drunken, sadistic, and depraved—who define the latter third of the film and move the action forward to its savage conclusion.

The Passion of the Christ might almost have been titled *The Beating of the Christ.* Jesus is beaten at his arrest in the garden, beaten as he is taken to the court of Caiaphas, beaten en route to the court of Pilate, scourged at length by Pilate's soldiers, and so endlessly on. One of the very first beatings leaves him with his right eye swollen shut, requiring Jim Caviezel, much of whose acting in the role of Jesus consists of soulful gazing, to make do with one soulful eye only. The makeup artists Keith Vanderlaan and Greg Cannom do their best to turn two hours' worth of beatings into a visible descent toward death, but they have a near-impossible task. The script requires Jesus to absorb so much punishment at the start that makeup must turn him into a physical ruin with perhaps forty-five minutes of the film still to run.

The true physiological monstrosity of crucifixion—the victim, delirious, dying by asphyxiation, ending his life with hideous gasps, like a man dying of asthma or drowning in mid-air—is not shown, and who would want to see it? Who would want to linger over the true obscenity of a shamed victim, his tongue lolling out of his dehydrated mouth, pulling himself up by his bound and nailed arms to prevent the *sedulum,* a saddlelike Roman torture device placed beneath his perineum, from grinding his groin to a pulp? Agony of this sort has never been portrayed in art; I doubt that it ever will be, any more than I expect or want the real horror of racist lynching ever to appear on an American movie screen. Crucifixion, which usually took days, killed Jesus in just three short hours; but would any audience remain in a darkened movie theater for even that long watching a life drain away drop by boring drop? Catholics stay in church that long at the traditional *tre ore* Good Friday service, but Hollywood will never ask so much.

No, for all its bloodiness, *The Passion* must stun more by the moral evil it suggests than by the physical suffering it portrays. Yes, it imports into the rather tame subgenre of the "Jesus movie" some of the techniques of the horror movie, even the "splatter movie," but these contribute rather little in the end. As the blood drips and the blows land by the scores, if not the hundreds, more begins to seem less. Still more—to the point of duplicating the excruciating boredom of the real thing—would have been still less.

One begins to long, in fact, for the interruptions, the flashbacks, that relieve the monotony. Thanks to the sensitive cinematography of Caleb

Deshamel, these include some of the most visually appealing moments in the film. At one moment a candlelit interior will recall Georges de la Tour, at another Christ's face at the Last Supper will suggest Rembrandt's famous head of Christ, at still another the cut and color of Mary's veils will recall a Bellini pietà, and so forth. Such allusions figure in the bloodiest scenes as well. When Christ's left hand contracts into a claw at the moment the nail pierces it, a few viewers, surely, will think of the clawlike hands of the crucified Christ in the deeply moving Isenheim Altarpiece of Matthias Grünewald.

These reminders and others like them hover, by choice or design, just below the threshold of visual consciousness. Nothing is ever copied or "quoted" exactly, yet the sneer on that soldier's face. . . . Have I not seen it somewhere before? Is it Brueghel? In most films, actors make you think of other actors and other people you know. In this film, scenes make you think, instead, of art you are sure you must have seen before, though you can't quite remember where. It helps, of course, that the film was shot partly on location in Matera, Italy, and that the Italian landscape, natural and built, is the visual backdrop to so much of the greatest Christian art. Rather than break new ground in costuming or setting, *The Passion* has chosen to continue an iconographic tradition.

This means, for example, that rather than walking with his arms lashed to the detachable crossbeam of a T-shaped cross, as scholars believe was likely, Jesus lugs a towering Latin cross like those seen in most classic paintings, though such a cross would in fact weigh as much as six or eight railroad ties and be so heavy that no man—in fact, no two or three men—could possibly lift it. When we see this baroque cross falling in slo-mo and striking the ground with an amplified, sepulchral "boooom" from the sound track, we are—to repeat a point made earlier—in the realm not of quasi-documentary realism, but of refined hyperrealism, the cinematic enhancement of inherited imagery. Real crucifixions did not come with background music.

Before concluding, it seems only fair to note, on the one hand, that with regard to *The Passion of the Christ* as a chapter in the history of Christian iconography, this film does *not* continue any of the anti-Semitic visual cues one reads about in Ruth Mellinkoff's 1994 landmark *Outcasts: Signs of Otherness in Northern European Art of the Late Middle Ages*. One observes here, in other words, none of the "typical distortions associated with Jews [in late medieval art]—enlarged eyes, hooked noses, enlarged mouths, and fleshy lips" (p. 128). On the other hand, the film must be said to break new anti-Semitic ground in its vivid representation of Matthew 27:25 ("His blood be upon us," etc.). Against the view that early Christian literary and artistic tradition sought to win favor in the Roman Empire by inculpating the Jews and exculpating the Romans for the death of Jesus, it must be noted that in the very earliest, thoroughly Roman depictions of the Passion, Pilate is always the central figure, while Jews, other than Judas, are secondary or altogether absent (see Gertrud Schiller's massive and comprehensive *The Iconography of Christian Art,* vol. 2, p. 65). Jewish agents grow more prominent in later depictions, but as it happens, artistic representations of Matthew 27:25 ("His blood be upon us," etc.) are essentially not to be had at any period. In exaggerating the Jewish role in the Passion story as much as it does, then, *The Passion of the Christ* may owe more to the shorter history of Western religious drama, as at Oberammergau, than to the longer one of Western religious art.

: : :

Time will tell whether this film will have any longer a life or any deeper an impact than its predecessors in the genre, all of which seem faded or eccentric failures in retrospect. The plot of the Gospel—good, beautiful man confronts evil, ugly establishment, loses everything, but then miraculously wins everything back in the end—is Christianity's supreme gift to Hollywood. Think of good, beautiful Tom Cruise in *Jerry Maguire.* Think of good, beautiful Paul Newman in *Cool Hand Luke.* The list is endless. Generation after generation, the old story keeps on coming; only the faces change. Even Steven Spielberg couldn't do his Holocaust movie until Thomas Keneally wrote *Schindler's Ark,* uncovering within that supremely intractable catastrophe a story that conformed more or less to the Gospel archetype. This is the deepest, most inescapable impact of the Gospel on American literary and artistic culture.

The Passion conforms to the archetype in principle but differs from most Hollywood examples of it by severely contracting the beginning and the end (confrontation and triumph) and greatly expanding the middle (suffering and loss). As a result, despite the length of *The Passion,* I suspect audiences who do not walk in with a developed theology to apply will walk out with a feeling of "Is that all?" This film offers indeed only the Passion of Christ and not the Gospel of Christ. Absent from this film are the Gospels' beautiful and consoling scenes of the risen Jesus's reunion with his disciples. The omission is surely defensible on artistic grounds. The fact remains that catharsis, as a result, is withheld. Millions will want to see this film, but few will want to see it twice.

Speaking personally, I regret the worsening of Jewish-Christian and Jewish-Muslim relations that I believe is likely to result from the scenes I have lingered over here. I fear the use that may be made of the film by Muslim anti-Semites such as the Syrian president, Bashar Assad. A Christian group delivered a copy to Yasir Arafat, who pronounced it to be without anti-Semitism. Afterward, his media spokesman commented: "The Palestinians are still daily having exposure to the kind of pain Jesus was exposed to during his Crucifixion."

Larger factors than any American film will surely determine both Jewish-Christian and Jewish-Muslim relationships, even in the period immediately ahead. More lasting, perhaps, as the film gradually fades away, may be a result of at least middling importance in Protestant-Catholic relations in the United States. I refer to the astonishing fact that in their embrace of *The Passion,* evangelical Protestants have celebrated a portrayal of Jesus that visually and theologically—in every way, perhaps, except in the wail, thunder, and thud of John Debney's deafening score—is flamboyantly, Counter-Reformationally Roman. This film is awash in Catholic piety and Catholic imagery that the forebears of today's evangelicals would have found religiously and aesthetically repugnant. *The Passion* has been embraced most warmly by Bible belt churches, where, to this day, the faithful kneel before crosses without corpses. What has come over them? And, having come, will it stay? Roman Catholic worship in the United States is far more Protestant in tone than it was before Vatican II. Will Protestant worship now begin to assume a more Catholic tone? Will this improbable film be the occasion for the return of the repressed blood-rite element in the archetypal Christian service that Paul speaks of?

It is astonishing, finally, that political conservatives should have embraced—during wartime—a film whose message is that when under murderous attack, one should not fight back but instead forgive one's attackers and accept one's death humbly as the will of God. Personally, I am inclined to think that a serious, life-challenging topic such as pacifism is rarely if ever addressed effectively in a film. New films knock down old films as bowling balls knock down bowling pins in successive frames. Even the most grandiose of "major motion pictures" asks so little of the filmgoer that the discussion almost never outlasts the hype.

Will this film be different? Perhaps it will be, but if it isn't, fear not: there will be a remake within the decade. Of that you can be certain. The Gospel is a story with legs—short ones, to be sure, but very, very sturdy.

2

The Good News of Mel Gibson's *Passion*

George M. Smiga

They were young. They were bright. They were interested. In April 2004 I found myself in a discussion with high school students from St. Joseph Academy, a Catholic school for girls. The session was part of a long-standing program of the City Club of Cleveland, whose members I had just addressed in a talk titled, "Is Mel Gibson's *Passion* Anti-Semitic?" For the last few months I had been busy, as had most of my colleagues, with speaking engagements born out of the promotion and release of *The Passion of the Christ*. Long accustomed to addressing a handful of stalwart believers in church basements, we now found ourselves speaking to hundreds, many of them spurred by the film to seek biblical and historical information for the first time. Our comments concerning the movie were largely critical. We were concerned about its historical inaccuracies, its limited theological perspective, and, as in the talk I had just presented, its potential for anti-Semitism.

Although the students from St. Joseph Academy had not noticed the anti-Jewish tendencies in the film, I could tell by their questions that they were absorbing the implications of such an insight and were grateful it had been pointed out to them. As we approached the end of our session, I decided to pose a more general question. I asked, "What did you think about the film overall?" There was a pause and a slight hesitation. Then one of the young women said, "We liked it. We liked it a lot." Her classmates nodded in agreement. Another continued, "We have religion classes regularly in school, and I often tune them out. But since I have seen this movie, when I hear the name 'Jesus,' I stop and listen. I want to know more about him." Anyone committed to religious education knows the significance of that statement. In the contest to communicate the Gospel, having someone ready to listen is not simply a hit but a grand slam.

Modern society revolves around the competition to "get the message out." Millions of dollars are paid for a thirty-second spot during the SuperBowl or the closing episode of *Friends*. No matter how worthy the content, success depends upon first stimulating interest. *The Passion* has seized the attention of millions of people. One of the highest-grossing movies of all time, it has created an opportunity to say a word about religion in American culture. People are listening.

Professional historians, theologians, and biblical scholars have largely concerned themselves with the film's inadequacies. With millions listening, surely we should not limit our comments to negative assessments. There are positive words to be spoken. Allow me to present three: a word about Jesus, a word about the Bible, and a word about God.

Jesus: Humanizing the Christ

In discussing *The Passion* people often remark, "Jesus is so human in this film," or "Jesus is really one of us." They speak as if in possession of some new information. Yet the humanity of Christ has been a central tenet of the Christian faith since the great councils of the fourth and fifth centuries. It is a central part of pastoral life for millions of Christians. I have preached it in hundreds of homilies and emphasized its importance in countless educational settings. Why, then, are so many who have seen the movie surprised at the humanity of Jesus? The answer to this question is both theological and cinematic.

Theologically, the orthodox teaching on Jesus is complex. He is understood to be one person with two natures, fully human and fully divine. The success of this dogma depends upon holding the two natures in tension, without folding one into the other. On the level of the ordinary Christian, however, this tension is frequently relaxed. Christians tend to choose one nature over the other, and it is the divine nature that usually wins. This inclination is nurtured by official faith statements such as the Nicene Creed, which is recited on a weekly basis in most liturgical Christian churches. Since the creed resulted from the effort to establish the full divinity of Christ, its description of his divinity is emphatic and repetitive:

> We believe in one Lord, Jesus Christ, the only son of God, eternally begotten of the Father, God from God, Light from Light, true God from true God, begotten, not made, of one being with the Father. Through him all things were made.

To balance this statement of divinity, the creed offers only two phrases to assert Jesus's humanity: that he took flesh through the Virgin Mary and was made human.

This creedal emphasis is reinforced by the devotional practices of many Christians. They address Jesus in their daily prayers, asking him to meet the needs of their lives. Therefore, although the orthodox teaching clearly insists upon a tension between the natures of Jesus, on a functional level many believers simply approach Jesus as God. Therefore, a confrontation with a human Christ can come as a surprise.

The cinematic reasons for the surprise, however, are as potent as the theological. Modern culture has become primarily visual. Although biblical scholars and historians still surround themselves with books, to the ordinary American, the text is dead. The Internet, television, and film have made news, entertainment, and education pictorial experiences. Seeing something determines its relevance and reality.

In such a culture, what pictures of Jesus are available to us? An Internet search on Jesus will result in thousands of hits. However, the majority of images are either great art from the thirteenth through the eighteenth century or sentimental pictures from the nineteenth and twentieth centuries. What *The Passion* has done is presented Jesus in the most sophisticated medium of our own time.

Film has its own language. People in the audiences that gathered to view the first "moving pictures" actually screamed when they witnessed their first close-up. To view an isolated head on the screen seemed unnatural and frightening. Today audiences intuitively understand that a close-up provides importance and intimacy to a character, because they have become literate in the language of the cinema. Perhaps the most effective images in *The Passion* are the close-ups of Jesus and his mother. To see these central characters of the Christian story presented in the same medium that brings us Brad Pitt and Julia Roberts not only gives Jesus and his mother a cultural authority, but also bestows upon them a reality that is inaccessible in other forms of expression. As a result, Jesus, his mother, and the love between them can for the first time seem "real." Despite the film's heavy theological overlay, Jesus as conveyed by the undeniable cinematic power of *The Passion* surprises the viewer with his full humanity.

If the authority of *The Passion*'s cinematic language has reified the humanity of Christ and contributed to a better balance between the divine and human natures, such a contribution should be welcomed. To those seeking to pass their faith on to the next generation, this is Good News.

The Bible: Shaping the Gospel Tradition

Since the Enlightenment, scholars have attempted to reconstruct the process by which the Christian Gospels were written. There is an academic consensus that the trajectory was a complex one in which earlier pieces of material were received by the evangelists and then reshaped to suite their audiences. In Catholic circles this understanding of gospel formation reached its most authoritative expression at the Second Vatican Council, when the bishops of the world stated:

> The sacred authors wrote the four Gospels, selecting some things from the many which had been handed on by word of mouth or in writing, reducing some of them to a synthesis, explaining some things in view of the situation of their churches and preserving the form of proclamation but always in such fashion that they told us the honest truth about Jesus. (*Dogmatic Constitution on Divine Revelation* 19)

Unfortunately, this creative process of gospel formation remains largely unknown to the ordinary believer, who continues to read the Gospels as simple historical accounts. Efforts to educate "the person in the pew" are usually frustrated by the limited interest in such academic matters and the difficulties of finding an effective way to explain the process itself.

The Passion has not only awakened an interest in the ordinary person to understand the Gospels more fully, but has also provided a vivid model by which the process of gospel formation can be illustrated. The film clearly uses the Gospels as a major source of material. Yet it is evident that Gibson has adapted the scriptural material in dramatic ways.

He has selected certain parts of the scripture for use, synthesized other parts, and added material, all in order to better address his audience. Gibson's directorial effort to adapt the scriptures for his purposes is a useful parallel to the editorial efforts of the evangelists, who adapted their own sources to form the Gospels. Calling *The Passion* "the Gospel according to Mel" is more than clever commentary. It highlights a significant insight: the Gospels, like the movie, are not dry historical reporting but creative adaptations of the tradition *according to* Matthew, Mark, Luke, and John.

The movie can therefore be used to illustrate the formation of the gospel tradition. For example, in Luke 22:51 we are told that when Jesus was arrested and the ear of the high priest's slave was cut off in the scuffle, Jesus "touched his ear and healed him." In the movie Gibson expands upon this scriptural material. Although nothing more is said of the slave of the high priest in the scriptures, he continues as a character in the film. The experience of his healing causes him to break from the others who have come to arrest and abuse Jesus and eventually leads him to become a disciple. By this elaboration upon the scriptural text, Gibson communicates to the viewer how a contact with Christ has the power to save, to change lives.

A very similar impulse to proclaim the power of Christ can be seen in the editorial activity of Luke himself when he shapes the scene of Jesus's arrest. All four Gospels recount the cutting off of the ear of the high priest's slave. Luke alone reports that Jesus heals him. The healing, then, is best understood as an elaboration on the part of Luke that enabled him to make an additional statement to his audience. Luke shapes his Gospel in such a way that the healing and forgiveness of Jesus are emphasized. Luke alone states that the power of the Lord was with Jesus to heal early in Jesus's ministry (5:17). Throughout the Passion narrative, only Luke tells us that Jesus reconciles Pilate and Herod (23:12), forgives those who crucify him (23:34), and grants paradise to one of the criminals crucified next to him (23:39–43). Like Gibson, who builds upon the sources available to him, Luke expands upon the traditions handed down to him so that his readers might know that even in his Passion Jesus was healing and saving others.

Both by the interest it has generated and by the process by which it was made, *The Passion* can assist in educating Christians on the nature of the Gospels and the creative work of the evangelists. The film is a gift, then, to every pastor or educator who wishes to bring the advances of biblical research to popular awareness.

God: Describing the Inexpressible

In the media buzz that surrounded *The Passion,* many people encouraged their family and friends to see the film. This was certainly true in my parish. Yet as a pastor I was concerned. Many churchgoers are not moviegoers. I realized that many elderly members of our parish who had not seen a movie since *The Sound of Music* were eagerly making arrangements with friends to view *The Passion.* As an avid film buff myself, I was accustomed to the *Terminator–Kill Bill* world of the modern cinema. But how would these innocent groups of the uninitiated respond to what Roger Ebert has called the most violent movie ever made? I imagined hordes of sickened believers fleeing from theaters in shock and disgust.

I was wrong. Regardless of previous movie experience, the vast majority of my parishioners who viewed the film informed me that it had deepened their faith. Some even told me how it changed their lives, leading them to give up smoking or to reconcile with an estranged family member. Instead of becoming paralyzed by or fixated upon the violence on the screen, most people of faith seem to have left the theater with a deeper appreciation of God's love. How can this paradoxical outcome be explained?

The answer lies in the metaphorical language of faith. The Christian tradition has long taught that God is totally other and that no language or image can adequately express who God is. Thus all knowledge of God is by way of metaphor. Every statement concerning God must be limited to saying that God is "like" some aspect of human experience. When we say "God is good," we are really saying God is like the goodness we can comprehend but at the same time so much greater than any human goodness. When we say "God is Father," we are really saying that God is like a father but also that no experience of human fatherhood could ever capture who God is. The classic recognition of this mode of religious language was expressed in 1215 C.E. at the Fourth Lateran Council. The bishops gathered there agreed that if we are to speak of God, comparisons with created realities are necessary. However, they insisted that no similarity between Creator and creature can be expressed without implying an even greater dissimilarity. Therefore, whenever we speak of God we must employ some image from our own experience. We then use the familiar human reality as a springboard from which we "jump" to some appreciation of God. The jump is always greater than we can imagine.

What *The Passion* placed on the screen was the brutal torture and death of Jesus. However, many people of faith saw more than that.

Because they brought to the movie a faith conviction that Jesus was divine and that he chose to suffer for their sakes, they "jumped" from a cruel human crucifixion to an experience of divine love. The concrete and common experience of human suffering became for many the vehicle through which they might touch, if only in part, the immensity of God's love. The movement was instinctual to most, unreflective. As believers they were simply accustomed to the metaphorical language of faith.

On this faith level, criticisms by professional historians and medical experts are irrelevant. Clearly the historical Jesus could never have endured the amount of violence presented in the film. He would have been dead many times over before reaching Calvary. In Gibson fashion, the violence is "over the top." Yet when the film is apprehended as a metaphorical expression, the excessive violence becomes a powerful means to appreciate a divine love that is also, truly, "over the top." The physical depiction of violence is exaggerated; the divine love to which it points is not.

Thus millions left *The Passion* overcome not by horror at the violence but by thankfulness for the love it revealed to them. To the extent that the film has provided a metaphor to describe the inexpressible love of God, it functions as a vehicle for Good News.

: : :

The Passion has divided church communities and society at large. Some claim it is the most historical account of Jesus's Passion ever made; others insist it is significantly the result of Hollywood's imagination. One viewpoint boasts that it is the most valuable evangelical tool of the century; another warns that it can fan the flames of anti-Semitism. Devotional analysis relishes the idea that the film flows from Gibson's deep religious convictions; cynical analysis points to a marketing savvy that knows the power of generating controversy. Amid the swirl of opinions and motives, this essay has attempted to locate three ways in which pastors and scholars can use the film to promote the Gospel.

There is no doubt that if we seize these opportunities, we will do so on Gibson's terms. He had the vision to conceive of this film and the clout to thrust it into the mainstream of American culture. Those of us who deal with the scriptures on a professional basis might feel miffed that this story of faith, which serves as the basis of our daily ministry, has now risen to national attention through the influence of a Hollywood star with no biblical or ecclesiastical credentials. No doubt, were we given the opportunity to tell this story in our own way, we would present it very differently. But it is Gibson's game, and our only choice is whether or not we will play. I suggest we take the field.

After all, there is nothing new about proclaiming the Gospel in the midst of conflicting voices. The apostle Paul, writing to the Philippians, recognized that others in his community were preaching God's word in ways quite different from his own. He went so far as to question their motives, claiming that some spoke out of goodwill but others out of envy or rivalry. Yet his final assessment of the situation is revealing: "What, then, is important? Only this, that in any and every way, whether merely for show or sincerely, Christ is proclaimed. In that I rejoice" (Philippians 1:18, author's translation).

One can question and criticize many aspects of *The Passion,* but one cannot deny that through it Christ is proclaimed. Therefore, when asked how I respond to the movie, I stand with Paul. I rejoice.

3

Tragically Heroic Men and the Women Who Love Them
Tod Linafelt

Filmmakers have quickly learned what the poets seem always to have known: that nothing amplifies the pathos of the tragic, violent death of a man more than the presence of a woman who loves him. Of course the man must be heroic, and the woman is often his mother, sometimes his wife. Occasionally both wife and mother are there to grieve over the hero's fate, which is made more tragic by the women's very presence. Although it may be true, *rationally,* that the violent death of any man who has yet to live out a full life is tragic in equal measure to the violent death of any other such man (and here, by the conventions of the scene, we are talking about men, not men and women), it is simply not true *emotionally*. A warrior, a soldier, a victim—these categories or types become more real to us, become fleshed-out human beings, when we are reminded that they are not just warrior, soldier, or victim, not just a casualty of war, but also some mother's son, some woman's husband, and perhaps some child's father. So from Homer and the Bible to Steven Spielberg and Mel Gibson, we find a surprisingly consistent, if flexible, "type-scene" in which a handful of elements are employed to shape our response to the work.

Consider, to begin with, the first great epic poem of Western literature, Homer's *Iliad*. Near the end of the poem—in Book 22, after the Greeks and the Trojans have been at war for the better part of a decade outside the besieged city of Troy—comes the death of Hector, the Trojan champion, at the hands of Achilles, the champion of the Greeks.

> . . . as Hector charged in fury brilliant Achilles drove his spear
> and the point went stabbing clean through the tender neck . . .
> . . . The end closed in around him,
> flying free of his limbs
> his soul went winging down to the House of Death,
> wailing his fate, leaving his manhood far behind,
> his young and supple strength.
> *(Fagles translation)*

Hector's father, King Priam, and his mother, Hecuba, watch from the city walls as Achilles, "bent on outrage, on shaming noble Hector," drags the corpse behind his chariot. The emotional tenor of the scene is heightened as the poem recounts the anguished response of father and mother, devoting (in the Greek) fourteen lines to Priam and seven lines to Hecuba. But clearly the emotional climax of Book 22, where the reader feels most keenly the full impact of Hector's death, comes when the scene shifts to Hector's wife, Andromache, to whom are devoted nearly eighty lines of poetry as she first learns of and then laments the death of Hector.

Initially Andromache, "weaving at her loom, deep in the dark halls," has no inkling of the events outside the city wall. Planning for Hector's return from battle—for he has always returned before, why not this time as well?—she calls to her serving-women to prepare for the hero a steaming hot bath. But hearing the wails of grief coming from the walls, she begins to suspect the worst.

> what if great Achilles
> has cut my Hector off from the city, daring Hector,
> and driven him out across the plain, and all alone?—
> He may have put an end to that fatal headstrong pride
> that always seized my Hector . . .

Andromache is propelled by this thought, "her heart racing, her women close behind," to the ramparts, from which vantage point she witnesses

the "ruthless work" of Achilles as he desecrates Hector's corpse. The
book closes with Andromache keening a lament over the death of Hector
and over the imagined fate of herself and her small child.

This excerpt from the *Iliad* gives us all the elements of a recognizable
type-scene, one in which women are portrayed as waiting, in vain, for
their men to return from war. We note, to begin with, that the woman
or women are fundamentally *passive:* they wait, and they react. We
note, too, that the place of waiting for the women, especially for Andromache in this case, is clearly identified as the *domestic* realm, with
all its comforts ("And she called to her well-kempt woman through the
house / to set a large three-legged cauldron over the fire / so Hector could
have his steaming hot bath / when he came home from battle"), which
contrasts with the brutal male realm of combat ("poor woman, / she
never dreamed how far he was from bathing, / struck down at Achilles'
hands"). In this domestic realm there are hints, although rarely more
than hints, of a *female solidarity,* a counterpart of sorts to the more celebrated male solidarity in battle. So the poetry moves from Andromache
calling to her serving-women to prepare the hot bath for Hector to the
final line of Book 22: "Her voice rang out in tears and the women wailed
in answer." And we note, perhaps most important for the type-scene,
that *motherhood* is invoked to great effect. Thus, Hector is not just a
warrior or a casualty of war, but also a mother's son: "noble Hecuba /
led the wives of Troy in a throbbing chant of sorrow: / 'O my child—my
desolation! How can I go on living?'" Likewise, Andromache's grief is
deepest when she considers the fate of their child, Astyanax: "the boy
only a baby, / the son we bore together, . . . Now what suffering, now
he's lost his father." Twenty-five of the forty lines comprised by her
actual lament are devoted to Astyanax.

Before looking at how filmmakers have appropriated this type-scene
(especially in *The Passion of the Christ*), I want to consider one more
example from literature, in this case the Bible, in order to show how the
basic elements of the type-scene may be employed while the type-scene
itself is dramatically transformed. The passage quoted below is from
the book of Judges, chapter 5, and is a poetic celebration of the death
of Sisera, chariot commander of Israel's archenemies, the Canaanites,
at the hands of a woman named Jael. The previous chapter of Judges
recounts Israel's defeat of the Canaanite army, with Sisera fleeing the
battlefield on foot and arriving at the tent of Jael, and in that chapter a prose version of the following scene is given. But here it is in
verse form:

Most blessed of women be Jael,
    the wife of Heber the Kenite,
    of tent-dwelling women most blessed.
He asked water and she gave him milk,
    she brought him curds in a lordly bowl.
She put her hand to the tent peg
    and her right hand to the workmen's mallet;
she struck Sisera a blow,
    she crushed his head,
    she shattered and pierced his temple.
He sank, he fell,
    he lay still between her legs;
between her legs he sank, he fell;
    where he sank, there he fell, destroyed.

Out of the window she peered,
    the mother of Sisera gazed through the lattice:
"Why is his chariot so long in coming?
    Why tarry the hoofbeats of his chariots?"
Her wisest ladies make answer,
    indeed, she answers the question herself:
"Are they not finding and dividing the spoil?—
    A womb or two per man, per hero;
spoil of dyed stuffs for Sisera,
    spoil of dyed stuffs embroidered,
two pieces of dyed work
    embroidered for my neck as spoil?"

So perish all your enemies, O LORD!
    But may your friends be like the sun as it rises in its might.
(Judges 5:24–31, NRSV slightly modified)

Notice first the elements of our type-scene: the violent death of a warrior (in this case Sisera); the presence of a woman (Sisera's mother) waiting at home for news from the battle; the contrast between the domestic realm associated with women (both Jael in her tent with milk and curds and Sisera's mother gazing out the window of her house) and the violent realm of war; the hint of female solidarity in the midst of the domestic realm (here, as in the *Iliad*, taking the form of serving-women who surround and respond to their mistress); and finally, the importance of motherhood in establishing a female character's relationship to the slain man.

All the elements of the type-scene we saw in Homer are present, then, in this biblical poem. But how drastically they have been transformed! The focus is on the death of male warrior, but as commander of the Canaanites he is hardly meant to be a hero to the reader. His death comes not on the battlefield but, pointedly, in the domestic realm (the tent of Jael, with milk and curds at hand), and he is killed not by a stronger, fiercer warrior but by a woman (who is of course anything but passive).

Most striking about the scene, however, is the abrupt shift in setting from Jael's tent, where Sisera has just been violently and gruesomely dispatched, to the home of Sisera's mother, who wonders why her son is so late in returning from the battle. Does she, like Andromache, begin to doubt that the man for whom she waits will return from battle after all? If so, then the deeply ironic answer she gives to her own questions—that Sisera is delayed because he and his soldiers are each taking "a womb or two" as spoil, in addition to the elaborate dyed and embroidered cloth that will be brought home to the women who loyally wait—is wishful thinking, a desperate last hope to forestall the onset of grief. If not, then we are left at the end of the scene with a mother living in a counterfactual world, one in which a murdered son is still alive and expected home at any minute. In either case, the poignancy of the scene is keen, and the reader cannot help but feel sympathy for this newly sonless mother.

What makes the biblical poem so fascinating, and indeed virtually unprecedented, is not that the poet employs a type-scene he or she must surely have known would elicit the sympathy of the reader, but that this sympathy is elicited not on behalf of a beloved hero and his bereaved mother, but instead on behalf of the enemy and the enemy's mother. The poem is not by any means free of pro-Israelite propaganda, as we see in its final, triumphalist line. And if on first reading one cannot help but feel for Sisera's mother, on second reading one cannot help but be repulsed by her coarseness: she imagines Sisera and his soldiers are off raping Israelite girls—one or two apiece—before they come home for their hot baths, and the fate of these girls warrants only a half-line of thought before she moves to imagine in much more detail her share in the spoil. But the sympathy elicited by the first reading is surely not entirely supplanted by the moral reprobation elicited by the second. The result is a richly imagined, morally ambivalent perspective on the world, a perspective that the poet achieves by both using and transforming the elements of the type-scene.

Probably the clearest use of this type-scene in a modern film can be found in Steven Spielberg's World War II movie *Saving Private Ryan* (1998). Indeed, it is the theme of a mother waiting at home for news of her child who is at war that grounds the movie and drives its plot. After an extended opening sequence in which the viewer sees first the slaughter and eventually the triumph of American troops in the invasion of Normandy (and, as with *The Passion of the Christ*, much was made of the supposed realism of the violence in this sequence), we learn of a mother back in Iowa who is about to receive death notices for three of her sons on the same day. The type-scene itself is set off as a sort of interlude, as the movie shifts from the war in Europe to the iconic midwestern American family farm. As with Andromache and Sisera's mother, this (nameless) mother is initially unaware of the bad news she is about to receive, and like them she is a passive character, one who waits and reacts. Her place of waiting, in keeping with expectations, is the home; indeed, her thorough association with the domestic realm is indicated by the only activity in which we see her engaged, washing dishes. Looking up from her work she sees a military vehicle approaching on the dirt road, and we know that she has begun to suspect bad news as she haltingly walks to the front porch to receive the visitors. When she sees a priest exit the car along with a military man, she collapses in grief on the porch. The scene ends.

Brief as it is, the scene nonetheless serves as the ground for the entire movie. For matching it is a scene in which General George Marshall decides, after learning that this mother has only one remaining son who is himself missing in the French countryside, to authorize a mission in which a small group of men will attempt to find that son, Private Ryan, so that he might return to his mother. Thus, it is the mother waiting at home, though we see her only briefly and she never speaks a word on-screen, that justifies what otherwise seems a hopeless and even irrational mission (why risk the lives of eight men to save one?) and that haunts the rest of the film.

Steven Spielberg may be a skilled director in many respects, but subtlety is not his strong suit, and in addition to an overreliance on clichés it seems to me that the movie suffers from a lack of moral complexity. That is, the mother-waiting-at-home theme is used to great effect in order to evoke the viewer's sympathy not only for Private Ryan but for the other American soldiers, as the men talk throughout the movie about mothers (and other women) that they have left behind in going to war. But it is only the American soldiers who are portrayed as having mothers that love them. It is only the American soldiers who are humanized with any reference to a home life. Indeed, it is only the American soldiers whose deaths are slow and painful and tragic. The German soldiers, on the other hand, appear only as targets in rifle scopes, who go down immediately when shot and never die painfully or tragically. Logically we know, if we stop to think about it, that these German soldiers must also have women and families who love them and are waiting for news of them. But in the movie we are not given the chance to stop and think about it, and the by-now-archetypal image of a mother waiting for her son to return from war is used, effectively if simplistically, to focus the sympathy of American audiences on "our boys" and to deny any such sympathies for the enemy.

The foregoing discussion may help us to get at part of what has made *The Passion of the Christ* such a powerful experience for moviegoers. Like Spielberg, Gibson has intuited, whether consciously or not, the truth that lies behind this type-scene, namely, that an audience's reaction to the death of a male hero can be made more sympathetic with the presence of a mother and/or wife who grieves over that death.

We may note several of the key elements of our type-scene in *The Passion of the Christ*: the violent death of a male hero; the presence of women who love him (not only Mary his mother, but of course Mary Magdalene); the essentially passive nature of the women in relation to the death of the hero; the association of the mother with the domestic realm (note especially the idyllic flashbacks of Jesus with his mother); a strong female solidarity between the two Marys (who are first introduced as living together and spend the rest of the movie comforting each other), which functions as a counterpart to the exclusively male solidarity of Jesus and his disciples. There are also interesting divergences from the standard form of the scene: although the hero is killed violently by soldiers, he is not himself a soldier; and although they are essentially passive, the women do not wait for news about the hero, but rather follow him throughout the movie and observe his fate for themselves. And rather than the scene's being a discrete part of a larger narrative, the movie itself is one very long version of the scene, with the death of the hero and the concomitant reaction of the women constituting the entirety of the plot. On balance, though, it seems to me that we can recognize *The Passion of the Christ* as an example in the history of this type-scene that I have very briefly traced here.

What becomes clear when we view *The Passion of the Christ* in terms of this type-scene is that the strong emphasis on Mary the mother of Jesus (who is present throughout the movie, far more so than in the Gospels themselves, and through whose point of view, more than that of any other character, we as viewers see events unfold) is due not only to traditional Catholic theology, which highlights her role as the mother of God and features a long tradition of Marian devotion, but also to the type-scene's penchant for juxtaposing motherhood to the tragic death of a heroic man. That is, in addition to theological reasons, there are good generic and aesthetic reasons for Gibson's fascination with Mary.

Allow me to unpack that last sentence a bit. I confess to being less affected than most viewers by the violence done to the character of Jesus. For all the talk of the gritty realism of the violence, it too often seemed Hollywood-fake to me: there was too much blood, the flayed skin seemed to wrinkle unnaturally and betray itself as latex, and the wounds seemed too obviously the product of the makeup artist. But I found that I *was* moved by the presence of Jesus's mother as she witnesses his torture and death. Mary's presence engaged my imagination in a way that the character of Jesus did not. I have a hard time imagining what it would be like to suffer that sort of physical abuse. It registers as pain, pain, and more pain, but there the imagination stops. What would it be like to be beaten by whips? Painful. And to be beaten again by crueler whips? Painful again. And to have a crown of thorns pressed into one's skull? Painful. And to have spikes driven through one's hands and feet? More painful still. There is little more to be said. Perhaps this is the numbing effect that some viewers describe feeling in the face of unrelenting violence: one can flinch or cringe only so many times. Or perhaps it is the problem with too literal a representation; not a failure of the imagination, but rather that the imagination is never truly engaged. We are not asked to imagine what it might be like for a body to be beaten incessantly, we are simply shown. We are not asked to imagine complex emotions or motivations, but simply pain.

With Mary, though, things are different. If few of us, certainly in mainstream American audiences, will ever have to endure such extravagant violence, all of us have (or will have in the future) dealt with the death of loved ones. And although we are spared public whipping and crucifixion, there many other ways that such deaths can be painful and tragic. So it is not so much of a stretch to put ourselves in Mary's place as it is to put ourselves in Jesus's place. And if the death of Jesus loses much of its potentially tragic nature by the fact that he so resolutely accepts and even moves toward it, that does not make Mary's experience of losing a son less tragic.

The presence of Mary functions, then, in much the same way that the presence of mothers has always functioned in our type-scene: it makes the death of the hero more tragic, it humanizes the hero by showing his familial connections, and it both focuses the audience's pathos and makes it more complex (rather than imagining just pain or death, we are asked to imagine grief, loss, regret, etc.). The film's use of Mary is,

I think, both effective and affecting. It is hard not to be moved when viewing the tragic death of a hero from the perspective of his mother.

We have seen that the sort of automatic sympathy generated by this type-scene can be mobilized in the service of a morally complex view of suffering, death, and war (as in Judges 5) or in the service of a much simpler, essentially propagandistic, morality (as in *Saving Private Ryan*), with of course a possible continuum between the two. So perhaps the final question to ask here is, where does *The Passion of the Christ* fall on this continuum? I have my own opinions on the question, naturally, but I think I will leave it to the reader to generate his or her own response. Likely there is not one easy answer to the question, with certain parts of the film coming down in one place and other parts coming down elsewhere, and with certain viewers responding in one way and others in another way. But this is the nature of interpretation, whether one is interpreting literature, art, movies, or even a political speech. What is it that moves us? Why does it move us? For what purpose does the author (or director, or speaker, et al.) want to move us? And can we understand why others might respond differently? The work of interpretation lies in the sorting out of these questions, and that is a work that each of us must undertake for ourselves.

4

Contexts: Theology, Devotion, and Culture

Vincent J. Miller

Much of the conversation about and critique of Mel Gibson's *The Passion of the Christ* has involved issues of context. Some argue that by focusing only on the last twelve hours of Jesus's life, the film fails to communicate the significance of his death. Others respond that Christian viewers bring their own religious context to the film. Still others raise the issue of the impact of the film. Whatever Gibson's intentions, they fear it will incite the anti-Semitism historically associated with Christian Passion plays. This essay considers the contexts of both the creation and reception of the film. The meaning of works of culture such as film arises from the interaction between the symbols and meanings that their creators use in making them and the expectations, concerns, and sensibilities of those who receive them.

In this essay I will consider three contexts. The first is theological. The past four decades have been marked by profound theological debates concerning how best to understand the meaning of Jesus's death. The second context concerns the popular devotional practices through which Christian believers meditate on the Passion of Christ. I will examine traditional Catholic devotional practices as well as more recent evangelical forms of religious imagination. The third context is the "culture wars" in contemporary America. Although the theological and devotional contexts are important to the film's production and to its reception among viewers, the broader cultural debate about the film has tended to subordinate these factors to the concerns and code words of the debate between cultural conservatives and liberals.

We must begin by noting the particular history of Christian meditation on the Passion. It did not become a dominant focus of theology, spirituality, or art until the late medieval era. Surprisingly, a review of Christian art through the ages reveals that the Passion was not a major theme of painting or sculpture prior to the thirteenth century. Crucifixes, of course, date back much further (although not to the first centuries of the church). Early crucifixes, however, portray the Christus Victor, the risen Christ reigning from the cross, rather than the dying Christ suffering upon it as a victim of torture. The twelfth-century crucifix of San Damiano in Assisi, Italy, which was so formative in the spiritual vision of Saint Francis (a great popularizer of a Passion-centered spirituality) is an informative example. Christ's face is placid, noble, and loving; it does not display pain. There is blood, but it serves much more as a symbol of God's grace showering the church (represented by the apostles gathered beneath the cross) than as a realistic portrayal of suffering. It is not until the sixteenth century, with northern German works such as Matthias Grünewald's Isenheim Altarpiece, that graphic depictions of suffering become standard. As John O'Malley observes, the Sistine Chapel has no representation of the Crucifixion in Michelangelo's cycle of paintings depicting the life of Christ. O'Malley argues that a Passion-centered spirituality grew from the late Middle Ages through the modern era and became a dominant motif in Catholic spirituality in the nineteenth century ("A Movie, a Mystic, a Spiritual Tradition," *America,* March 15, 2004). Thus, like so much of what is understood to be "traditional" in Catholicism and Christianity, spiritualities focused on the Passion are only a few centuries old.

Theology and Jesus's Passion

If the past five centuries witnessed an ever-growing focus on the Passion of Christ as a touch point for theology and spirituality, the twentieth century was a time in which Christian theology undertook a major rethinking of its understanding of Jesus Christ (or, to use the technical term, Christology). This rethinking has produced tensions within the churches. Gibson's film is located on these fault lines.

In order to understand the present theological context, we must first consider its history. It is interesting that a Christian theme as central as how Jesus saves (soteriology) has not been a topic of firm doctrinal definition. Belief in the saving power of Jesus's death is, of course, quite ancient in the Christian tradition, but the details have long remained unspecified. Although the great Christological dogmas defined in the first five centuries of Christianity established that Jesus was both divine and human, often by arguing that such an understanding was necessary in order to understand that Jesus *could* save humankind, they did not define precisely *how* he does so.

The most influential thinker on this matter in Western Christianity—both Catholic and Protestant—is the eleventh-century archbishop Anselm of Canterbury. Anselm viewed the problem of salvation in terms of overcoming the offense against God caused by sin. Employing the feudal legal logic of his day, Anselm argued that since sin was an offense of finite creatures against an infinite God, the offense itself was infinite. This resulted in an infinite debt to God that had to be repaid. Humans, as finite creatures, could never atone for or offer "satisfaction" for this debt themselves, and God, out of justice, could not simply forgive it. This situation could only be remedied by one who was both divine and human—Jesus Christ. As human, he could act on behalf of finite creatures. As divine, he could satisfy the infinite offense of human sin against God. He did so by accepting death, which, as a sinless being, he did not have to suffer. Although it has been understood in different ways by different Christian denominations, this notion of satisfaction has dominated Christian theology in the West for the intervening nine hundred years.

This understanding of salvation focuses attention on Jesus's suffering and death. Jesus's Passion is *the* means by which humankind is freed from bondage to sin and death. For this reason, this theology marginalizes other elements of Jesus's life that other ancient theologies considered to be salvific. Many theologies have emphasized the Incarnation itself—the very act of God's becoming human—as a decisive moment in salvation history. Other Christian traditions focused on Jesus's saving work as a divine teacher. Thus, his public ministry—both his preaching and his actions—is part of his saving work. A third element, the Resurrection, was the most central and primordial focus of salvation. It, not the Passion of Christ, was the focus of Christian liturgy and piety until the late Middle Ages. In terms of the concerns of this essay, one could say that atonement theologies greatly narrow what is considered to be the relevant context for understanding Jesus's death. The Passion is the decisive saving act of God in cosmic history, in which Jesus offers himself freely to atone for the sins of all. The specific historical causes of his death are rendered unimportant; they are merely the proximate means for him to achieve his suffering and death.

It is precisely this broader context that the theological renewal of the past half century has attempted to recover. It was spurred to do so by two historical factors: the rise of historical critical biblical scholarship and the church's coming to terms with Christianity's central role in the history of anti-Semitism.

For more than two centuries scholars have applied the tools of critical historical scholarship to the Bible. Of the many results of these studies, one in particular is relevant to theological reflections on the context of Jesus's death. They clarified a point that is obvious in the Passion narratives but easily overlooked: Jesus was executed by the Roman authorities as a political insurrectionist. Whatever theological depth is read into the title displayed on his cross, "King of the Jews," and whatever salvific power is ascribed to his death, the historical Jesus was executed by an occupying imperial power anxious to quell political unrest.

The second factor that has influenced reflection upon the meaning of Jesus's death is the church's attempts to come to terms with its long and deep complicity in anti-Semitism, which grew through centuries of pogroms against Jews in Europe, often associated with Good Friday remembrances and Passion plays, to a horrific climax in the Nazi Holocaust. In light of this history, "Who killed Jesus?" and "Why did they do it?" became more than mere academic questions. For this reason, special attention has been given to historical research concerning the diversity and complexity of the first-century Judaism in which Jesus was formed and acted. Numerous groups and theologies contested for the allegiance of the various classes and for power in the politics of Roman occupation. Jesus was rejected not by "the Jews" but by specific factions among the Jewish religious and political authorities.

Twentieth-century theology broadened the focus of Jesus's saving work and thus placed the Passion within a broader context. Theologians recovered the ancient emphasis on Christ as saving teacher by considering the elements of his preaching and his prophetic actions that brought him into conflict with the religious and political authorities of his day. Although Jesus's preaching of the "Kingdom of God" was not directly political in the sense of calling for armed rebellion against the Roman occupiers and their Jewish collaborators, it was clearly and pointedly political in a way that threatened the status quo. The central term in his preaching the "Kingdom of God" was the Greek *basileia*, "empire"—

the same word the Romans used to describe their own empire. Jesus's association of this term with the God of Israel, a historically jealous and politically active deity if ever there was one, was certain to make Judea's Roman occupiers uneasy. Likewise, his preaching and practice of a kingdom where outcasts were not only welcome but preferred guests of God had an appeal for the lower classes that was bound to bring him into conflict with the religious authorities. Thus, Jesus's execution as a political criminal, his Passion, is intrinsically tied to the content of his preaching and ministry.

This perspective offers a different way to imagine Jesus's attitude toward his death. Atonement theologies tend to portray Jesus as playing out his role in a divine script wherein he must suffer and die to save the world. More recent theology picks up another thread, equally present in the Gospels—Jesus's interpretation of the opposition he encounters as opposition to the kingdom of God. Jesus of Nazareth is the one who remains faithful to God's Kingdom, even when it becomes clear that to do so will lead to his own demise. From this perspective, Jesus saves the world through his faithfulness as much as through physical suffering.

These attempts to incorporate broader context into understanding how Jesus saves humankind provide not just a more complex theology, but one that is more directly tied to discipleship. Atonement theologies tend to make discipleship as abstract as their portrayal of Jesus's suffering. Christians should submissively embrace the "crosses" that life brings and obediently accept their suffering as Jesus did. Such a view is always in danger of distorting Christianity into a masochistic celebration of human suffering. Suffering is often far from redemptive. It is simply the destruction of human persons. Such suffering should be challenged, not embraced. In *Passion of Christ, Passion of the World,* the Brazilian liberation theologian Leonardo Boff fears that such a view of suffering is profoundly ambiguous. It can serve to "mask over the injustice of the practices of precisely those who manufacture the cross and death of others" (3). It discourages people from seeking to identify and overcome the local causes of suffering and oppression.

Jesus's pursuit of God's cause of justice brought him into conflict with the powerful, and he suffered the fate that prophets encounter in a sinful world. So it remains today, as Gandhi, Martin Luther King, and Archbishop Oscar Romero have shown with their lives. From the perspective of this theology, following Jesus entails embracing one's cross—not because suffering is intrinsically redemptive, but because some suffering is tied to working for God's cause of justice in a world still burdened by the selfishness, fear, and violence of sin.

This account of various theologies of Jesus's Passion helps us locate Gibson's portrayal. He clearly employs an atonement or satisfaction theology to interpret the Passion. He draws from its assumptions by focusing on the final twelve hours of Jesus's life, with only limited flashbacks to his active ministry. Little attention is given to detailing the specific reasons the Romans and the Jewish authorities opposed him. Like the hyperconservative traditionalist movement of which Gibson is part, the film shows little interest in engaging the theological work of the past four decades. Thus, the film can be read precisely as an argument about context—that traditional atonement theologies provide all the meaning necessary to understand Jesus's Passion. Gibson signals as much with the epigraph that opens the film, which quotes Isaiah 53: "He was wounded for our transgressions, he was bruised for our iniquities; upon him was the chastisement that made us whole, and with his stripes we are healed." Contemporary Christologies might prefer the passage from Isaiah 61 that marks the beginning of Jesus's public ministry in the Gospel of Luke: "The Spirit of the Lord is upon me, because he has anointed me to preach good news to the poor. He has sent me to proclaim release to the captives and recovering of sight to the blind, to set at liberty those who are oppressed."

Devotional Practices and Religious Imagination

The theological context clarifies the film's understanding of the Passion. It also is helpful for understanding the anxieties of theologians and religious leaders about the film. Many religious believers, however, responded to the film not with suspicion, but with religious engagement. Whether or not they shared the film's theological assumptions, they related to it as a spiritual meditation. Thus Richard Alleva's insightful comment in his review for *Commonweal* (March 12, 2004) that "Gibson has elected to make a ritualistic work rather than a dramatic one, a cinematic equivalent of following the stations of the cross on Good Friday." Although his opposition between drama and ritual might deserve some questioning (drama is in fact one particular class of ritual), he provides insight into the interpretive context many bring to the film: various traditions of spiritual meditation upon the Passion of Christ. I will consider both Catholic and evangelical spiritual practices and their presence in the film and in its reception.

In his review, Alleva suggests the obvious Catholic ritual parallel: the Stations of the Cross. These are a form of devotional practice that evolved in the fifteenth century as a way of recreating pilgrimages to

Jerusalem: devotees would walk the path Jesus was believed to have taken on his way to the Crucifixion. Depictions of the stations can be found in most Catholic churches. They serve to aid meditation on fourteen moments in Jesus's journey, from his being condemned to death by Pilate to his being laid in the tomb. Clearly, Gibson's film employs much from this tradition, but curiously, it ignores elements of it as well. The film's Passion sequence ends with the penultimate station, Jesus being taken down from the cross. There is another devotional practice that explains more of the content of the film—the rosary.

The rosary originated as a practice that the illiterate laity could substitute for the monastic practice of reciting the 150 psalms over a four-week period. Originally the rosary involved saying the Lord's Prayer or Our Father 150 times. The rosary in its current form evolved from the melding of that practice with devotional texts that offered brief evocations of scenes from the Bible as the basis for meditative prayer. A rise in devotion to Mary led to the eventual substitution of the Hail Mary prayer for the Our Father as the primary repeated verse. The rosary is prayed by repeating the Hail Mary as a mantra ten times while meditating on one of fifteen mysteries. The mysteries are divided into three groups of five: the Joyful, the Sorrowful, and the Glorious. The Joyful mysteries are based on the events surrounding Jesus's birth and childhood and are drawn from the Gospel of Luke. They set up the implied perspective of the meditations: Mary's witnessing the mysteries that God works through her son. In the words of that Gospel: "She kept all these things, pondering them in her heart" (Luke 2:19). The Joyful mysteries emphasize the incarnation: the Annunciation of the angel to Mary that she will conceive a son by the Holy Spirit; her Visitation to Elizabeth, her cousin and the mother of John the Baptist; the Nativity or birth of Jesus; the presentation of the infant Jesus at the temple; and, finally, Joseph and Mary's finding of the young Jesus at the temple teaching the scholars. The Sorrowful mysteries involve Jesus's suffering and death. Their scenes are drawn from the Passion narratives: Jesus's agony in the Garden of Gethsemane, his scourging, the crowning with thorns, carrying the cross, and his Crucifixion. The Glorious mysteries begin with the Resurrection and continue with the key elements of the post-Resurrection narratives in the Gospels: Jesus's Ascension into heaven and the sending of the Holy Spirit to the disciples at Pentecost. The Glorious mysteries are rounded out with two Marian mysteries: Mary's Assumption into heaven and her coronation as queen of heaven and earth.

In contrast to Protestants, Catholics long had little or no tradition of reading the Bible. Nevertheless, Catholics had a widespread, shared, basic understanding of the key events in the gospel stories. They gained this knowledge through the rosary. Although the practice has declined, the canon of biblical events portrayed in the rosary still forms the basis of biblical literacy for many Catholics. Churches and schools are named for the various mysteries—Annunciation, Nativity, Visitation, and so on—and the mysteries continue to provide shared touch points for Catholic preaching.

Gibson uses this canon of key scenes in the film. He opens with the first of the Sorrowful mysteries, the agony in the garden, proceeds through the rest, and concludes by briefly invoking the first of the Glorious mysteries, the Resurrection. But the resonance goes deeper than merely invoking these canonical scenes. Gibson portrays Mary as the primary witness of Jesus's suffering, just as the rosary frames the mysteries of Christ's life within Mary's experience. She first appears in the film starting from sleep, distraught, as Jesus undergoes his agony in the garden and arrest. She is present at the trial scenes. She is similarly linked to Jesus mystically during his scourging and mockery as she cries out and presses her body against the stone floor beneath which the soldiers torture him. She follows him while he carries the cross, and she witnesses his Crucifixion. While the final scene at the foot of the cross is clearly Gibson's attempt to offer his own cinematic version of the pietà scene, it is also the final framing of the entire Passion cycle within Mary's gaze. The scene ends with her staring directly at the audience. Gibson draws many of these extrabiblical elements from the writings of two visionary nuns, Maria de Agreda and Anne Catherine Emmerich. Agreda's *Mystical City of God: The Divine Story of the Virgin, the Mother of God* follows the Marian structure of the mysteries of the rosary and is likely one of the primary connections between the rosary and Gibson's film.

Beyond illuminating some of the inspiration for the screenplay's choices, the rosary also gives insight into how Catholics might be inclined to approach the film. The rosary and spiritual practices like it train people to engage with portrayals of the key scenes of the Passion as the basis for spiritual meditation. As Alleva notes, the requirements of this form of engagement are very different from those for drama. Character development, plot, suspense, surprise—none of these are required for ritual engagement. The needs for a ritual film are less extensive: the basic symbols and elements of the scenes need only be presented in a recognizable and respectful fashion. The viewers synthesize them into their own religious understanding.

Reading the film in terms of the rosary provides the possibility of seeing a hidden theological context for its presentation of the Passion.

Whether or not the film presents the Incarnation as more than the prerequisite for the satisfaction Jesus worked on the cross, by quoting the Sorrowful mysteries, and giving such a prominent role to Mary, the film also invokes the more Incarnation-focused Joyful mysteries as well.

One of the problems hindering the renewed Christology from having a broader impact is that it has not been tied to popular devotional practices. John Paul II addressed this in 2002 by proposing five additional mysteries for the rosary. These "Luminous" mysteries focus on the life of the adult Jesus. The central mystery—his preaching of the kingdom of God—corresponds well with the theological concern to link Jesus's Passion with his preaching and ministry.

Evangelical Christians were enormously influential in the success of the film. To it they brought their own devotional and imaginative resources. Theologically, evangelicals by and large share in the Anselmian tradition, interpreting the Bible from the perspective of the history of its reception through Aquinas, Luther, and Calvin. Thus, their perspective on the Passion is similar to Gibson's. They also share his suspicion of the revisionist claims of contemporary theologians (although, insofar as these arguments are biblically based, evangelicals would be much more receptive to them than Catholic traditionalists). It is precisely the biblical literalism of evangelical Christianity that is relevant to the film. The film's hyperrealism can be understood as the visual equivalent of biblical literalism. Jim Caviezel's acting, his interpretation of Jesus, is nearly irrelevant to the film. He is merely the canvas on which the Passion narratives are depicted—literally so in the extended scourging scene. The film was widely lauded by evangelicals for depicting God's love for humanity. But this depiction was effected precisely by the graphic portrayal of Jesus's torture and execution. What mattered was not the artfulness of the film, but its claim to literally represent what Christ underwent in his Passion. Such a spiritual imagination is perfectly suited for cinema in these days of near-perfect special effects. Traditional Roman Catholic devotional meditations did not rely on such literal visual depictions. Art served to focus and inspire the imagination, but it did not provide the full content of meditation as does the all-encompassing spectacle of contemporary cinema. This is not to deny that the film was artful, or to argue that evangelical spiritual practices are less sophisticated or meaningful than traditional Catholic ones. It is merely to note that the film, when understood in the context of devotional art and practice, represents a new moment in that history—a new moment that is curiously compatible with the emergent form of Christian belief in this age.

The Culture Wars

This brings us to the final context relevant to understanding the film—
the so-called culture wars currently taking place within the United States.
In some ways, this might be the most important context for the film's
meaning. Yet the historical and theological subtleties are secondary to
the film's primary function as a marker in these culture wars. Those on
the side of cultural conservatism tended to support the film enthusiastically, whether they were Christian or not (witness Michael Medved).
Likewise, progressives and liberals tended to voice concern or openly
criticize the film. These ranged from the atheist cultural critic Christopher Hitchens's dismissal of the film as emblematic of all Christianity
("leave it to the psychos who like this sort of thing") to the more refined
concerns voiced by mainstream Jewish organizations, Christian theologians, and other religious groups. I will consider two elements of this
context: the claims for the historical accuracy of the film and the tension between the right to articulate one's own religious vision and the
responsibility for the broader social impact of that vision.

I have talked about the positive evangelical reception of the film in
terms of the claims made for its historical and biblical accuracy. Such
claims have accompanied the film from Gibson's first public discussion
of the project. He repeated them in his *Prime Time* interview with Diane
Sawyer: "Critics . . . don't really have a problem with me in this film,
they have a problem with the four Gospels. That's where their problem
is." Various essays in this book discuss how the picture of Jesus Gibson offers has been challenged by widely accepted historical research.
In the current culture wars, such critical reconsiderations are frequently
dismissed as instances of "revisionist history," a term implying that history is being reworked to suit the needs of a politically correct agenda.
It must be admitted, as critics pointed out long ago, that historical re-
constructions of Jesus tend to look a lot like the historians doing the
reconstruction. Yet such revisions are also driven precisely by a responsibility to the full truth of the Christian tradition, by the claims of the
past upon the present. What is most striking about the advocates of
the film's historical and biblical accuracy is how untroubled they have
been by the many nonbiblical events presented in the film. These include
Jesus's avant-garde genius in furniture design, his dramatic swing over
the side of the bridge while being held by the chains of the temple guard,
his mother and Mary Magdalene mopping up the blood from the floor
after his scourging, and the raven plucking the eye from the criminal
on the cross beside Jesus, not to mention the extended role given to

Satan. The Resurrection coda to the film provides the one perspective the Gospels refuse to offer: a spectator's view of the moment itself. Many of these nonbiblical elements are drawn from the writings of Agrade and Emmerich. Needless to say, the mystical visions of Catholic nuns are sources that evangelical Christians would view with great suspicion under normal circumstances. Yet in the context of the culture wars, it is not so much actual historical and biblical accuracy, but the *claim* of it that matters. Claims of accuracy function primarily to legitimate popular religious assumptions. Indeed, such claims serve to protect these assumptions not only from the erosions of secular modernity, but also from the challenge of correction by the fullness of the biblical evidence and the broader understanding of the Christian traditions.

The question of historical accuracy and the need for critical revision of traditions overlap with the second aspect of the culture wars relevant to the film: the tension between a community's right to express its beliefs and its responsibility for the social impact of those beliefs. This tension appeared in the concerns Jewish and many moderate and progressive Christian groups expressed about the film's anti-Semitic potential. The response of the Right took one of two forms. Many simply asserted that since anti-Semitism was a sin, a true telling of the gospel story could not be anti-Semitic. Others openly challenged the pluralistic assumptions of the critique. Religions should not be required to change their beliefs to suit the concerns of others. It is worth noting in this regard how the responses differed among more highly organized religious traditions. Both the National Council of Churches and the U.S. Catholic Bishops took the problem seriously and responded to the film with educational programs. The latter group provides a good illustration of the issue. As a highly institutional and international religious tradition, Roman Catholicism could not deny the historical connection between performances of the Passion and anti-Semitic violence. That is why it reissued its 1988 *Criteria for the Evaluation of Dramatizations of the Passion.* These go so far as to state that if it cannot be shown "beyond a reasonable doubt that the particular gospel element selected" will not "have the potential for negative influence on the audience," then it should not be used. In the abstract context of the contemporary culture wars, such an injunction sounds like extreme political correctness. But for a community that remembers its own complicity in anti-Semitic violence, it is an obligation in service to morality and faithfulness to its own tradition.

5

Mel Gibson's Lethal *Passion*

Bruce Chilton

The decor of my local cinema might make you think you were sitting in a suburban mall, but it lies next to rich fields in the Hudson River Valley. The spot mixes an idyllic view of the Catskill Mountains with the ambition of an uneven economy. An invitation to review *The Passion of the Christ* brought me to the Lyceum 6 in Red Hook, New York.

I have seen fine films there, but my expectations were not high for that Saturday matinee. Mel Gibson's claims of divine inspiration seemed unbalanced to me, and his critics sounded shrill. My assignment to review the film cornered me into doing what I had resisted for weeks. But I am glad I went. Nothing I had heard during the weeks beforehand, whether from Gibson's boosters or his detractors, prepared me for what I saw.

This film has nothing at all to do with authenticity or plausibility.

The Passion of the Christ is a medieval Passion play rendered in celluloid. Gibson shows considerable skill in making this transition, but he also indulges himself in some of Christianity's most hate-filled excesses. He has fashioned a blunt instrument of propaganda, edged with artistry, whose visceral power gives his film the potential of becoming his most lethal weapon of all.

Medieval Passion plays amused their audiences and at the same time drew them into the sufferings of Christ. These performances involved flights of fancy and superstition: perfidious Jews, assorted demons, buxom Magdalenes, gargoyle-faced demons, and the like. But they also offered vivid realizations of how Christ, by following the way of the cross, was transformed into his resurrected glory. The intent was to open the path of Christ to all believers as well as to entertain them.

That pattern of transformation was embedded in Christian theology long before the Middle Ages. In the fourth century Cyril of Jerusalem made Jerusalem a site of international pilgrimage by urging Christians to follow the way of the cross in the city where Jesus died. Cyril's Via Dolorosa was the roughest of approximations. Jerusalem had been destroyed and rebuilt several times between Jesus's death and the fourth century, and the holy sites that were identified then—and are venerated to this day, sometimes with calculated naiveté—are dubious in archaeological terms.

But archaeology aside, the cross for Christians has always been a symbol, not just a particular identifiable scaffold of execution. The exact location of Jesus's death is not a question on which mature faith will stand or fall. In the Gospels Jesus himself tells his followers, "If anyone would follow after me, let him deny himself, take up his cross, and follow me" (Mark 8:34). Even before Jesus's death, the cross features in his teaching as the emblem of suffering mortality. The Passion in the Gospels reflects the liturgical practice of Christians during the first century: they recollected Jesus's suffering during Lent as they prepared new believers for baptism and committed themselves afresh to walk in the footsteps of Christ. The Passion is at the heart of Christian identity, and Gibson is astute as well as pious—somewhat in Cyril's entrepreneurial style—in focusing on that.

The pace of Gibson's film is courageously slow throughout, so the viewer can see and reflect on the beautiful tableaux that are created: beads of Caravaggio-like images strung on a thread of relentless pain and violence. In medieval style, Satan plays a prominent role, calibrated so that the film embodies the doctrines of the Catholic Reformation (also known as the Counter-Reformation) to which Gibson is committed. The opening scene features Satan mocking Jesus in Gethsemane, ridiculing the belief that one man can suffer so as to expiate the sins of others.

Jesus's psychic pain is at its height at this point. In fact, the film reaches its climax within three minutes or so of its beginning; everything that follows the opening is denouement, excruciating but inevitable. This is a very brave dramatic gamble, a knowing reversal of Aristotle's principles of tragedy—and it succeeds. Gibson front-loads the drama of his film and then prolongs its impact by means of a calculated choreography of human pain. Jesus's hands tremble manically in Gethsemane, as they will later during his pitiless flogging, because the Savior of the Counter-Reformation knows everything that is going to happen to him in advance, and he has to embrace that pain as his personal payment for the sins of the world. Once that all-important transaction is accomplished, salvation is secure. If Jesus fails, all is lost.

This theory that Jesus personally and literally pays for the sins of the whole world has crossed over from the Counter-Reformation to become one of the "fundamentals" of Fundamentalism. That is presumably why Billy Graham and Jerry Falwell have taken up positions in support of the film, even though it frequently and blatantly contradicts the Gospels. Both of these famous preachers illustrate how far people who call themselves evangelicals have abandoned fidelity to the Bible as a principle. According to the logic of pop-culture Christianity, if you say you believe the right thing, you can make up the facts—and the Bible—as you go along.

The trouble with this medieval payment theory, championed by Anselm, archbishop of Canterbury (who died in 1109), is that any comparison between Christ's sacrifice and commercial value is deeply flawed. Why should God pay himself with his own Son's blood to forgive the sins of humanity? Can't God forgive what he likes, when he likes? What interest can the Creator of the universe have in payment at all? Sometimes this dubious transaction is portrayed rather as a bribe that gets Satan to let go his hold on Adam's progeny. That is the version of this bizarre teaching that Gibson prefers. It is a preference that links Fundamentalists and Catholics who rebel against Vatican II (concealing their rebellion under the label "traditional Catholicism").

In contrast, many Christians since the first century have worshipped Jesus in view of his *sacrifice* rather than any payment. In the classic theology of the church, Jesus's offering draws human admiration and divine favor into an unbreakable knot of love, not a calculation on a financial ledger. Medieval Christians cheapened this ancient teaching because they believed, following barbarian custom, that only fines could expiate wrongdoing. The modern trivialization of Jesus's sacrifice amounts to a theological free ride: if you believe enough, you get as a benefit what you could never have earned on your merits. Jesus pays, you collect the dividend.

Gibson makes Jesus the bait that will lure Satan into trading away his power. Satan will succeed in killing God's Son, but at the cost of his own authority. Jesus pays off the principal and the interest on humanity's primordial debt, robbing Satan of his due. As Jesus lies on the ground in his prayer to God in Gethsemane at the opening of the film, Satan releases a snake. It crawls lasciviously over the Savior's body, adumbrating the torture that is to come. But once he is on his feet again, Jesus crushes the snake's head and marches out to meet his tormenters. The bait has been taken, the climax attained, the bank of sin nullified; everything else that happens in the film is the screeching, flashing agony of the gates of hell shutting over Satan himself, mangling Jesus's body in the process.

That literally serpentine scene in Gethsemane is, of course, not in the Gospels, and its basis is light-years from history. Satan and his snake are imported from medieval imagination—Anselm's theory marinated in gothic fantasy and packaged in Hollywood's glitter. The scene represents an elaborate interpretation of Genesis 3:15, where Eve is told that her seed will bruise the head of the serpent who seduced her into eating the forbidden fruit and that the serpent will snap at her seed's heel. Jesus becomes Eve's son, undoing Adam's fall. That is allowed in a Passion play, as are all the scenes Gibson invents from legend and imagination. And as is the case in any Passion play, the artistry consists in what is invented, not in fidelity to the Gospels. History is beside the point.

Still, you do have to wonder why Gibson multiplies the Jewish tormenters of Jesus in scene after scene. Satan weaves in and out of their midst as Jesus is betrayed, mocked, beaten bloodier and bloodier, and denied. Satan's hairless face and head somehow seemed familiar to me, but I could not quite place him (or her, since the role was played by a woman) at the beginning of the film. I lost my curiosity about that for a while, diverted by the baroque portrayal of the violence inflicted on Jesus by the high priest Caiaphas and his colleagues.

Some commentators have seen this brutality as gratuitous, and it all does have the feel of the last few minutes of *Braveheart* stretched out over a couple of hours. But violence is crucial to Gibson's approach to making this film. He diverts our conscious attention with suffering. We are taken up with our own visceral responses to his bloody images while he delivers his message softly in his subtitles. He is both the good cop and the bad cop of an interrogation of the audience. The more concerned you are with controlling your own emotional and physical reactions to the beatings inflicted on Jesus, the less you notice about Gibson's portrayal of Jesus's Jewish tormenters. They are all opulently but darkly dressed; their interior corruption is manifest. If we have any doubt about the moral standing of the high priesthood, one of Caiaphas's colleagues wears an eye patch. *Ben-Hur* meets *Pirates of the Caribbean*.

These vivid images really do tip into camp from time to time. Gibson comes up short in his bid to achieve Inquisitorial stature. Judas hangs himself by taking the rope off a dead and rotting donkey, a rope big enough to pull a barge. He ties himself to a tree overhanging a cliff. I was left wondering how he got up there: did Satan levitate him? Caiaphas seems to sleepwalk through the action, a stock villain driven by no specific complaint against Jesus, miming hatred, finally whimpering in his destroyed temple after the Crucifixion, when an earthquake—the cherry on a big cake of pseudo-history—destroys the place.

Herod Antipas wears a wig and has kitted out his palace as a brothel. One of his hookers—a black woman—casts a sympathetic look at the battered Jesus in the only gesture toward political correctness that Gibson allows himself. Pilate, on the other hand, is a wise but ineffectual ruler, who not only asks, "What is truth?," as he does in John's Gospel (18:38), but takes up the question in a private seminar with his wife.

Pilate's wife plays a pivotal role in this film. She tells Pilate right off the bat that Jesus is a "holy" man and does what she can to intervene in the proceedings against him. When she can't stop the execution, owing to Caiaphas's manipulation of the crowds with the Pharisees (with whom he is supposed to be allied, despite being a high priest and not of the Pharisaic party), she hands out big sheets of linen to Jesus's mother and Mary Magdalene. That way, they can mop up huge quantities of blood after Jesus's scourging. Likewise, Veronica is later placed on the Via Dolorosa to have her famous piece of linen imprinted with the bloody image of Jesus's face. Reliquaries of nails and a crown are also conveniently left by the cross, so that they can be "discovered" during the fourth century. The film could be described as a prolonged advertisement for reliquary kitsch.

By the time Gibson's Jesus finally died, the people sitting near me had been reduced to loud weeping and gasping on several occasions, so effective are his violent images. Some in the audience even stopped eating their popcorn and drinking their Cokes for a little while. Jesus, however, pursues the resolve forged in the crucible of Gethsemane, so they can go back to eating and drinking while he is raised from the dead.

At the Resurrection Jesus stands apart from the altarlike stone on which he has been laid in his monumental tomb. The burial, by the way, completely eliminates the role of Joseph of Arimathea, which is central in the Gospels: an opportunity to portray crucial sympathy by one of Jesus's contemporaries in Judaism is squandered. In any case, Jesus's immaculate linen shroud trembles in the breeze, awaiting shipment to Turin. He stands—his face, butt, and punctured right hand in profile. He marches out of the tomb much as he marched out to his tormenters in Gethsemane, but to the martial beat of a drum. He has paid, and it all sounds very much as if someone else is about to pay, as well.

As a Passion play this film is a hokey but respectful meditation on the death of Jesus. The music sustains the stately pace through what amounts to the Stations of the Cross that Cyril developed in Jerusalem and that Christians still use for devotion today. The score is derivative, sounding faintly like some of the music for *Gladiator*, but it comports well with the film's tableaux and occasional bursts of violence and splattered blood. Acting in this case requires no comment, because there is no room for it in between static images and violent outbursts, most of which involves flaying latex skin.

The camerawork is more successful in effecting the aim of a Passion play. We look on the action, appalled and uplifted by the various characters. The blind hatred of Caiaphas, the crazed disorientation of Judas, the mute betrayal of Peter, the dithering goodwill of Pilate, the magnificent loyalty of Jesus's mother, the smoldering devotion of the Magdalene, the chaste quasi-conversion of Pilate's wife, the sadistic pleasure of the Roman soldiers, the clueless cross-bearing of Simon of Cyrene all reflect and heighten our own responses. We ask, as we should, where we would be and where we are in this action. As the film's deliberate rhythm proceeds, Jesus himself looks up from his agonies to fix his gaze on the characters and on us, so as to underline that question.

As I looked into his face and his latex wounds, however, I found myself more and more distant from this Jesus and his torments. The action finally became so removed from any reality that the film lost its way. The power of this Passion play is dissipated and finally undermined by its claim to authenticity. Much has been made of the "Aramaic" spoken in this film alongside Latin. In fact, the Semitic-language scenes are a mixed brew of Aramaic, Hebrew, and Syriac, with grammatical mistakes in all three. The Latin is pretty good, but to have Jesus conversing learnedly with Pilate in that language is just too funny for words. There is not a word of Greek in this film, not even in the *titulus* on the cross, although John 19:20 specifies that the charge against Jesus was written in Greek as well as in Latin and Aramaic.

But this mistake is no lapse. Gibson uses the conversation between Jesus and Pilate to preview the future that the Counter-Reformation desired: a Latin-speaking extension of the Roman Empire into the world of spirit. Pilate and Jesus together, and then Pilate with his wife, provide the only moments of tranquil power in the midst of mob violence. What is wrong with Pilate in this portrayal is not that he is corrupt and violent and anti-Semitic (all of which is historically true), but that he lacks backbone. Jesus is there to give him that, and Pilate's wife is present to help with the transplant. The fact that prefects of Pilate's lowly rank were not permitted to bring their wives with them on postings is as lost on Gibson as the simple truth that, as prefect, Pilate lived in Caesarea Maritima, not Jerusalem.

Only Latin counts, not Greek—only Roman Catholicism, not Orthodoxy. Protestantism's concern for biblical accuracy does not worry Gibson, and in his view Roman sympathy outweighs Jewish sympathy in importance. There are, to be sure, Jews who care for Jesus, chiefly his mother and the Magdalene. Dressed as peasant versions of Dominican sisters, they both have unique insight into Jesus.

Jesus's mother is with him in Nazareth in a truly peculiar flashback, in which Jesus, pottering in his shop like a suburban householder in Los Angeles, completes a handsome but unusually high table in a Swedish contemporary style. He predicts he will make chairs tall enough to make it serviceable, prophesying the use of kitchen tables around which his followers will presumably one day sit and discuss this film with admiration.

The Magdalene does not have big breasts, but a pouty mouth signals her earlier profession: she is the woman taken in adultery in John 8, and her big earrings mark her as a prostitute. This identification, of course, contradicts what is said about both Mary Magdalene *and* the woman taken in adultery, a triumph of "pious" imagination over the biblical text. This synthetic Mary Magdalene is nearly stoned by a ring of people carrying rocks, much as in the stoning scene in *Monty Python's Life of Brian,* rather than by being thrown from a cliff and crushed with a large rock, a method both the New Testament and the Mishnah describe.

When Jesus is about to be crucified, the Jewish crowd does turn back in his favor, if inarticulately and half-heartedly, and the beloved disciple John is sympathetically portrayed. But on balance the power of the Romans makes their support of Jesus more magnetic than Jewish sympathy, and even one of the sadistic soldiers who tormented him converts at the end, awed as much by Jesus's mother as by Jesus himself.

In the scourging scene, I finally realized who Satan reminded me of. Although the Gospels place this scene in the praetorium, Gibson locates it in a square with easy access for disciples, high priests, and the two Marys—the virgin and the whore—to mop up copious quantities of Jesus's blood. Satan makes his way among Jewish high priests and sadistic Roman soldiers. This time alone among his several cameo

appearances, Satan is carrying a child, a truly ugly tot with a face somewhat reminiscent of the children who taunt Judas prior to his suicide,
seeming sometimes to be demons. The child is bald and hairless, his head
shaped like Satan's.

I was transported to the *Austin Powers* series my sons are fond of:
Dr. Evil and Mini-Me incarnate, assisting at the torture of Jesus. In consideration of the weeping popcorn chompers around me, I did not laugh
aloud. But reflective silence only confirmed my conviction that this is the
funniest Jesus movie since *Monty Python's Life of Brian.*

Monty Python tried to be funny, and succeeded, because *Brian* was
not about Jesus at all, but about Brian. Putting this Cockney hero into
situations like those Jesus faced, under obviously phony historical circumstances, makes for brilliant parody. In Gibson's case, the parody
is equally powerful, but pathetically unintentional. By mixing together
the genre of the Passion play with the pretension of historical accuracy,
Gibson has inadvertently made his Passion play into pious vaudeville.

Claims that this film reflects the Gospels or history, or that it even
comes close, are cynical when they are not hopelessly ill informed. Critics who treat *The Passion of the Christ* seriously have confused their profession with self-promotion. Had this film been directed by Mel Brooks
instead of Mel Gibson, we would have had something to watch with
pleasure. But Gibson's *Passion* is libelous farce, poor art, inept theology,
and an incentive for credulous viewers to confuse Christian faith with
hatred. After I went home, I watched *Die Hard* with my younger son
and felt morally restored. If I am going to be entertained by violence, I
prefer it served like a dry martini: straight up, and without any pretense
of nutrition.

6

Jewish Crowd and Roman Governor

John Dominic Crossan

John was an eyewitness—is that not history? Matthew was there, is that not
history? The historians that have come since are somehow given more credibility
than Luke, and Mark who were right [there]. . . . In fact, these four testimonies
are what all Christians base their faith on, are these four testimonies. This is
what it's based on! If you don't take it from there, what do you got? That's it.

Mel Gibson, from an interview by Raymond Arroyo,
"The World Over Live," *Roman Catholic Eternal Word Television*,
January 23, 2004

I focus here on one single word in the New Testament stories about the death of Jesus and on how it is interpreted
in Mel Gibson's film *The Passion of the Christ*. I leave
aside for now much larger problems with his decision to
increase the brutality of the already extremely brutal 1833
script *The Dolorous Passion of Our Lord Jesus Christ according to the Meditations of Anne Catherine Emmerich*,
or his cinematic creation of religious pornography in his
film's rapturous hymn to a savage God. But I start over
forty years ago at Oberammergau because the experience
of its Passion play has always been constitutive for my
own response not only to the danger of Passion drama
but also to the meaning of "gospel truth."

Problem of the Crowd

In 1960, while doing post-doctoral study at Rome's Pontifical Biblical Institute, I was sent by my religious order as priest-chaplain with a group from the United States on a pilgrimage to various Roman Catholic shrines across Europe, including Fatima, Lourdes, Lisieux, Rome, and even Monaco for Grace Kelly! The Oberammergau Passion Play, that year in its second postwar production, was unchanged since Hitler saw it twice in 1930 and 1934, before and after becoming chancellor of Germany. It has been performed on special centenaries and every decade since 1634 in avowed gratitude for the village's deliverance from plague. About it, Hitler said admiringly: "There one sees in Pontius Pilate a Roman racially and intellectually so superior, that he stands out like a firm, clean rock in the middle of the whole muck and mire of Jewry."

I have always recalled one most striking detail from that day—apart from how cold it was in a five-thousand-seat theater open above the stage to the late-September air of the Bavarian mountains. That detail was the crowd shouting for Jesus's Crucifixion before a reluctant Pilate. And "crowd" (*ochlos*) is the focus-word of this article.

I knew, of course, the story as text, but something new happened when I first saw the story as drama. The play took about six hours, split on either side of a long lunch break. At the start, on Palm Sunday in early morning, I watched a huge crowd, with children conspicuously present, reenact the (anti?)triumphal entry into Jerusalem. At the end, on Good Friday in late afternoon, I watched that exact same crowd, overflowing the huge stage at Oberammergau, reenact the scene before Pilate. First they shouted for Jesus, and then they shouted against him. Palm Sunday was all enthusiastic acceptance, but Good Friday was all savage rejection. No explanation was given for that change of attitude. Whatever one wishes to say about the story as either history or Gospel, it was inept as visual drama.

I do not hint for a second that my lifelong study of the historical Jesus was consciously generated by that experience, although such logic is always beguiling as one looks backward after the fact. I do know that my first scholarly journal article was titled "Anti-Semitism and the Gospel" (*Theological Studies,* 1965) and that the crowd scene before Pilate was one of its major points. I had long ago lost my offprint of that article but reordered it from DePaul's Interlibrary Loan Department when Mel Gibson's film appeared. In the section titled " 'The Mob' at Jerusalem during the Passion," I concluded that "the evidence explicitly and definitely points against any representative Jerusalem crowd shouting for

Jesus's death; it is quite possible that the crowd before Pilate was interested primarily in Barabbas as a rebel hero, and in Jesus only insofar as
He became a threat to Barabbas' release." I still hold to that position
today and, in what follows, intend only to spell it out in even greater
detail. But first I return to Oberammergau.

In 2000 I went to Oberammergau once again. Was it improved by the
many changes requested by both American Jewish and Roman Catholic
groups? Yes and no. *Yes,* because, for example, that infamous verse in
Matthew 27:25 where "the people as a whole answered, 'His blood be
on us and on our children!'" is now completely absent. The question
is, how many viewers hear its absence or note its omission from their
German or English scripts? And *no,* because, even in the new script,
which allows some argumentation for and against Jesus among both
authorities and crowds, that distinction is totally lost in the staging as
drama. Who can see, hear, or count in the shouting crowd before Pilate
that three groups (Crowds A, B, and C) shout forty-one times against
Jesus while one group (Crowd D) shouts three times for Jesus? I could
do so only because I had studied the script. That improved 2000 version
only served to emphasize for me the problem of the "crowd" as the core
problem of any Passion story, play, or film. It is also, of course, a core
problem for any thoughtful reading of the New Testament Passion text
itself.

In what follows I do not raise any questions about radical historicity,
about whether the open paschal amnesty, the Jesus-Barabbas choice, the
shouting crowd, and the reluctant Pilate are Markan parable or Roman
history. For here and now I focus only on the narrative logic of the gospel
story and ask this simple question of Mel Gibson as director: Granted
that you have collapsed four Gospels into one, shortened that one to
execution only, and interpreted that execution as *passio* or suffering,
how did you decide the identity, purpose, and number of that crowd
before Pilate? If you reply that the "crowd" is straightforward gospel, I
rephrase my question.

In reading the text, you can leave undecided what number makes
a "crowd," but in staging a play or directing a film, you must decide
how many extras to employ (fig. 2). How was that decision made, and
why was it made in that way rather than in some other way? The term
"crowd" is obviously relative to time and place, situation and occasion.
If we say, "Two's company, three's a crowd," we know the precise situation involved. If we say, "There was a crowd of dignitaries in the Oval
Office when the bill was signed," we can probably guess it involved
fifteen to twenty people. If we say, "The crowd jumped to its feet and

FIGURE 2 The crowd before Pilate and Jesus in Jerusalem. Still from *The Passion of the Christ* (2004).

roared its approval," we could mean 75,000 people at a football game. Situation rules the identity, purpose, and number of any "crowd."

Identity of the Crowd

What is that "crowd" before Pilate? The Oberammergau play begins on Palm Sunday morning, but the Gibson film begins on Holy Thursday night. It lacks, therefore, that entire sequence of preceding days. Mark's Gospel, by contrast, indicates each of those days quite separately and repeatedly notes that the "crowd" is so much in favor of Jesus that the high-priestly authorities are unable to move lethally against him. Jesus, in other words, is saved by that crowd's supporting presence.

Sunday starts in Mark 11:1. "Many people [*polloi*] spread their cloaks on the road, and others spread leafy branches that they had cut in the fields. Then those who went ahead and those who followed were shouting, 'Hosanna! Blessed is the one who comes in the name of the Lord! Blessed is the coming kingdom of our ancestor David! Hosanna in the highest heaven!'" (Mark 11:8–10). That Palm Sunday enthusiasm is noted again on each of the three succeeding days.

Monday starts in 11:12. Even after Jesus's action in the temple, "the chief priests and the scribes . . . kept looking for a way to kill him; for they were afraid of him, because the whole crowd [*pas ho ochlos*] was spellbound by his teaching" (Mark 11:18).

Tuesday starts in Mark 11:20. The tension between those who are for Jesus and those who are against him is reiterated that day as a threefold climax. First, after Jesus praised John the Baptist, "they were afraid of the crowd [*ochlon*], for all regarded John as truly a prophet" (11:32).

Next, when "the chief priests, the scribes, and the elders . . . realized that he had told this parable [of the Evil Tenants] against them, they wanted to arrest him, but they feared the crowd [*ochlon*]. So they left him and went away" (12:12). Finally, "the large crowd [*polus ochlos*] was listening to him with delight" (12:37).

Wednesday starts in Mark 14:1. "The chief priests and the scribes were looking for a way to arrest Jesus by stealth and kill him; for they said, 'Not during the festival, or there may be a riot among the people [*tou laou*].'" In other words, they have given up their plan to eliminate Jesus because the crowd is too much on his side. But, of course, since Jesus will depart at the end of the festival, that means they have given up completely. And that is precisely why Judas is so important. (I speak again within narrative logic and bracket for historical actuality.) "Then Judas Iscariot, who was one of the twelve, went to the chief priests in order to betray him to them. When they heard it, they were greatly pleased, and promised to give him money. So he began to look for an opportunity to betray him" (Mark 14:10–11). It is Judas who tells them that Jesus can be taken at night away from the crowd and, presumably, swiftly eliminated before the crowd's support can be mobilized. That, of course, is why the Gibson film starts with a nighttime arrest and an apostolic traitor. Does no viewer ever wonder why those elements were necessary as the start of the film? But if Mark 11–14 emphatically insists on that pro-Jesus "crowd," whence comes his anti-Jesus "crowd" in Mark 15? Are we speaking of the same "crowd"?

Purpose of the Crowd

What is the purpose of that "crowd" before Pilate? Watch very carefully the sequence of verses in Mark.

First, Mark says that Pilate had established an open Passover amnesty: "at the festival he used to release a prisoner for them, anyone for whom they asked" (15:6). The word "open" means that the crowd rather than the governor chose the individual to be released.

Second, Mark notes that "a man called Barabbas was in prison with the rebels who had committed murder during the insurrection" (15:7). They were, in other words, Jewish freedom fighters, like that Scottish hero of *Braveheart* and that American hero of *The Patriot* from the days when Mel Gibson glamorized rather than caricatured such individuals. In The *Passion of the Christ*, however, Barabbas is depicted as a loutish buffoon, which in dramatic terms serves to increase the savagery of the crowd in preferring him to Jesus.

Third, "the crowd came and began to ask Pilate to do for them according to his custom" (15:8), and, since the choice was theirs to make, we must presume that they themselves asked for Barabbas. This three-verse Markan sequence is quite clear. The "crowd" comes up to request freedom for Barabbas; they come, that is, *for* Barabbas and not *against* Jesus.

Fourth, confronted with the unwanted possibility of Barabbas's release, Pilate offers them Jesus instead. "He answered them, 'Do you want me to release for you the King of the Jews?' " (15:9). That makes good narrative sense. He knew Barabbas was a violent rebel and had therefore rounded up his followers with him in 15:7, and two of them would die beside Jesus in 15:27 (in the Greek, as rebels, not thieves). He also knew that Jesus was a nonviolent resister and therefore made no attempt to round up or execute his followers. Pilate, in other words, had got it exactly correct from a Roman administrative viewpoint. He may have considered Jesus innocent but, more likely, he simply considered Barabbas the far more dangerous criminal and wished to release, if possible, the lesser threat.

In summary, Mark has two quite separate uses of "crowd." One is that pro-Jesus "crowd" throughout chapters 11–14 and the other is that directly pro-Barabbas and only indirectly anti-Jesus "crowd' in 15:6–9. But, if all indications are that the former crowd is quite large (since it can deter high-priestly action), how big is that latter crowd before Pilate?

Size of the Crowd

Whether one takes Mark's Barrabas/Jesus story as fictional or factual, parabolical or historical, how big should we imagine his "crowd" to be? Granted, of course, that "crowd" size is always relative to the situation and occasion under discussion, how many people were in it? Three background factors facilitate decision on that crucial point.

First, at any of the major feasts thousands of Jews concentrated in a rather small area in and around the temple. But at Passover they did so to celebrate deliverance from ancient Egyptian bondage while under present Roman control. From an imperial viewpoint, the atmosphere was that of a tinderbox, the toleration for disturbance was zero, and the governor came up from Caesarea on the coast to ensure order in Jerusalem and the temple.

The historian Josephus, for example, records two serious riots during Passover. One, described in *Jewish War* 2.10–13 and *Jewish Antiquities* 17.213–18, took place in 4 B.C.E. when the "vast crowd pelted with stones" the soldiers of Archelaus, son of Herod the Great, and he "let loose upon them his entire army," which, "falling unexpectedly upon the various parties busy with their sacrifices, slew about three thousand of them and dispersed the remainder among the neighbouring hills." The other, described in *Jewish War* 2.224–27 and *Jewish Antiquities* 20.106–12, took place under the procurator Cumanus between 48 and 52 C.E. when the pilgrims, after a soldier's crude insult, "picking up stones, hurled them at the troops." The result was a massacre: "such violence was used as they pressed round the exits that they were trodden under foot and crushed to death by one another; upwards of thirty [*or:* twenty] thousand perished, and the feast was turned into mourning for the whole nation and for every household into lamentation."

Second, two contemporary Jewish authors portray Pilate with characteristics that flatly contradict the equivalent ones in the Gospels. One is his method of dispensing justice, the other is his method of handling crowds.

The philosopher Philo's *Embassy to Gaius* describes Pilate as "a man of a very inflexible disposition, and very merciless as well as very obstinate." It speaks of "his corruption, and his acts of insolence, and his rapine, and his habit of insulting people, and his cruelty, and his continual murders of people untried and uncondemned, and his never ending, and gratuitous, and most grievous inhumanity." Pilate was "exceedingly angry, and . . . at all times a man of most ferocious passions" (301–3). He is Philo's poster boy for bad governors.

Josephus records, in both his *Jewish War* 2.172–77 and *Jewish Antiquities* 18.55–62, that an unarmed crowd came before Pilate's tribunal at coastal Caesarea to demand that he remove from Jerusalem the pagan images on his military standards. He surrounded them with soldiers "three deep," and they were saved from slaughter only by a willingness for martyrdom. But the next time they tried the same nonviolent resistance, Pilate had them infiltrated by soldiers dressed "in Jewish garments, under which they carried clubs," and "many of them actually were slain on the spot, while some withdrew disabled by blows." Finally, according to *Jewish Antiquities* 18:85–95, the Syrian governor, Vitellius, removed Pilate from office and sent him back to defend himself before the emperor Tiberius in Rome. You can probably guess for what offense. His soldiers attacked a Samaritan crowd on Mount Garizim. The high priest Caiaphas, by the way, was removed from office at the same time; that ended his ten-year collaboration with Pilate, a collaboration ultimately judged unwise even by Roman imperial interests.

Third, the purpose of that Markan crowd was to request amnesty for one whom they may have considered a heroic freedom fighter but whom Pilate considered a murderous bandit. In that situation, they themselves could easily have been arrested at least as Barabbas's sympathizers if not as his actual followers. Recall, for example, that in Mark 15:43 (only), Joseph of Arimathea needed "courage" even to request the dead body of Jesus from Pilate. That "crowd" needed to appear peaceful, respectful, and very, very polite.

When, therefore, I put together the dangerous context of Passover, the volatile character of Pilate, and the hazardous purpose of the request, my best historical reconstruction concludes to a Markan "crowd" (*ochlos*) of definitely less than a dozen people. But it is also absolutely clear that when later Gospels copied their Markan source, they both changed the purpose and expanded the size of that original (very small) crowd.

Change of the Crowd

Notice how both Luke and John retell Mark so that they come up *against* Jesus rather than *for* Barabbas. In Luke, the Markan sequence is reversed so that "the chief priests and the crowds [*ochlous*]" in 23:4, or "the chief priest and the rulers and the people [*laon*]" in 23:13, are already there accusing Jesus. Watch the sequence: "Then they all shouted out together, 'Away with this fellow! Release Barabbas for us!' (This was a man who had been put in prison for an insurrection that had taken place in the city, and for murder.) Pilate, wanting to release Jesus, addressed them again; but they kept shouting, 'Crucify, crucify him!' " (23:18–21). Similarly, in John, Pilate himself raises the issue of amnesty: " 'But you have a custom that I release someone for you at the Passover. Do you want me to release for you the King of the Jews?' They shouted in reply, 'Not this man, but Barabbas!' Now Barabbas was a bandit" (18:39–40). You could scarcely tell from those changes that the crowd came up originally *for* Barabbas and not *against* Jesus and became anti-Jesus only when Pilate tried to switch prisoners on them.

Increase of the Crowd

You can see the process of expansion most clearly in Matthew. He starts by accepting Mark's "crowd" (*ochlos*) in 27:15, but it becomes "crowds" (*ochlous*) by 27:20. He reverts to "crowd" in 27:24, then expands it exponentially to "all the people [*laos*]" in 27:25. And, of course, as everyone knows, John changes all those options to "the Jews" (18:31,

36, 38; 19:7). Those expansions, however, must only be read and should only be understood to mean: *all the Jewish* (John) *people* (Matthew and Luke) *in that very small crowd* (Mark).

I submit that, apart completely from any questions of ultimate historicity, the narrative logic of Mark and the sequential changes in Matthew, Luke, and John demand that anyone dramatizing a Passion story based on "the Gospels" ask inaugurally those basic questions about the identity, purpose, and size of the crowd before Pilate. If a director decides to fill the streets of ancient Jerusalem and the screens of our modern cinemas with a Jewish crowd totally and inexplicably against Jesus, what inferences will global audiences take from that presentation? That all Jews of Jerusalem, of Israel, of the Roman Empire, or of all time and place were and/or are against Jesus?

The question is not about Mel Gibson's father or Mel Gibson's faith. The question is not even whether he is anti-Semitic or his film is anti-Semitic, although, comparing it with Oberammergau's classic play, his film heightens exponentially that contrast between the noble Aryan Pilate and the ignoble Jewish crowd. Hitler would certainly have applauded the Gibson Passion film even more enthusiastically than he did the Oberammergau Passion play, and for the same anti-Semitic reason. Nonetheless, the question is this: as a conscientious Christian who knows full well the theological anti-Judaism and ethnic anti-Semitism that have arisen from the Passion story across two millennia, what did Mel Gibson do to cauterize that continuing venom in making this film? Does the film evince careful responsibility or depraved indifference to its possible or even probable results?

7

Gibson's Mary Magdalene

Jane Schaberg

Not much to say, at first glance, and even on second viewing, about the portrayal of Mary Magdalene in *The Passion of the Christ*. The legend of her as a beautiful, reformed sexual deviant is alive and well. The apocryphal texts are ignored. The Christian Testament passages concerning her at the empty tomb are omitted from the script, and her presence during *The Passion* is overshadowed by that of Mary the mother of Jesus. My book *The Resurrection of Mary Magdalene: Legends, Apocrypha and Christian Testament deals with* three aspects of her image. In this essay, I will apply them to Mel Gibson's portrayal of her.

Scholarship

Gibson had said up front and often that he has no truck with scholars—what do they know? I had no expectation, therefore, that insights of the last quarter-century of feminist scholarship on Mary Magdalene would be in evidence. That scholarship takes seriously the presence of women in the Kingdom of God movement associated with Jesus and takes seriously their participation and agency. My own position is that it was a movement grounded in the apocalyptic and wisdom traditions of Judaism, egalitarian not in any ideal sense, but in the sense that some women and men struggled to live out a belief in their equality before God.

Feminist scholarship does not take the Christian Testament texts at face value as representing history "as it was," but rather sees them as male-authored, male-centered texts, whose perspective involves ignoring, distorting, and suppressing the contribution of women, and whose gaps, silences, and discrepancies we must learn to read in order to reconstruct history. These texts are wonderful, and they are flawed. Passages about the Crucifixion and the empty tomb and about the appearance of the resurrected Jesus to Mary Magdalene are crucial for reconstructing the role of women in the creation of the Easter faith. Gibson's decision to ignore the contributions of feminist scholarship, and of Christian Testament scholarship in general, was a decision to deny Mary Magdalene a strong and central role in the movie as a prominent witness of the Crucifixion, burial, and empty tomb.

The Vatican

Gibson has said also that his Catholic sensibilities are pre–Vatican II. This warns the viewer that Mary Magdalene's "rehabilitation" by the church will be ignored. In 1969 the Roman calendar was changed. It no longer describes her as "Penitent" and no longer uses for her feast day the readings from Luke 7 (about a "woman in the city, who was a sinner," who comes uninvited to the house of Simon the Pharisee, weeps on Jesus's feet, dries them with her hair, anoints them with perfume, and is forgiven, says Jesus, because she has "shown great love") and from John 12 (about Mary of Bethany, Lazarus's sister, who anoints Jesus before his death). Officially, Mary Magdalene is no longer confused or conflated with these other biblical women, who in the streams of legend were also often conflated with the woman caught in adultery of John 9, the Samaritan woman of John 4, and others. Gibson ignores this directive. The Vatican, in its reported praise of his movie, ignores it too.

The Legendary Magdalene

Gibson's portrayal follows the legendary trajectory, more than 1400 years old, that conflates Mary Magdalene with unnamed women from the Gospels, thus giving her a dramatic biography and the reputation of a redeemed whore. One motive for such legend-making is understandable: it rounds out her character. In the Christian Testament texts, she

FIGURE 3 Flashback of Mary Magdalene as the woman caught in adultery (John 8). Still from *The Passion of the Christ* (2004).

appears out of nowhere in the story, at the cross of Jesus. The reader of the Gospels of Mark and Matthew is told at that point that she and other women, some named, some not, have been with Jesus all along, from Galilee. John gives no explanation of her presence. Only Luke 8:1–3 mentions her and others in the ministry section of his Gospel, preparing for their presence at the cross: "The twelve were with [Jesus] as well as some women who had been cured of evil spirits and infirmities: Mary, called Magdalene, from whom seven demons had gone out, and Joanna, the wife of Herod's steward Chuza, and Suzanna, and many others, who provided for them [some manuscripts read: for him] out of their resources." Gibson and his co-screenwriter Benedict Fitzgerald have decided not to go the route of depicting her seven demons, her healing, or her possible wealth. (The "androgynous" character of Satan is more than enough female demon.) Mary Magdalene's female companions have been disappeared.

To quickly explain her presence and in essence give her something like a "call" to follow Jesus, the movie bypasses some of the scenes used in legends. It does not use the story of Jesus being anointed by a woman before his death (John 12, Mark 14) or that of his being anointed by the "sinner" (Luke 7). Instead, Gibson's choice is to conflate Mary Magdalene only with the woman caught in adultery (John 8:2–11), who is saved when Jesus writes on the ground and insists that whoever is without sin cast the first stone. According to the law referred to here (Leviticus 20:10, Deuteronomy 22:22), both the man (married or unmarried) and the woman (married or betrothed) should be put to death; witnesses are told to cast the first stones in Deuteronomy 17:7. (For information about the rationale for this law [safeguarding the "nuclear family"], interpretations, prosecution, means of execution, and the use of the term "adulteress" as a metaphor for apostasy, see Elaine Adler Goodfriend's article, "Adultery," in the *Anchor Bible Dictionary*.) The fact that no guilty man is mentioned in the scene in John 8 is perhaps a touch of realism.

This passage is not in most early manuscripts of John. It interrupts the teaching of Jesus in the temple and is regarded as a non-Johannine bit of floating tradition. It floats into the movie as a flashback. Helping Mary wipe up the incredible amount of blood Jesus has shed at the scouring, Mary Magdalene, kneeling on the stones, flashes back to Jesus writing in the dirt. The camera's perspective is ground level, and as he writes, the stones slip from the hands of the men in the crowd and crash to the ground; the woman's hand then snakes out toward Jesus as his hand reaches down and lifts her up. The viewer sees her dirty embroidered sleeve, her weeping face, her dangling earrings. This ground-level perspective is very effective in conveying her abjectness and Jesus's relationship to her as superior to inferior, powerful to powerless. For the sake of this perspective, Gibson makes interesting changes in the text he is interpreting. In the movie Jesus stands up from his writing and then glances down at Mary Magdalene, at which point she crawls to him for mercy and forgiveness; but in the biblical text the woman has been standing all along, before the crowd and before Jesus, who rises to speak to her.

Mary Magdalene's identity and character are established in this scene by that crawling, those embroidered sleeves, and those earrings, and by being saved from sin and death. She is a forgiven adulteress. She dresses from now on in black with a white headband, as does Mary the mother of Jesus. Watch, however, how only Mary Magdalene's black veil falls off when she mops up the blood (and remembers how close she came to being stoned as an adulteress). Her trademark long, wild hair remains uncovered until the cross is raised upright. Her head is unveiled again at the deposition. In the procession to Calvary, the neckline of her black dress falls lower than that of Mary the mother's.

The Erotic and the Mother

Is there an erotic charge between Gibson's Jesus and Gibson's Mary Magdalene? Not that I could see. The imbalance between them at the stoning scene and the blankness with which Jesus regards her (the few times he even looks at her) dispel any notion of a romantic association, any suggestions of *The Da Vinci Code*. At least, the relationship is not romantic on Jesus's side: he is busy dying, busy with tragedy. In all of his flashback memories, he is unpartnered. The role written for his mother and the casting of a stronger actor (Maia Morgenstern) in that role tell us that his strong erotic bond is with his mother, not with Mary Magdalene. His mother is the one who kisses his crucified feet, bloodying her mouth. The scene in which many viewers identify with her emotionally is the one in which, remembering him falling as a little child, she runs to him as he falls under the cross. In the painterly scene of the deposition, the removal of Jesus's body from the cross, Mary his mother is at his head, Mary Magdalene at his feet, John in the middle. John's hand moves up the thigh of the corpse. (Compare the depositions by Titian, Tintoretto, Botticelli, Giotto, Raphael, and others reproduced in Susan Haskins's work *Mary Magdalene: Myth and Metaphor*.) Psychoanalytical interpretations of infantile attachment and underlying homoeroticism are certainly in order.

In *The Passion*, Mary Magdalene seems to be cast as the daughter of Mary the mother, as her sidekick and supporter. Mary the mother is the central focus of Mary Magdalene's concern and care. In making Mary Magdalene the constant companion and helper of Mary the mother, who is of greater visual and dramatic interest, Gibson underlines the fact that Mary the mother has greatly eclipsed Mary Magdalene in Christian theology and spirituality. He has not replaced Mary Magdalene with Mary the mother, but he has given precedence to Mary the mother. In *Mary Magdalene, the First Apostle: The Struggle for Authority*, Ann Graham Brock has shown that some ancient Syriac traditions about the empty tomb make Mary the mother prominent and reduce Mary Magdalene to "the other Mary." Other ancient texts that are translations or adaptations from an original text actually replace Mary Magdalene with Mary the mother of Jesus. Brock calls this "a strategy for eliminating the competition" for apostolic authority. That is, Mary Magdalene is diminished or eliminated and replaced by the unthreatening figure of Mary the mother, depicted as submissive and deferential to Peter. Brock considers such diminishment and substitution to be a deliberate and systematic tactic. It is a clue both to the politics of the original texts and to the politics of the adaptations. This strategy from the second to the sixth century continues in works of spirituality down to the twenty-first century. The film should be seen as part of this spectrum.

In *The Passion*, the two Marys, joined by the disciple John, rush from the courtyard of the high priest's house to Pilate's headquarters, up and down the streets on the way of the cross, to Calvary, jostled by crowds. The mother is always prominent in the trio, almost always in the center of the frame and given the most close-ups. Mary Magdalene is behind her or to the left of the frame. At Calvary she hangs back while John (understood by Gibson, but not by most scholars, as the disciple Jesus loved) and Mary walk forward to stand together at the foot of the cross to hear the words "Woman, behold your son" and "Behold your mother" (John 19:26–27). A family has now been created: God the father, Mary the mother, and Mary Magdalene, John, and Jesus as siblings of a sort.

There is a fascinating confusion in the four canonical Gospels' descriptions of the Crucifixion concerning who was present. Mark lists three women by name—Mary Magdalene, Mary the mother of James the younger and of Joses, and Salome—and mentions many other women who had come up with Jesus to Jerusalem. Matthew lists Mary Magdalene, Mary the mother of James and of Joseph, and the mother of the sons of Zebedee, along with many women who had followed Jesus from Galilee. Luke writes of the women who were following with him from Galilee (see Luke 8:1–3) and all those (masculine in the Greek) known to him; then Luke names Mary Magdalene, Mary the mother of James, Joanna, and the other women with them at the empty tomb. But John places at the Crucifixion "his mother and his mother's sister Mary the wife of Clopas and Mary Magdalene," and the disciple (masculine in the Greek) whom Jesus loved. It is not clear whether John is referring to two, three, or four women, since the Greek does not punctuate. In *The Death of the Messiah*, Raymond E. Brown reasons that there are four (a traditional three plus the mother), and also that the mother of Jesus and the beloved disciple have a predominantly symbolic (not historical) role. Gibson's film, like many paintings of the Crucifixion, privileges an abridged Gospel of John over the Synoptic Gospels. Already in John the mother has begun to edge out Mary Magdalene, no longer named first but last there, and to whom no words are spoken.

Beauty and Knowledge (Gnosis)

Monica Bellucci's beauty is the signature of the legendary Magdalene. Asked on a talk show why he chose her for the role, Gilson replied simply, "Because she's beautiful." As she has almost no lines, Bellucci's expressions are her primary script. They range from alarm to concern to stagy fear to wariness to a kind of curiosity to sadness. Not revulsion, nausea, or rage. She is never "ugly" or grim in grief, unlike Mary the mother, whose vein pulses in her forehead, whose eyes are puffy, who looks driven nearly insane. Many of Mary Magdalene's expressions are, in fact, difficult to read, difficult to put a name to. Puzzlement seems to be a main ingredient. And lack of courage. She looks down and covers her face repeatedly so as not to see, uttering little sobs. She covers her ears so as not to hear when the crowd shouts for Barabbas, and again when it calls for crucifixion. In contrast, the mother of Jesus looks with knowing horror on the events; she does not turn away, does not hide her face, but stares at the tragedy and, full-faced, at the camera. It is she who has a psychic connection with Jesus below in the dungeon, she who holds and comforts the weeping Mary Magdalene after the scourging.

Gibson's Mary Magdalene is not a knower, not a gnostic. She is not the Magdalene praised in the apocryphal Dialogue of the Savior 139:12–13 as "a woman who had understood completely." She is not one who sees the light (Gospel of Philip 64:5–9), who is "blessed beyond all women on earth" for her spiritual understanding (Pistis Sophia I:19), and in whom resides "a virile and courageous mentality" (Acts of Philip VIII:3).

The Christian Testament gives Mary Magdalene no lines to speak in the Passion narratives. Gibson breaks with this tradition when she shouts to a Roman soldier that he should stop the Jewish crowd that has arrested Jesus in secret. A colleague of the high priest shuts her up, telling the soldier, "She's crazy." It is significant that she appeals to Rome, not to the Sanhedrin. This is her only real action, her moment of initiative. But here she becomes one of the many swirling, ineffectual characters, three in the Sanhedrin "trial" alone, who try to stop the proceedings. Watching from her windows above the street, Pilate's wife, Claudia, is a spectator like Mary Magdalene, but Claudia has a more interesting, more beefed-up role, as does Satan. These two characters know the truth.

Resurrection

As the stone is shifted and light pours into the tomb, the risen Jesus— naked, with see-through holes in his hands—stands and walks forward. Where does *The Passion* take the viewer in imagination when the screen goes black and the credits roll? It seems clear that if anyone besides Jesus will have a powerful role after the Resurrection, it will be Mary his mother, not Mary Magdalene. In fact, some of the Syriac traditions mentioned above and widespread popular piety substitute Mary the mother for Mary Magdalene at the empty tomb. As the first to whom the risen Jesus appears, his mother becomes the primary witness to the Resurrection.

But I think perhaps the viewer is not meant to imagine even that. What is significant about the Resurrection in this film is that it happens without human insight. The Resurrection, that is, is separated from the Resurrection faith (a separation that does not occur in the Gospels, which do not imagine the Resurrection itself). It is all about Jesus, only about Jesus.

Another Film Magdalene

We can understand Gibson's Mary Magdalene better by comparing her to another film Magdalene, Denys Arcand's in his 1989 film *Jesus of Montreal.*

The Legend: No film has yet been made without use of the legend. Arcand's *Jesus of Montreal* is the story of a small troupe of five professional actors, all friends, hired to perform a Passion play on church property. The actor in the role of Mary Magdalene (Mireille, played by Catherine Wilkening) is not a professional prostitute, but a model. Some of these friends share an apartment; the sexual arrangements are unclear. This Magdalene is grateful to Jesus (Daniel Coulombe) for saving her from having to strip for a job in a commercial.

Discipleship/Companionship: Jesus of Montreal is unique among Jesus movies in its presentation of the movement as a group of friends (two women and three men) engaged in a joint project, an egalitarian community. Their conflict with church authorities and with forces in the advertising industry leads to the cancellation of the play they have been hired to do and the accidental death of the actor playing Jesus. The Magdalene encourages Jesus and the others when they meet opposition: "What's with you guys? You can't let it get to you. You saved me; you can't let me down. What we have here is precious. We have to keep going." Not only is she a full member of this troupe; she is a leader with insight and courage.

At the Crucifixion: In *Jesus of Montreal,* only the two women jump into the ambulance with him when the Jesus character is injured, and they stand around an operating table as the efforts to save him fail. They make the decision together to donate his organs.

Empty Tomb and Resurrection Faith: Arcand's Magdalene actor runs in a dark tunnel from the light, her clothes billowing, to tell the others. Resurrection as presented here is ambiguous, mysterious: it has to do with seeing, and perhaps with a continuance of community. The movie's final, visually interesting scene is a return to the subway platform where Coulombe fell dying. An escalator rises and descends against a black wall. Two women sing Pergolesi's *Stabat Mater* for money to music from a boom box. These women, who appeared in the film's opening scene singing the same song in the church, are not, I think, the two actors of the original troupe. Are they an idealistic new troupe or promoters of a compromised theater company? Perhaps the music indicates they represent the tamed Mary, mother of Jesus. Mireille, as we will see, may be the only one who understands, the one who carries the meaning of the Resurrection.

Jesus of Montreal is a film that works against kyriarchal ideology, against patriarchal religion. After the death of Coulombe (Jesus), the actors playing disciples are approached with a marketing idea: to found a theater company in the name of the dead and now famous Coulombe, with the one who plays Peter as founding president. The show-business lawyer agrees this can be done—"Yes, and turn a profit." Then Mireille says quietly, "Excuse me." The camera follows her as she calmly walks out of negotiations and up a stairway. She walks alone and silent in the dark outside on the church terrace above Montreal, the city lights below her. The camera follows her as she closes her eyes and leans on a railing, turning her back to the camera and the audience. She is gone away, and she is alone, but the viewer is drawn out with her.

Arcand offers a deep and pessimistic criticism of the corporate business world, with its buying and selling, its exploitation of women, its sentimental superficiality, its enthusiasms and fads. It is a criticism of clerical culture as well, as part of that business world. The official church in this film is afraid of Jesus, afraid of the modernization of his story, afraid of scholars. It demands restrictions, modifications, the old script, comfort. Arcand is saying that the real community, the real church—if there is one—is elsewhere. Or at least it tries to be elsewhere, was for a time elsewhere, might be somewhere again. Mary Magdalene/Mireille is the silent spokesperson for this hope.

Gibson's Magdalene, in contrast to Arcand's, is conventionally cast, her role unsubtly diminished. She is a woman of the past, of the old script, and of a partial script. While his Mary Magdalene is almost a marginal character, women are not marginal to *The Passion*. But their elevation (as grateful, beautiful follower, as grieving mother) does not disturb any stereotypes, does not upset traditional Christian "family values." Arcand's is truer to the Christian Testament texts, with their problems and their powerful potential to be reread in liberating ways. Without a role at the empty tomb, Gibson's Magdalene is associated only with Jesus's suffering, not with the transcendence of suffering.

Arcand's layering of past and present, acting and reality, shows how the Passion and Resurrection narratives can be dramatized in new and different ways, taking historical criticism and feminist interpretation into account and featuring a complex and challenging Magdalene. But *Jesus of Montreal* was not designed for and did not reach the mass audience. It demands much of the viewer emotionally and intellectually and rewards multiple viewings. *The Passion* is deliberately uninfluenced by scholarship and by even moderately changing views of women. Financed by Gibson himself and a work, he says, of religious zeal, it does reach a mass audience, not exactly by pandering to market values but by reinforcing orthodox fundamentalism, with its ageless and powerful forms of sexism. These two approaches to filming will surely produce conflicting film views of Mary Magdalene in the future.

Some Final Thoughts about Blood

What does all that blood in *The Passion* have to do with Mary Magdalene? All that sadomasochistic violence, men beating and then killing a man. Nancy Jay, in *Throughout Your Generations Forever,* theorized that sacrifice is men's "remedy for being born of women . . . birth done better." A major means of disempowering women, it "establishes intergenerational continuity between males that transcend[s] dependence on childbearing women." Gibson sees the death of Jesus as a sacrifice that is inevitable (God's will), meaningful, and vicarious. "He was wounded for our sins," reads the prologue on the screen. There are many depicted as sinners in this movie (the chief priests, the Jewish crowd, Judas, Peter, soldiers, maybe even Pilate). Mary Magdalene above all, for those who know her legend, represents sinners, sinners who repent. But she is not the character through whom the suffering is focused for the viewer in *The Passion.*

All those tears. In the theater, the woman to the left of me and someone down on the right sobbed throughout the flogging and the way of the cross. Mary Magdalene and all the others who protest the Crucifixion are shown as powerless to prevent it, to stand against the powers of the state and religion. They can only weep. They do not, cannot, say "never again" in righteous rage. Women as mothers and companions support men. Bad men kill and good men are killed, and women mop up the blood. Then the solitary good man, whose God is his sacrifice-demanding Father, triumphs. This, says *The Passion,* is the way things are.

Excuse me. The Resurrection faith, as I understand it, says no to this—this theology, this version of history. And the moment of the Resurrection faith's initial insight or revelation—omitted by Gibson—is associated with Mary Magdalene.

8

Mel Gibson, Bride of Christ

Mark D. Jordan and Kent L. Brintnall

While laboring one night to understand the mystery of Christ's death, Mel Gibson began rummaging in a library he had purchased from a failing convent. A book leaped from the shelf into his hands: *The Dolorous Passion of Our Lord Jesus Christ*. It was an English version of the life and selected visions of Anne Catherine Emmerich (1774–1824), an Augustinian nun from the vicinity of Munster, Germany. Once miraculously delivered, the book opened Gibson's eyes. "Amazing images," he later enthused to Peter Boyer in the *New Yorker*. "She supplied me with stuff I never would have thought of." Or ever read in the canonical Gospels, which lack both the coherence and the florid detail of the nun's recital. It was Emmerich's book, and not the New Testament, that provided the overarching framework for Gibson's film *The Passion of the Christ*. Gibson's screenplay and directorial inspiration came primarily not from the gospel writers, but from a German visionary who carried on her body multiple wounds from the Passion of her Divine Spouse.

Gibson chose his source wisely: Emmerich's visions of the Passion are cinematic. No other word will do. They are strong on images and weak on words. She frequently claims not to hear what someone is saying and not to remember a sequence of events, but her eye for visual detail is unerring: gesture, facial expressions, costumes, hair styles, décor, even color temperature are registered with precision and exactitude. Emmerich privileges the visual record, willingly interrupting the flow of the narrative to describe what she sees from her vantage point, as in "a glance at Jerusalem" on the night of Jesus's arrest (pp. 145–50 in the TAN edition). Her visions are recorded as an "allegorical and historical drama," divided, like a screenplay, into "scenes" (26). Particular points in the visions were often clarified for Emmerich by the appearance alongside them, split-screen fashion, of a child who would display the appropriate iconographic features or scriptural captions (230).

Taking his cues from Emmerich's cinematic imaginary, Gibson foregrounds the practice of witnessing. Audience members are positioned alongside Emmerich, who regularly inserts herself when recounting her visions: "I saw" or equivalent phrases occur hundreds of times in her text. In the same way, Gibson's camera almost never offers point-of-view shots and only rarely operates as a mere narrational presence. Instead, Gibson's camera positions the audience as an engaged spectator to the unfolding drama of pain. Near the beginning of the film, for example, when Satan confronts Jesus in the garden, the camera is situated as an independent witness within the scene. The absence of an establishing shot to fix the coordinates of the setting and the use of a highly mobile camera leave the viewer disoriented and adrift. Moreover, the camera never aligns itself with the point of view of any character on screen; its vantage point is always slightly different from that of the disciples, Jesus, or Satan. Gibson's frame remains in motion throughout the film, roaming through crowds or spaces as if it were a person straining to see the events. With Emmerich as his model, Gibson prevents identification with any character or stable location in the diegetic space even while he emphasizes an experience of immediate presence before unrolling events.

To be only a witness, however, satisfies neither Gibson nor Emmerich. They understand themselves and their audiences as participants in the suffering of Jesus. Emmerich's life is more striking even than her visions of Christ's passion; her suffering, like that of many great visionaries, outdoes Jesus's. Anne Catherine studied mainly "in the school of suffering and mortification," "in the school of the Cross" (6, 10). As a young girl, she slept on planks laid out on the ground to form a cross (6). Sometimes troops of souls suffering in purgatory would wake her up so that she could pace out with them the Stations of the Cross in deep snow. She had "the habit of praying for long hours before pictures of all the stages of Christ's painful Passion, or before wayside crosses"

(24). When she was in her early thirties, Anne Catherine asked to be allowed to feel something of what Jesus endured on the cross (16; cf. 236, note). Her hands and feet were immediately pierced by terrible pains. Full bodily assimilation of the Passion was accomplished only later. In 1812, during successive visions, she was marked by multiple crosses on her chest and then, finally, by the full stigmata in hands, feet, and side (17–19). Anne Catherine's wounds bled again on dates associated with Christ's death. Toward the end of her life, her stigmata would open on the "real anniversary of the Passion" rather than on the liturgically determined date of Good Friday. "Her suffering body itself was to preach Jesus crucified" (23).

Although his film gives rise to (somewhat) less intense bodily experiences than do Emmerich's visions, Gibson follows her in presenting his Passion as a devotional text, not beholden to historical accuracy, meant to help people experience the salvific love of Jesus the Christ (as he says in the foreword to a collection of photographs from the film). Through his vivid depiction of brutal suffering, Gibson provides his viewers not so much an interpretation of the gospel accounts as an overwhelming share in Jesus's torture. On the few occasions when he provides a point-of-view shot (twice from the perspective of Jesus, once from that of God, all in extremely unusual angles), the experience depicted is intense suffering or grief. As part of this emphasis on direct experience of the Passion, many of the film's narrative details are not explained. Without prior acquaintance, parts of the story would make little sense. During the course of the movie, a mixed-gender trio attends carefully to the trial, torture, and Crucifixion. Jesus's mother, Mary, and his disciple, John, are named in the film. The third member of this human trinity is not. Informed viewers will identify this woman as Mary Magdalene, whom the canonical Gospels—and more emphatically Emmerich's visions—present as witness to both Crucifixion and Resurrection. A flashback within the film identifies this woman as the one caught in adultery whom Jesus saves from stoning. Again, viewers who know the conflations of Christian tradition will assume that this event is part of the life of Mary Magdalene, though the assumption is not warranted by the Gospels. Gibson's beautiful, elliptical flashback involving this character is legible only to audience members already familiar with the canonical texts. The emphasis, then, is on affective experience rather than narrative comprehension.

Gibson and Emmerich's narratives are produced for those already incorporated by faith into Jesus's life. They gesture toward the scriptures without committing themselves to an accurate rendering of textual details, discrepancies, or omissions. Emmerich's editor, the poet Clemens Brentano, is clear on this point. Emmerich "had never read the Old or New Testaments, and when she was tired of relating her visions, she would sometimes say, 'Read that in the Bible,' and then be astonished to learn that it was not there" (35). Her visions frequently make fantastic splices between the Passion and other biblical events. We learn, for example, that the room in which the Last Supper took place had been used to train King David's captains, to shelter the Ark of the Covenant during the building of the Temple, and to hide the prophet Malachi while he wrote "his prophecies concerning the Blessed Sacrament and the Sacrifice of the New Law" (65). The chalice used by Jesus to "institute" the "Holy Eucharist" had originally been given by Melchizedech to Abraham after being carefully preserved on Noah's ark (70–71). To say that there is no scriptural evidence for Emmerich's connections understates the point. The same is true of Gibson, whose deviations from biblical sources have been fully demonstrated by many others. Such demonstrations, however, are curiously misdirected. Emmerich's visions and Gibson's movie are meant to be engaged neither as the reproduction of biblical texts nor as commentary on them, but as the "complete" Passion toward which the biblical narratives only point. They show more than the canonical texts because they intend to stage a direct connection with the events for the faithful observer-participant. The best adjective for the experience is not biblical or evangelical, but "Catholic"—according to both precise and idiosyncratic senses of the term.

The most Catholic correction that Emmerich brings to the canonical Gospels comes in her depiction of Mary. In both accounts, Mary articulates her desire to die with Jesus during his Passion. Refused actual death, she shares Jesus's Passion during his trial before Annas and Caiaphas, his imprisonment by the Jewish council, his scourging, and his way to Golgotha, and while he hangs on the cross. Gibson continues to follow Emmerich faithfully but goes further in privileging the role of Mary. While Emmerich's Mary is the victim of frequent fainting spells, Mary's strength and tacit approval propel Gibson's drama forward. When Jesus collapses during his flogging, an exchange of glances with his mother enables him to pull himself up and endure more. The blows resume only after Mary gives a slight nod. When Jesus falls under the weight of the cross, Mary rushes to him, comforts him, and gives him the strength to continue. By exchanging glances with Caiaphas and Satan during the scourging, on the way to Golgotha, and during the Crucifixion, Mary seems to register her understanding of the events and then to give her permission for them to proceed. Again, and following

Emmerich, Gibson develops Pilate's wife as a spectator and interpreter of Jesus's death. Like Mary during the scenes of Jesus's torture, the Roman wife serves as an interpretive locus for the film's audience throughout the trials. Her reactions are our reactions; her response, ours too. In the film, near the end of Jesus's flogging, Pilate's wife and Mary meet. In silence, they exchange knowing looks (after all, would ardent spectators need words?), and Mary receives from Pilate's wife the towels with which she will mop up Jesus's precious blood. Those who send Jesus to die and those who mourn his death are linked by powerful, compassionate, understanding women. Indeed, so far as Emmerich credits Mary with inaugurating the Stations of the Cross (200–201, 266), episodes from which are the main scenes in Gibson's film, Mary through Emmerich becomes yet another (female) coauthor of *The Passion*.

Emmerich, like Mary, is a female witness to the suffering of Jesus. Like Mary, she is not a dispassionate one. Emmerich is watching not just any suffering, but the suffering of the man she most often calls her "spouse"—a "celestial" or "divine" spouse, to be sure, but also "beloved," "tender," and "adorable." In traditional Catholic spiritual theology, every nun is the bride of Christ, but Emmerich seems to have staked a particular matrimonial claim. In a moment of acute pain, she is consoled when Jesus says, "I have laid thee on my nuptial couch, which is a couch of suffering; I have given thee suffering and expiation for thy bridal garments and jewels" (42). Emmerich as faithful bride accompanies Jesus more steadfastly than Mary or any of the disciples. When he is alone in the garden of Gethsemane she is there, weeping and praying with her "Heavenly Spouse" (102, 114). When the foot of the cross drops into the hole prepared for it, Emmerich is absorbed in gazing on his body in close-up, from an angle no one else could reach; she praises details of his physical beauty before concluding that his body had become "one wound" (278–79).

Aligning himself with Emmerich in astonishingly precise terms, Gibson emphasizes the hole prepared for Jesus's cross—another narrative detail absent from the Gospels. He then focuses his camera in extreme close-up on Christ's eyes and body, giving the cineplex spectator access to details that no one at the foot of the cross could have seen. The hyperreal and very red criss-crossing on Jesus's body marks him as a single, open wound. By echoing Emmerich's narrative to this extent, has Gibson (knowingly or unknowingly) situated both himself and his audience as the bride of Christ? If so, then Gibson and the male spectators who have accompanied him in his cinematic veneration have undergone a notable gender reassignment. Gender shifts of this sort have been studied

in film genres that foreground violence. As Carol Clover argues in *Men,
Women and Chain Saws,* some of the pleasure for male spectators of
slasher films—and Gibson's *Passion* must be counted as a slasher film—
is a masochistic gender-blurring. Or think of what Lee Clark Mitchell
finds in the Western genre: the hero's costume draws explicit attention to
the contours of his body in a way that feminizes him, while the violence
in which he participates as agent and object establishes his masculine
bona fides. Indeed, as Steve Neale argues so convincingly about film
style generally, directing violence against the male body is a common
strategy for deflecting male erotic investment in the spectacle of male
beauty. As a heartthrob star of violent action films (the *Lethal Weapon*
and *Mad Max* series leap to mind), Gibson has endlessly acted out this
connection between sadism and the erotic display of the male form. As
William Luhr observes about *The Man without a Face* and *Braveheart,*
Gibson has worked hard to establish a link between masochism and
heroic masculinity in the previous films he has directed. *The Passion of
the Christ,* then, is hardly Gibson's first Jesus movie. As Elvis Mitchell of
the *New York Times* confessed: "When I heard that . . . Gibson would
direct a film adaptation of the life of Jesus, my first thought was, 'What
took him so long?' "

Gibson will admit none of this, of course. The erotic energy perme-
ating Emmerich's visions and radiating more traditionally from the crucified body of Jesus is deflected and contained by his film. For example,
The Passion betrays considerable panic about male nudity. Contrary to
historical warrants and cinematic precursors (like Martin Scorsese's *The
Last Temptation of Christ*), Gibson's Jesus is not crucified in the nude.
Again, and contrary to scriptural warrant (Mark 14:51–52), when a
follower of Jesus is fleeing the garden and has his robe torn from him,
he is not left naked. John dutifully attends to Mary and watches Jesus
affectionately, but never touches him—and certainly never reclines his
remarkably beautiful face and body near that of Jesus, no matter what
the scriptures say (John 13:24–25). The most explicitly homoerotic display in Gibson's film is the scene of Herod's living quarters. They are fur-
nished with stylishly dressed, cosmetically swathed eunuchs who minister to a notably effeminate Herod. This is a space of decadence in which
Jesus's humiliation is intensified and prolonged. By casting a female per-
former in the role of Satan, Gibson's only explicit blurring of gender is
made to coincide with the zenith of evil.

Just as Gibson seeks to contain homoerotic energy, he also deviates
from Emmerich whenever her visions threaten to unleash female power.
In Emmerich's experience of the Last Supper, Mary the mother of Jesus

floats into the room to receive Communion "in a spiritual manner," just as Jesus had earlier told her to do (72, 84; cf. 74, 77). Mary is also the first to share the joy of the Resurrection, when the "soul" of Jesus appears to present her to the patriarchs of Israel, whom he has just brought out of hell (353). In Gibson's depiction of the Last Supper, by contrast, Mary is nowhere to be found. Gibson intercuts the meal with his depiction of Jesus being nailed to and raised on the cross. Although women's reactions to Jesus's torture and suffering are the audience's cues for interpreting events in most of the film, at the altar/table John's face becomes our guide. When Gibson links Jesus's bloodied body on the cross to the body and blood received in Eucharistic celebration, John is the only witness. While Gibson foregrounds women as witnesses to the suffering of Jesus, when it comes to understanding that suffering theologically and reenacting it liturgically, the economy is exclusively male. Something similar happens in Gibson's depiction of the Resurrection. Here Emmerich's visions are consistent with the testimony of the canonical Gospels: the first witnesses to the Resurrection were women. But when Gibson's Jesus rises and prepares to exit the tomb, no witnesses are present in the frame. Is the audience meant to be inserted as first witness to the Resurrection? If so, are they to become women? Or is this rather Gibson's need to displace women as the exclusive first witnesses to the Resurrection? And from the angle of which gender are we to observe that Jesus is clearly naked in this scene? The ambiguously gendered audience is given a clear view of the line of the bare buttocks of the glorified and, to use Emmerich's language, "adorable" Jesus.

From the miraculous inception of his devotional project, Emmerich was Gibson's companion on the Via Dolorosa. With her, through her, Gibson becomes Christ's bride. With Gibson, in turn, the audience is wedded to the Savior. But Gibson's film conceals the gender reversals of its own veneration and refuses the gendered position of its main source. Gibson carries with him, as a relic, a patch allegedly snipped from Emmerich's religious costume. This relic from Emmerich's habit—her bridal gown—came to Gibson, like the book of visions, in a miraculous way. He happily carries and displays the patch, but refuses to wear the gown. He wants both to become the bride of Christ and to dominate the marital relationship—and only then to bring in an audience for a real man's movie about the heroic suffering of his comrade, Jesus. Gibson's co-author, Anne Catherine Emmerich, had more consistent notions about her images. She may, in the end, elude Gibson's control.

Part Two: Ethical and Theological Responses

9

No Pain, No Gain?

Paula Fredriksen

Rose was beautiful, and she was rich. She also loved Christ. When her father pressured her to marry the wealthy boy next door, Rose refused. She stopped eating. She cut off all her hair. She even rubbed broken glass into her face. Finally, her father relented, and he asked Rose what she now wanted to do. (Her would-be fiancé had vanished.) "Oh, father," Rose said, "just let me build a hut in the middle of the garden, and live there by myself." Rose's father built her hut, and there Rose lived, scarcely eating, and sleeping at night on a bed of broken bricks. She died young and went straight to heaven.

In 1957, in St. Rose of Lima's church in Warwick, Rhode Island, the nun instructing us held the roomful of six-year-olds riveted. We also heard of gallant martyrs, both ancient and modern (with communist Russia or China assuming the role played earlier by Rome). But Rose was different. Her suffering was voluntary—indeed, it was self-inflicted. Rose had embraced her pain, my teacher explained to us, in the imitation of Christ.

Why recount such things to first-grade children? Because we were preparing for our first Holy Communion. We had to understand the significance of Christ's sacrifice, the meaning of his body and blood, which we were about to receive. Christ had saved us not through his death so much as through his *suffering*. And he had suffered a lot—more, indeed, than any other human being had ever suffered or could ever suffer. *Think!* Sister exhorted. *The saints suffered horribly. But their pain was only for their own sin. Christ suffered for the sins of each and every one of us. How many sins is that? How much pain must he have felt? If he had not been God, he could not have endured!*

My grandmother's church, in a working-class Italian suburb of Boston, embodied this same message. The pains of the saints and martyrs visually intertwined with those of Christ, as the niches filled with their painted plaster representations (Saint Sebastian, covered with blood and arrows; the Madonna of the Seven Sorrows, her breast pierced by seven daggers) alternated with oil paintings of Christ stumbling through the Stations of the Cross. Lined with these images, the walls of the church converged on the altar, which held the Body of Christ. And over the mystery of the sacrament was suspended its visual and historical counterpart: Christ in agony, dying on his cross.

All of which brings us to Mel Gibson's most recent effort, *The Passion of the Christ*. Pumping up the gore—computer-generated flying flesh, Hollywood make-up artistry—Gibson has pulled off a cross-marketing coup. He has taken this now somewhat old-fashioned, quintessentially Roman Catholic fixation on blood and pain and sold it to millions of Sun Belt Protestants. It seems likely that at no prior point in American history have so many Baptists known the date of Ash Wednesday.

The Christ that Gibson is selling is not the Christ of the first-century scriptures, though elements of his story are drawn from them. The first-century Christ, presented primarily in the four Gospels, redeemed humanity not through his suffering, but through his death and Resurrection, which promised his return. The evangelists mediated historical traditions about Jesus's life and teachings, interpreting these through their own understanding of Jewish scriptures. Their meditations on their ancient sacred texts in particular shaped their presentations of the edges of Jesus's life, his birth and his death. The many narrative details of the Gospels' Passion stories deliberately echo various verses from the prophets and the Psalms. The evangelists' point: Jesus died and was raised according to the scriptures. The matching of recent event to ancient prophecy established, for the evangelists and for their communities, the authority of their stories.

Gibson missed the evangelists' point. His opening screen flashes a verse from Isaiah 53: "He was wounded for our transgressions; by his stripes we are healed." What served as prophetic authorization for the Gospels' proclamation Gibson takes as an invitation to explore, in lurid and lingering detail, how a human body would look if pulped, pummeled, and flayed. Part of this orientation, I know, comes from the Catholicism of his childhood. Part of it, as he has repeatedly claimed, comes from the visions of an early-nineteenth-century stigmatic nun, Anne Catherine Emmerich. (Knowing what my catechism classes were like in twentieth-century Rhode Island, I can only imagine what hers were like in eighteenth-century Westphalia.) Part of it, of course, is just Gibson's favorite visual vernacular, on display from *Mad Max* through *Braveheart* and beyond.

Gibson's Christ is a theological figure whose origins lie not in first-century Judea, but in late-medieval Europe. It was then that Jesus's Passion—a long catalog of sensational tortures and torments—was invented. Pious readers amplified the Gospels' scant accounts of Jesus's execution by turning to the Old Testament and taking lines from Psalms and the prophets as allegories of Christ. What began as spiritual imagery turned, over the centuries, into narrative descriptions that filled tracts and inspired illustrations. Thus, for example, a line from Psalm 109, "He shall drink from the brook in the way," became associated with the figure of Jesus. The idea eventually turned into Jesus's being dragged over a bridge and/or thrown by his captors into the brook of Kidron mentioned in John's Gospel (18:1). The image, woven into medieval narratives, made its way into Emmerich's visions, and two centuries later Jim Caviezel's Jesus dangled in chains off the side of a stone bridge on his way back from Gethsemane. Such staging has nothing to do with "being true to the Gospels," as Gibson seems to think. It has everything to do with medieval embellishments of gospel texts.

Grisly narratives detailing the torments of godly humans in order to inspire their lesser coreligionists to repentance are not a Catholic monopoly. Years after my childhood encounter with Saint Rose, wrestling with the huge liturgy of Yom Kippur, I struggled through *Eyleh ezacrah*, a long and lurid description of ten Roman-era rabbinic martyrdoms. Flayings, dismemberments, and beheadings, torture and flame: déjà vu all over again. Voluntary self-mortifications to the same end—flagellation especially—have concentrated the penance of the pious, in Judaism to a lesser degree, to a greater degree in Catholic Christianity and in Shi'ite Islam. This sensibility that combines pain and penitence crested in late-medieval Europe. It deeply affected, indeed altered, earlier Western ideas of redemption in Christ.

FIGURE 4 Jewish soldiers bringing Jesus before the high priest. Still from *The Passion of the Christ* (2004).

Thus, whereas the early church held that Christ's death and Resurrection redeemed the faithful, the medieval church and much of later Catholicism affirmed that Christ saved us through his uniquely terrible suffering. That theological idea dominates Gibson's movie. All the rest is window dressing. *The Passion*'s costuming, like its music, is lushly theatrical (fig. 4). The Bad Guys wear black, their Jewishness coded by prayer shawls, big noses, and bad teeth. The Jewish soldiers who form the arresting party look like visiting Romulan dignitaries, or extras from the chorus of *Nabucco*. The faces of the two Marys are framed by nun-like veils. (I half expected Monica Bellucci to whip out a rosary along the Stations of the Cross.) And Gibson's much-touted use of ancient languages, like the high quality of his celluloid gore, was a nod to verisimilitude, not real history. His Pilate chatted in Aramaic; his Jesus (at this point, I confess, I groaned aloud), in perfect church Latin. Greek—the actual linguistic medium of the first-century Roman Empire and the language of the original Gospels—simply disappeared.

Why did so many evangelical Protestants buy into this late-medieval Catholic stuff? They were aided by the movie's narrative blandness. Relentlessly visual, its story and characterization are slight. It has no plot, no character development. We are never told why Jesus has to die, or why Caiaphas so desperately wants him to die, or why Jerusalem's Jews so insist on his death. The film is actually a series of biblical-movie set pieces, strung together with lots of slo-mo sequences and spongy music. (And some shots—Roman troops marching briskly in formation; Pilate from his dais trying to reason with a Jewish mob—simply seem silly after *Monty Python's Life of Brian*.) What makes Gibson's movie weak as story, however, might be precisely what makes it so effective as a commercial interdenominational hit. Viewers without a particular theological orientation may well be slightly bored when they are not nauseated by the relentless bloodletting. But viewers of quite various theological orientations can all find support in Gibson's tableaux for whatever message they want, because they are the ones filling in all the blanks that he left.

Gibson's marketing targeted evangelical communities, and he hired the marketing mavens of Christian industry to push seeing his film as an act of religious commitment. In the months before the movie's release, Outreach, the firm Gibson hired, produced promotional materials— door hangers, banners, signs, posters, study guides, and other such spin- off tchotchkes—in flood-tide quantities. Outreach also made 250,000 movie-related DVDs and mailed them out to ministers throughout the country. Its Web site (www.thepassionoutreach.com) coordinated a na- tionwide campaign, enlisting churches to promote the movie. Pastors were encouraged to purchase Outreach's materials, to show the DVD trailer to their congregations, to hang movie banners in front of their buildings, to purchase tickets *en bloc,* and to solicit volunteers from their communities to walk neighborhoods while praying that God, working through Gibson's film, would reach souls with the message of the cross. This marketing campaign, as intended, drove ticket sales way up. *Passion* apologists spun the movie's carefully nurtured commercial success as an index of popular piety. Criticizing it thus became tantamount to criticizing not only the Gospels and Christianity, but also God-fearing Americans everywhere.

Evangelical churches in particular served as Gibson's premier agents. Gibson shone the light of his celebrity upon these churches, asking humbly that they help him to spread the truth of the Gospel. He also positioned himself as a pious warrior pitted against secular, sinful— indeed, anti-Christian—Hollywood. And he himself also crossed over, reinventing himself in the tropes of the born again. His script, he main- tained, was simply and directly based on the Bible (*sola scriptura,* in the language of the Reformation). His message, he insisted, was all about Jesus, love, and forgiveness. He himself had been a sinner, once lost but now found, once slave but now free. He was just a regular guy, called to witness to what he had to believe, because it's just what's in the Bible. In brief, to sell both himself and his film, Gibson morphed into a Protestant-style pre–Vatican II Catholic. And, amazingly, it worked. Who would have thought that so many Protestants would so enthusiasti- cally endorse this kind of medieval Catholic Passion play, assembled and tirelessly promoted by a man who believes that even his Episcopalian wife could have difficulty getting into heaven unless she converts to his church? *Extra ecclesiam nulla salus.*

What about *The Passion* and the Jewish Question? By January 2003 Gibson had already complained to the television talk show host Bill O'Reilly that his movie had "a lot of enemies." "Do you believe it's because you're making a movie about Jesus?" O'Reilly queried. "I think there are a lot of things," responded Gibson, "that don't want it to happen." Later that spring, Gene Fisher, interfaith officer for the United States Conference of Catholic Bishops (USCCB), contacted Icon, Gibson's production company, about having the movie's script reviewed by an ad hoc committee of scholars. Gibson was trumpeting the fidelity, historical and scriptural, of his film, and Fisher was offering him some free—and confidential—feedback. Fisher and Eugene Korn of the Anti-Defamation League (ADL) assembled an ecumenical group of professors, which I was invited to join. On April 17, 2003, Fisher informed William Fulco (the person who had translated the script into Aramaic and Latin, and our main contact on the Icon side) that he had received a copy of the script. On April 24, Fisher and Gibson spoke. Icon received our report in early May. Unbeknownst to all of us, we had handed Gibson his next round of ammo.

Gibson's lawyers threatened to sue the USCCB and the ADL, claiming that we knew we had worked with a stolen script. (In fact, we did not know, and based on Gibson's communications with us, we could not have known that was what he thought. Further, the fact that Fisher let Icon know immediately once he'd received the script indicates that Fisher had not thought the script was stolen: if he had, why would he have contacted Icon?) Next, someone at Icon leaked our confidential report to Zenit, a conservative Catholic news agency. Zenit in turn not only referred to our report as an "attack," but singled out the one identifiably Jewish name in the authors' roster for special treatment. Catholic criticisms were effaced or simply ignored. From that point on, the spin was in: *The Passion,* Icon apologists insisted, is the movie that the Jews do not want you to see. First the Jews went after Christ, and now they're going after Gibson.

Pundits have castigated the ADL and the Simon Wiesenthal Center for feeding Gibson's publicity machine. But both Abraham Foxman of the ADL and Rabbi Marvin Hier of the Wiesenthal Center were in a lose-lose situation. Silence would have implied consent; speaking out fed the PR machine. Icon's spin was already in place, and as its handling of our ecumenical report—drafted by a majority of Catholics—clearly demonstrated, Icon was not going to let articulate Christian voices of protest confuse its presentation of an us/them, good guys/bad guys, Christian/Jewish brawl.

So is Mel Gibson an anti-Semite, and is the film anti-Semitic? My response is: who cares? The only thing that matters is that the film is inflammatory, and that its depiction of Jewish villainy—exaggerated well beyond what is in the Gospels and violating what historical knowledge we have of early-first-century Judea—will give aid and comfort to anti-Semites everywhere. Indeed, Arab countries bent their own censorship rules, allowing and even endorsing *The Passion,* precisely because "the film is anti-Semitic" (so said Mustafa Darwish, former president of the Egypt Censorship Authority, to the Western press, as reported in the *San Francisco Chronicle,* April 1, 2004). "I encouraged [allowing] the movie," explained Mohiy el-Din Abdel Aleem, an Egyptian professor of media and journalism, "because it withholds from the Jews their claims that they are innocent of Christ's blood."

Islam teaches that Jesus was not crucified and did not die in Jerusalem. *The Passion*'s lurid anti-Jewishness, not its theology or its simplistic presentation of first-century history and politics, created its appeal to the Muslim market. Christian viewers, meanwhile, could see in Gibson's movie an endorsement of old-time religion. "JEWS KILLED THE LORD JESUS. 1 Thess 2:14–15. SETTLED!" proclaimed the marquee of Pastor Maurice Gorden's Lovingway United Pentecostal Church, in Denver, the very day the film opened. Did Pastor Gorden think this thought prior to February 25? Probably. Did Gibson's movie cause Gorden to inculpate Jews this way? Probably not. But the excuse Gorden gives for his sign is similar to excuses that Gibson has offered repeatedly in defense of his simple, polarizing script. Gibson's relentless self-promoting and slick fundamentalism created the atmosphere wherein Gorden could feel comfortable publicly broadcasting his view—a view that stands at the core of Christianity's long and toxic tradition of violent anti-Judaism.

Further, if Christians believe (as they do) that Jesus died for all humanity, because of all humanity's sins, then Christians obviously and easily think in terms of intergenerational corporate guilt. That's why this theological position, invoked frequently to deflect questions about the film's anti-Semitic potential, actually backfires. If all Christians at all times are guilty for the death of Christ, then why shouldn't all Jews be, too? And unlike Christians, Jews do not have the courtesy to be grateful, which is why Christians since at least the fourth century have felt moved to teach Jews a lesson. The centrality of the idea of corporate guilt in Christian theology is also why Gibson's personal position on anti-Semitism does not matter. Given the dramatic content of his movie, he's a carrier.

What happens next? The furor will quiet down. The film will be consigned to the limbo of Blockbuster. Churches will continue screenings at rallies as a tool of evangelization. (How Emmerich would feel about Gibson's retailing of her visions to make more Protestants I hate to think.) Gibson the Noble Victim will cash in, reaping the full reward of his nine-month publicity campaign. And let's face it: Gibson's virtuoso orchestration of public attention turned Ash Wednesday 2004 into a holy day of obligation for all sorts of fundamentalists who flocked, if not to Mass, then at least to the cineplex. That's a real Hollywood miracle.

Finally, Gibson and his minions, I must note with gratitude, have certainly educated me. The vicious e-mails that my colleagues and I have received, the hateful Web sites that this movie has spawned, and the angry displays of muscular piety prompted by this phase in America's culture wars have left me humbled and remorseful. With what conviction can I remain amazed by the literalism, the anger, and the defining power of hate in Islamic fundamentalism? With much less excuse, we have plenty of our own homegrown varieties right here.

10 Christ's Passion: Homoeroticism and the Origins of Christianity

Susannah Heschel

Mel Gibson's film is a classic example of colonialist rhetoric that uses first-century Palestine as an allegory for contemporary American conquests in the Middle East: the
triumphant empire whose rule of brute, destructive force
is masked by a pretense of moral and political superiority. In the film, the colonized are the Jews, whose religious
degeneracy reaches its zenith in their failure to recognize
Jesus as the Messiah, which in turn legitimates their colonial domination by Roman troops and the theological colonization of their scriptures by Christian religious leaders.
As is typical of most colonialist narratives, Gibson titil-
lates with plenty of violence, racism, and homoeroticism.

The ostensible focus of the film is the Jews, but in their
moral and sexual degeneracy and their inability to recognize Jesus as their savior, they are stand-ins for today's
Muslims, unable to understand the blessings of the Christian West. The film's gaze, however, is identified neither
with the Jews nor with Jesus, but with Pilate and Claudia, who represent the new American empire of George
W. Bush. This is one reason for the film's lack of appeal
in Europe, where the politics are different.

The anti-Judaism of the film lies not only in the repugnant Jews it portrays, but in its theological discourse regarding Christianity's relationship to Judaism. Throughout the film, homoeroticism is used to allow Gibson to achieve his religious goal: dissociating Christianity from its progenitor, Judaism. If Judaism is portrayed exclusively through male actors, most of whom are homosexual or at least sexually deviant, they cannot constitute a mother religion. Christianity is presented not as the product of Judaism, but as the moral and political powerhouse that conquers and colonizes Judaism. Using the story of Christian origins to depict a scenario of colonialism is not surprising. Christianity has been implicated in Europe's massive imperialist projects ever since the Roman emperor Constantine's conversion in the fourth century, to the point that by the 1930s European colonies and ex-colonies covered 84.6 percent of the land surface of the globe. In addition to its political power, however, Christian theology is also a colonizing theology.

In the domain of religion, Christianity colonized Judaism theologically, taking over its central theological concepts of the Messiah, eschatology, apocalypticism, election, and Israel, as well as its scriptures, its prophets, and even its God, and denying the continued validity of those ideas for Judaism. Indeed, no other major world religion has colonized the central religious teachings and scriptures of another faith and then denied the continued validity of the other, insisting that its own interpretations are exclusive truth. Through the Christian doctrine of supersessionism, Judaism came to function in Christian theology as the other whose negation confirms and even constitutes Christianity. Yet Christianity's colonization of Judaism is not a conquest in which Judaism is destroyed or sublated, but one that is reflected by Paul, who writes in Romans 11:28: "As regards the gospel, they are enemies of God for your sake; but as regards election they are beloved, for the sake of their ancestors." Enemies of Christianity, deniers of its faith, Jews are beloved for having unwittingly provided the very basis of Christianity. Without Judaism's concept of election, there would be no Christianity, yet by refusing to accept Christianity, the Jews become enemies who must be forced to submit. In its theological structure, then, Christianity created a colonialist model that provided an easy validation for subsequent geographic colonial ventures. At the same time, in colonizing Judaism, Christianity was unable to erase it; Judaism is taken within, becoming the unwilling presence inside the Christian realm, a presence that is deeply troubling and gives rise to a variety of strategies within Christian theology to contain, redefine, and, finally, exorcise that presence. The colonization is more than the transformation of Christianity into a state religion under Constantine and the colonization of Jews as people. It is also a matter of Christian theological discourse colonizing Jewish ideas with Christian scriptures and doctrinal traditions.

The odd and striking configuration of the film is its coupling of homoeroticism and anti-Semitism. The homoeroticism stems from the desperation of an agenda of Christian theological anti-Judaism. Theologically, the film attempts to defeat the old conundrum of Christian origins: if Christianity is the daughter religion of Judaism, what is new and original in its message? How can Christianity be the daughter religion of a religion as repugnant as Judaism (a repugnance reinforced by Christian teachings)? Moreover, if the Jews themselves failed to recognize Jesus as their promised Messiah, how can Christianity be said to have emerged from Judaism?

Gibson's filmic answer is to deny the possibility that Judaism is the mother religion of Christianity by representing Jews in the film only as men; by literally eradicating Jewish women he is metaphorically eradicating the possibility of theological motherhood. The result is a weirdly all-male presence on screen, punctuated only by Claudia, the wife of Pontius Pilate, and the two Marys, neither of whom is identified as Jewish or as practicing Judaism. Jewishness as represented by males in the film is repugnant and sexually deviant, deeply rooted in Western anti-Semitic stereotypes. In the one lingering sharp profile shot of a Jew toward the opening of the film, the hooked nose is clearly prominent. Why is Jesus the Jew not shown with such a nose? The exchange of money between Judas and the Jewish priests is a scene of money-grubbing—Judas dives for the silver coins as they fall to the floor. The smirking faces of the priests are matched by their overfed bodies (Jewish fat is a recurrent motif in the film), stringy black hair, and shifty way of walking—the priests actually waddle. All this is in contrast to the Romans Pilate and Claudia, who move with grace and ease, gliding. They are lean, clean, tall, elegant, quiet, gentle, and dignified. Claudia wears a white veil and seems to exemplify the association of purity with compassion—after all, her compassion for Jesus is that of someone who perceives his religious significance, not that of a disciple or family member. The film dwells on the Roman leaders less to exalt Rome than to provide a contrast to Jerusalem's Jews, a mob that demands the death of Jesus because, the priest proclaims, he broke the Sabbath. That, in turn, is yet another violation of the Gospels, since nowhere is this accusation made against Jesus at the trial. Nowhere in the Gospels does Jesus himself violate the Sabbath; he simply debates whether the acts of his disciples constitute a violation of the prohibition against work. Even

Pilate fears the Jews (another historical falsity). He is shown taking a big swallow to express his fear, and then explains that he is worried that if he denies the Jews' lust for Jesus's blood, they will destroy him. This, too, is entirely fanciful.

The film's anti-Semitism is not only a matter of replicating old stereotypes, though it does that well. The real juice of its racism lies in its narrative. The film's story of Jesus is racist not simply because of its images, but because it creates Jesus as the anti-race. That is, Jesus emerges from the Jews to become a non-Jew, a Christian. By retreating emotionally, spiritually, and physically into a solitary experience of horrific death, Jesus cleanses himself not simply of this world but of his environs, a religious purification that rids the Christian of the Jewish. That Jewishness is neither wholly carnal nor spiritual, but an undefined threat that can purge either body or soul and enter the one through the other, polluting the body through a corruption of the mind. Purity of the self can be achieved through a Christianization of the self, a removal of the Jewish, just as purification from the Jewish marks the creation of the Christian. The racism is produced by the narrative of the Christian story, not by the particular images of Jews.

What theological anxieties is the film trying to suppress? The anxiety over Jesus's identity, long a problem for Christian theologians, is clearly represented in the film. His identity is not entirely clear: is he a Jew or a Christian, masculine or feminine? He is shown in no positive connection to the Jews of the film, nor to Jewish institutions, such as temple and synagogue, despite the Gospels' attestations. The uncertainty of identity is precisely what makes him so susceptible to interpretation and also to gender politics: he is wounded, pierced, bleeding, victimized, and vulnerable, all classic attributes of the feminine. Is he indeed a man? A similar question can be asked of his Jewishness: after witnessing how the Jews repudiate him, turning him over for torture and death, demanding as a mob that Jesus, rather than a convicted murderer, be put to death, we can well ask: is Jesus indeed a Jew in this film?

The disavowal of Jesus's Jewishness is reinforced by the film's homoerotic politics, which Gibson undoubtedly did not intend but which emerge almost inevitably through the denial of Judaism as Christianity's mother religion. The film's Jews are uniformly male: the temple leaders, scribes, and Pharisees are all large, adult male members of the establishment. The women around Jesus are, like him, deracinated, showing no recognizable Jewishness. Jewish women have been excluded from the film in order to suggest metaphorically that Christianity has no Jewish mother that gave birth to a daughter religion. There is, instead, a homoeroticism that is inflected by race and leaves Jesus's sexuality ambiguous. The opening scene in the garden, filled with fog and dusk and sleeping men, has a gothic, dreamlike quality, and out of the mist rise Jesus and his disciples, as if discovered in the midst of secret activities. Satan is an androgyne, appearing first as a male, later as a mother (indeed, nursing a hideous infant with the face of an old man), and while Jesus is praying, a snake slithers out of the devil to penetrate him. The two Marys (mother and Magdalene), who also never indicate any Jewish identity, cling to one another, suggesting a homoerotic love enabled by their relationship with Jesus. Jesus and John have an intimacy that is delicate and gentle; when John clasps Jesus's thighs at the end of the film and gazes into his eyes, it is the firm, possessive gesture of a lover.

Gibson's Jews are its repugnant sexual deviants. Herod, king of the Jews, is a vulgar transvestite engaged in a lewd, drunken, bacchanalian orgy with a group of transvestite cohorts. The Jewish priests are a homosocial clan of physically unattractive men; they are stout and bloodthirsty, with yellowed teeth and gruesome sneers. Barabbas is horrific, a one-eyed monster who sticks out his tongue at the Roman soldiers and wiggles it in a lewd suggestion. The only "normal" heterosexual couple in the film is Pilate and Claudia, and it is with them, not Jesus or the Jews, that American viewers are to identify. It is their conversion that is the central event of the film: their recognition, as people of wealth and immense power, that Jesus is a special religious figure. They are the film's George and Laura Bush, leaders of the American empire, and it is them that Gibson wants Americans to identify with and to follow as an example of the religious conversion of the mighty empire. America is to be a Christian country and, through its empire, bring Christian "values" to the rest of the world—implicitly, the Muslims, who are lurking in the film's imagination as today's version of first-century Jews. As treacherous as the Jews were in Jesus's day, and as frightening as they were to Pilate, Christian America now faces the repugnant, violent Muslims of the Arab world who cannot understand Bush's American message of democracy and morality. They must be colonized to be converted, suppressed to be rendered safe.

The film's Jesus emerges from its cauldron of sexual deviants who surround him. His character suggests an undefined or perhaps innate asexuality, but his eroticism is expressed in the sadomasochism of the beatings he endures and to which his body silently responds with jerks and spasms. Gibson creates Jesus's manliness by showing him taking the flaying without screaming and then arising from his death shorn of his Jewishness and all the violence he experienced, reborn a Christian, if not a clear heterosexual; after all, his major love interest in the film is his mother, hardly a normative heterosexual passion.

The conundrum of Jesus's originality raised by the specter of his Jewishness has been central to the debates between Protestant and Jewish historians engaged in the historical reconstruction of Christian origins. Its revival today by Gibson is also stimulated by contemporary American politics. The film reflects and reestablishes the Christian hegemonic moment of the United States. Gibson's Jesus does not go to the synagogue or the temple, nor does he signify his Jewish loyalties in any recognizable fashion. A Jewish Jesus cannot be allowed to appear in the film because Christian hegemony cannot be established if historical truth forces Christianity to admit it is derived from Judaism. There can be no hegemony of Jesus if his teachings are shown to be neither unique nor original but shared with the Judaism of his day. Yet simply eliminating the Jewishness of Jesus is not sufficient; Gibson goes further by portraying the Jews as irrationally seeking the destruction of Christianity in the name of their religion.

Every era invents the Jesus that meets its needs. Gibson's Jesus is not simply the product of his own religious imagination; he is an expression of the contemporary American cultural moment and a response to the long Christian conundrum of whether Christianity is the daughter religion of Judaism. We might ask why Americans today want a film about the Passion of Jesus and not about his birth, miracles, preachings, or Last Supper, which constituted the topics of earlier films about Jesus's life. Put another way, the cultural demands of today's American colonialism have to rewrite Gibson's Scottish rebel fighting against British domination, in his 1995 film *Braveheart,* as Jesus. To contextualize Muslim terrorism against the West, the film presents a Jesus who is tortured rather than a Jesus who is the leader of a political liberation movement. The torment of Jesus in Gibson's film—a detailed account of torture found nowhere in the scriptures—brings the gruesome, prolonged, gory horror of medieval Catholic Passion fantasies together with those of Hollywood horror movies. That it has won particular acclaim from American Protestant evangelicals, where Bush has his strongest supporters, should not be surprising; theirs is a political alliance, not a theological one. This American Jesus of the twenty-first century creates and sanctifies the right-wing memory of the horrific events of September 11, 2001—the Passion of Christian America—when innocent, defenseless Americans were attacked over and over in a most brutal fashion, in an unthinkable, unprecedented, unwarranted assault that killed thousands of innocent people and left thousands of families bereft.

In reacting to those events, Americans did not embrace the hundreds of millions of people around the world who expressed their sorrow for us and their solidarity with us, nor did we turn inward and engage in a national effort at religious self-examination and atonement. Instead, we immediately declared war and looked for targets. We first bombed one of the poorest, most primitive countries on earth, Afghanistan, in a failed bid to capture Osama bin Laden, and then we turned against on an old enemy, Iraq, which had no known connections to the terrorist acts. Rage and war were the responses of our government, which claims it is waging war to create peace.

What acts have been committed in the name of Jesus's Crucifixion, as opposed to his teachings of love and generosity? Think of the wars, massacres, crusades, and burnings that have been stimulated by rage over his death, and imagine what we Americans might do with our passion if it is elevated from an unconscionable political assault to an act of religious martyrdom. Gibson throws down the gauntlet: the Passion is a metaphor for Christian America, bloody and violent, and the Christian colonization of Western civilization is a justification for America's colonization of the Middle East. Yet we may well wonder how this film will reflect on us, once it is seen in Muslim countries. Will American imperialism be linked to Christianity? Will the film evoke as much anti-Americanism as anti-Semitism? The question we ought to be asking ourselves as Americans is whether we can identify with the sufferings of another people. That is, after all, the premise of multiculturalism, but in the world of Gibson and Bush there are friends and there are enemies, and there is no turning the other cheek. Those who tortured Jesus to death are not the friends; after September 11, on which side are we going to place Muslims and Arabs?

One of the most common criticisms of Gibson's film has been the charge that the film deviates markedly from the text of the Gospels. Its account of the death of Jesus does not follow the Gospels' accounts; thus, some critics have concluded with a note of triumph, the film cannot be said to depict the end of Jesus's life with any historical accuracy. The false assumption, of course, is that the Gospels give a historically accurate account of Jesus's death, and that a disparity between film and Gospel will undermine Gibson's claims of Christian credibility. Yet such criticisms misunderstand the film's significance. It is a film of religious evocation, not historical instruction. That is clear from the adoration of the film by members of evangelical Protestant communities, who demand fidelity to the literal text of scripture and who have traditionally been opposed to the Catholicism whose traditions underlie Gibson's script. An alliance between the two is, of course, possible because their religions have become a matter of politics, not theology. And while proclaiming a passionate defense of the state of Israel, much to the delight of right-wing Jews, evangelical Christians are engaging in a holocaust of mischief that Jews have failed to recognize, but for which the Gibson film serves as a prime stimulus.

The film's anti-Semitism is located not only in its stereotypes and in its proclamation that the Jews are responsible for the death of Jesus, but in its Holocaust envy. Gibson wants the millions who have seen *Schindler's List* and who flock to the Holocaust Museum in Washington, D.C., to pay attention now to the Christian Holocaust: the death of Jesus. In the Crucifixion, Gibson is seeking to outdo in horror and suffering the many Holocaust films that have been seen by mass audiences and that their directors had hoped would inspire compassion for Jewish suffering. Part of the problem is that the Holocaust has no simple-minded, redemptive message, and that is what Gibson hopes his film will provide.

Holocaust envy has also been driven by the Christ envy expressed by some Jewish writers on the Holocaust. Long before Hitler, Jewish writers and artists used the Crucifixion to describe Jewish suffering: "Mir kumen tsu kholem di yidn vos hengen af tslomin; I dream of the Jews hanging on crosses," wrote Uri Zvi Greenberg in 1923. Marc Chagall's painting *The Crucified* (1944) depicts a village with fully clothed Jews hanging from a series of crosses. Later, the Holocaust came to be invoked as a crucifixion and the Crucifixion as a mass murder. For example, there is Elie Wiesel's famous image in *Night* of three Jews hanging on the gallows at Auschwitz, the middle victim a young child who is so light that the drop fails to break his neck, and so he dies slowly and agonizingly. An anonymous voice asks, "Where is God now?" And another answers, "Where is He? Here He is. He is hanging here on this gallows." In the appeal to Christ imagery that emerges from the passage, the suffering of the Jews is expressed by reference to the Crucifixion and by claiming superiority to it: the six million Jews are the greatest victims, not the single Jew Jesus. Such comparisons are reinforced by insistences that the Holocaust is a singular, unique, incomparable event.

Just as the Holocaust has become the point of reference for human suffering of the twentieth century, Gibson wants Christ's Passion to be the template for the future. Yes, six million Jews died, but, he suggests, in interviews and by letting his father's Holocaust denial become public knowledge, the flaying of Jesus far exceeded the suffering in the gas chambers of Auschwitz. Perhaps what he wants, in addition to creating a violent night at the movies, is to forge a template of cultural memory that will abide in our minds, haunting us, and through which we are now supposed to negotiate the long, terrible conflict that awaits us with the Muslim world.

That the film engages in a Holocaust tit-for-tat was confirmed for me when I saw a book entitled *The Passion of Jesus Christ,* written by a Minneapolis pastor, John Piper, being distributed outside the theater by a local evangelical group. The book opens with a chapter comparing the Crucifixion with Auschwitz and asks whether Auschwitz might lead to "an understanding of Christ's passion." Piper writes, "Is there a way that Jewish suffering may find, not its cause, but its final meaning in the suffering of Jesus Christ?" By comparison to Gibson, Piper's question sounds almost philo-Semitic, at least leaving a small space for Jewish experience.

Most worrisome about the film is its divisiveness. Its proponents argue that true Christians will be moved and inspired by the film, while those who find it offensive or dull reveal their lack of Christian salvific grace. While the film's opening epigraph is taken from Isaiah 53, perhaps a more appropriate verse would be 1 Corinthians 1:18: "For the message about the cross is foolishness to those who are perishing, but to us who are being saved it is the power of God." While Gibson might hope that the film will inspire its viewers to convert to Christianity, the film's primary goal is something different: to reveal those in its audience who are saved and those who are not. The film is a precursor to the "rapture," the instantaneous translation into heaven of saved Christians that precedes the Second Coming, according to premillennial dispensationalists. Those who are not saved will remain behind to suffer the apocalyptic tribulations. Like the promised rapture of the future, the film is supposed to expose us: those who are saved and those who are damned.

The revival of this sort of gnosticism in an era of fascism, terrorism, and nuclear weapons is the most dangerous role religion can play. With only a slight twist, the verse from Corinthians gives perfect justification in the name of God to kill people if they view the cross as foolishness. Even as Samuel Huntington tried to frighten and enrage us by inventing a "clash of civilizations," this film is creating a dangerous and ugly culture divide among Americans and among Christians.

11 Mel Gibson's Passion

Richard L. Rubenstein

With the extraordinary success of *The Passion of the Christ,* Mel Gibson has demonstrated that he is one of those especially empowered individuals who in the twenty-first century have the resources to challenge and conceivably alter long-established institutions. Unlike his father, Hutton Gibson, a marginal sectarian who has bitterly opposed Vatican II and the post–Vatican II church, the younger Gibson may be able single-handedly to reverse much of the recent work of Vatican II, especially in the field of Catholic-Jewish relations, through his mastery of powerful media such as the cinema and related digital media.

Briefly stated, Gibson's film reminds us that on the fundamental issue of how human beings relate to divinity, there is an unbridgeable chasm between Jews and Christians. There is, for example, in Judaism nothing remotely like the ritual of Holy Communion, in which the believer partakes of the true body and blood of the Savior. One of the strengths of *The Passion of the Christ* is that it makes the difference between the traditions unmistakably clear. That gulf was evident in the very different reactions most Christians and Jews had to the film. To the best of my knowledge, no film has ever depicted Christ's sufferings as graphically or as explicitly as Gibson's. Jews who saw the film viewed the graphic depictions of Jesus's suffering with great discomfort. This was certainly my reaction. The violence appeared gratuitous and excessive and had no redeeming feature. By contrast, it was precisely the excessive violence that had a redeeming feature for many, if not most, Christians.

Gibson offers his rationale for the film's extreme violence at the very beginning of the film, which is introduced with the biblical verse, "He was wounded for our transgressions; he was crushed because of our iniquities. *By his stripes were we healed*" (Isaiah 53:5, italics added). Christians have traditionally interpreted the verse to refer prophetically to the Passion of Jesus and its redemptive consequences. The verse gives context and legitimacy to the film's unending depiction of the suffering and pain inflicted upon Jesus. According to the New Testament scholar Paula Fredriksen, Gibson's Christ is a theological figure who saves "not through dying so much as through endless, unspeakable, unbearable suffering." Writing in the *New Yorker* in September of 2003, Peter J. Boyer relates that Gibson had been told by friendly audiences that *The Passion* was too violent and that seeing Jesus subjected to such an unending series of brutal assaults would "have a numbing effect on the audience, detaching them from Christ's pain." Gibson acknowledged the possibility but nonetheless kept the violence and brutality in the film.

Gibson's instincts were on target. If Christ atones vicariously for the sins of humanity, and if Christians are healed "by his stripes," then the more pain inflicted on Jesus in the film, the better. His torment constitutes a surrogate for the chastisement each and every sinner deserves at the hands of a just, righteous, and gracious God who nevertheless accepts Christ's pain as atonement for their sins. Moreover, the sacrificial character of Christ's Passion is emphasized in a scene near the end of the film in which the temple is torn asunder, symbolizing divine rejection of the temple, its priesthood, and the sacrificial system over which the priests presided. The film thereby dramatizes a crucial Christian teaching that only Christ's atoning sacrifice, and not the temple sacrifices, could save Israel and humanity. While there is no warrant for this scene in scripture, Gibson's version is symbolically consistent with traditional Christian teaching on the meaning of Christ's sacrifice.

Watching *The Passion*, I could not help but think of another recent depiction of alleged Jewish villainy, the presentation on TV networks throughout the Muslim world starting November 6, 2002, of *Horseman without a Horse*, an "historical" series based on the notorious forgery *The Protocols of the Learned Elders of Zion* that purports to show the existence of a secret international Jewish conspiracy aimed at securing worldwide domination and power. The series covers the Middle East from 1850 to 1948 and offers "proof" of an alleged Jewish plot to dominate the world, starting with the founding of the state of Israel. The unprecedented use of the *Protocols* in a television series reaching perhaps as many as 200 million Muslims continuously for forty-one days constituted a radical escalation of both the scope and the intensity of anti-Jewish propaganda in the Muslim world. The Nazis used a widely circulated print edition of the *Protocols* as an important legitimation of their plan to exterminate the Jews because of their alleged role as a hidden enemy within Christian Europe. The producers of *Horseman without a Horse* possess a far more effective propaganda medium, one that combines visual and dramatic power and is capable of influencing millions with varying degrees of literacy.

The paradigmatic image of Judas is what links *The Protocols of the Elders of Zion* and *Horseman without a Horse* with Gibson's film. In the film, not surprisingly, Judas is depicted as an especially repugnant archetypal Jew. The ascription of betrayal and treason as fundamental Jewish characteristics, which figures so prominently in *The Protocols,* has its roots in the image of Judas Iscariot betraying his master for money with a kiss. The moral of the Judas tradition is simple: no Jew can be trusted. Even his seeming virtue is only a demonic disguise for the betrayer's role. He may seem like a good citizen, a valued intellect, an unselfish patriot, but one can never be sure whether a betrayer lurks beneath these postures. And the story, imparted in the context of sacred times and seasons, is absorbed into the child's religious imagination before he or she is capable of critical reflection.

The image endures. When Alfred Dreyfus, the only Jew on the French General Staff, was unjustly accused by his colleagues in 1894 of having betrayed France's military secrets to Germany, he was identified with Judas. In the aftermath of Germany's defeat in World War I, the Judas story and the *Protocols* contributed greatly to establishing the credibility of the widely held belief that Germany's defeat was not due to the superior strength of the Allied military forces, including the entry of fresh troops from the United States into the war, but to a "stab in the back" (*Dolchstoß*) by Germany's internal Jewish enemies. Before and during World War II, the *Protocols* served as an implicit justification for the extermination of the Jews. German nationalists took the *Protocols* as "proof" that (1) the Jews were the hidden domestic force that had betrayed Germany and brought about her defeat and (2) the Bolshevik revolution was the result of a Jewish conspiracy to enslave the world and destroy Christianity. Such beliefs helped to render credible to the Nazis the conviction that genocide was a moral necessity. In his diary entry for May 13, 1943, the Nazi propaganda minister, Josef Goebbels, reported a conversation with Hitler concerning the *Protocols* in which Hitler expressed the belief "the *Protocols* were absolutely genuine." Hitler drew the conclusion that "there is therefore no other recourse left for modern nations except to exterminate the Jew" ("Es bleibt also den Modernen Völkern nichts anderes übriges, als die Juden auszurotten").

Both Gibson's depiction of Judas and his depiction of nonbelieving Jews as ugly and despicable also call to mind the role defamation of the Jews has played in the history of Christianity. The defamatory tradition has served to discredit any possible Jewish interpretation of the career of Jesus that runs counter to the accepted Christian narrative. The implicit symbolism of the defamatory tradition helped to cast doubt on the credibility of any possible Jewish challenge. Like Judas, neither the Jews nor their narrative was to be trusted. From the Christian perspective, an entire civilization had been erected on the basis of that tradition's story. Too much was at stake to permit a Jewish challenge to stand.

The film's unrelievedly sadistic brutality, culminating in the most graphic depiction of the Crucifixion ever presented in the cinema, seemed to me to border on the obscene, but, as a Jew, I am expressing a distinctly minority opinion. I was also reminded of the fact that in pre–Vatican II Europe, Holy Week was always a dangerous time for Jews. The recollection of Christ's suffering and Crucifixion, especially on Good Friday, elicited the temptation to avenge that most terrible crime on those who in the Christian religious imagination were regarded as its perpetrators. For most Christians throughout history, Christ's Crucifixion, blamed entirely on the unbelieving Jews in the film, was no ordinary homicide. It was the murder of God, the fountainhead of all goodness, order, and structure. The deicide accusation placed unbelieving Jews squarely in the camp of Satan, as does Gibson's film. To make his point, Gibson, without scriptural warrant, inserts into the narrative an arguably hermaphroditic Satan, played by a female actress, and seven demonic young Jewish boys. Because of our inability to accept the lordship of Christ, my people have traditionally been cast in the role of the most despicable of villains in the primary narrative of Western civilization.

Gibson's *Passion* has enormous dramatic power and emotional impact. One need not read the Gospels or even go to church to get its message. Like the video version of the *Protocols,* it has reached hundreds of millions of people, and subsequent DVDs may have additional scenes and dialogue. In the film Gibson depicts the high priest exclaiming in Aramaic, "His blood be upon us and our children" (Matthew 27:25) Gibson reluctantly omitted the translation of this line from the subtitles. However, given the success of the film and his indifference to Jewish concerns, there is nothing to prevent him from including the omitted subtitles in any forthcoming DVD. Contemporary media have greatly enhanced the ability of their possessors to distribute an owner's message with potentially explosive effect.

Nevertheless, I do not believe that Gibson's primary intention was to create an anti-Semitic film, even though the anti-Semitic message is one of the film's principal by-products. An intriguing article by the reporter Jean Cohen in the *Jerusalem Post* (March 12, 2004) sheds an interesting light on Gibson's motivation for producing the film. His father, Hutton, is an unreconciled, extremely right-wing Roman Catholic traditionalist who sired eleven children and was bitterly opposed to both the Second Vatican Council of 1962–65 and the Vietnam War. Fearing that his sons might be drafted to serve in the war, he moved his family to Australia, his wife's birthplace. In the summer of 1974, Mel, then eighteen years old, had an argument with his father and flew from Australia to Israel, where he stayed for a time at Kibbutz Degania, near the Sea of Galilee. According to Cohen, at the kibbutz young Gibson met and became close friends with Jamie Whittier and Claude Delancey. The latter testify that Gibson began to attend Sabbath services, to observe the Sabbath in accordance with traditional Jewish law, and to insist on eating only kosher food. One way or another, Gibson was apparently fated to be a true believer.

Within six months, young Gibson was taking conversion classes and had informed his family that he intended to remain in Israel as an Orthodox Jew. Given his father's religious commitments, this was the ultimate act of filial rebellion. In response, Hutton Gibson threatened to disown him. He also told Mel that Jesus had brought an end to Judaism as a valid religion, and that no son of his would become "a kike." Initially, Mel stood his ground. By the time Hutton arrived in Israel in November 1974, Mel had adopted the name Moshe and had begun to dress in the traditional black garb of Israel's most conservative Orthodox Jews. He also observed the practice of putting on *tefillin* (phylacteries) for morning prayers.

To get his son to return home, Hutton told Mel that his mother was suffering from cancer and had asked him to return immediately. Upon his return, his father and his brothers locked him in his room and cut him off from all contact with the outside world until he abandoned his plans to convert to Judaism. Gibson held out for two and a half weeks and then agreed to return to Catholicism—that is, to his father's distinctive version of Catholicism. Not long thereafter, Gibson began to denounce Jews and Judaism to anyone who would listen, although he later learned to be more discreet. His familial rebellion was at an end. The paterfamilias had restored his unquestioned authority.

Hutton Gibson's religion is hardly that of the Roman Catholic mainstream. He is one of the best-known contemporary traditionalists. The elder Gibson claims that Vatican II was "a Masonic plot backed by the Jews" (see Christopher Hutton, "Is the Pope Catholic . . . Enough?," *New York Times Magazine,* March 9, 2003). He also claims, in a letter to Prakash John Mascarenhas, that the post–Vatican II church is "not a Church but an apostasy" whose "official worship is idolatry." Like his fellow traditionalists, he is openly contemptuous of all of the popes who came after Pius XII, calling them heretics and asserting that "anyone who recognizes a heretic as pope joins that 'pope' in his heresy." According to the Hutton Gibson, the alleged destruction of the church by the post–Vatican II popes is a sign of the apocalypse. As soon as the destruction is complete, the world will end. Moreover, he sometimes depicts himself as single-handedly delaying that terrible day: "I figure that as long as there's one [true] Catholic in the world, it hasn't finished. So I'm trying to keep it going" (see Wendy Grossman, "Holy Father," *Houston Press,* July 24, 2003).

The alleged descent of an institution as ancient and durable as the Catholic church into such catastrophic heresy requires an explanation. Not surprisingly, the elder Gibson has found the source of such consummate villainy: the Jews, who he alleges are seeking to take over the church in pursuit of "one world religion and one world government." In effect, Gibson's accusation is yet another rehash of *The Protocols of the Elders of Zion.*

Casting the Jews as cosmic villains seeking world domination usually involves either denying the Holocaust ever took place or declaring that the Jews got what was coming to them. Hutton Gibson has chosen Holocaust denial. Historians of the Holocaust estimate that between five and six million Jews were murdered by Nazi Germany. The elder Gibson claims that they simply left Poland and settled in "the Bronx and Brooklyn and Sydney and Los Angeles."

But is there any connection between the elder Gibson's views and the film Mel Gibson has produced? Gibson has made no secret of the fact that, like his father, he is a traditionalist Catholic. While in Rome making the film, he attended Mass daily but took care to find a traditionalist priest, preferably one ordained before Vatican II, who would say the traditional Latin Mass. Gibson also holds the view traditional before

Vatican II that *extra ecclesiam nulla salus*—outside of the church there is no salvation. When queried whether he believes that non-Catholic Christians are disqualified from eternal salvation, Gibson replied: "There is no salvation for those outside the Church. . . . My wife is a saint. She's a much better person than I am. . . . She's, like, Episcopalian, Church of England. She prays, she believes in God, she knows Jesus, she believes. . . . And it's just not fair that she doesn't make it, she's better than I am. But that is a pronouncement from the chair. I go with it" (in Peter J. Boyer, "The Jesus War," *New Yorker,* September 15, 2003). The younger Gibson's commitment as a "traditional" Catholic has even involved financing at great personal expense the building and support of a "Traditional" Catholic church in his own community.

Among the achievements of Vatican II was a new openness to ecumenical dialogue with other religious communities, Christian and non-Christian. Especially noteworthy was the promulgation by Pope Paul VI on October 28, 1963, of *Nostra Aetate,* the church's declaration of its relationship with non-Christian religions. The document expressed approval of "fraternal dialogues" with Jews. This constituted a radical departure from earlier methods of imparting information about Christianity to Jews. The earlier methods included disputation and compulsory Jewish attendance at sermons by priests who used the occasion to denounce the "evils" of Judaism. In the Papal States the forced sermon remained in effect as late as the middle of the nineteenth century. In a disputation, one seeks to prove the truth of one's own religious claims and the falsity of one's opponents. By contrast, dialogue allows for mutual respect and understanding.

One of the most important results of Vatican II was the radical transformation of the church's relations with Jews. Nevertheless, the reforms of Vatican II hardly met with unanimous approval. A conservative wing of the church regarded the whole project of *aggiornamento,* bringing the church "up to date," as anathema. The dissenters regarded the reforms of Vatican II as undermining the fundamental strengths of the church. From the perspective of the sociology of religion, the conservative reaction was both predictable and inevitable, as indeed has been the worldwide rise of fundamentalism in other traditions. The church's willingness to enter into ecumenical dialogue was especially threatening to conservatives. If, as most Catholics believed at the time, membership in the Roman Catholic Church was the *only* way a person could gain salvation, then dialogue could serve no useful purpose. Representing truth, the church was seen as having neither reason nor need for dialogue with traditions it regarded as mired in error. After the death of

Pope John XXIII on June 3, 1963, the curia succeeded in moderating some of the reforms proposed by the council. Nevertheless, Vatican II represented a radical break from the past.

Most of the dissenters eventually accommodated. A small number, including Hutton Gibson, refused all accommodation. Rejecting the authority of the council, John XXIII, and Paul VI, his successor, they left the church altogether and invoked the term *sede vacante* (literally, "the seat is vacant") to describe the current condition of the church. The term is normally used for the situation in which a pope has passed on and a new one has yet to be elected. However, sectarian traditionalists such as Hutton Gibson argue that the papal throne has been empty since the passing of Pope Pius XII in 1958 and that John XXIII, Paul VI, John Paul I, and John Paul II were heretical antipopes.

So Gibson was unlikely to be moved by critics who suggested that there is a connection between traditional Christian anti-Judaism and the Holocaust. Gibson rejects the well-researched connection, arguing that "modern secular Judaism wants to blame the Holocaust on the Catholic Church. And it's lie. And they have been working on that one for a while" (quoted in Boyer). In reality, no responsible scholar, Jewish or Christian, blames the Holocaust on the Catholic Church. They do hold that Christian anti-Judaism, especially the deicide accusation, was an important contributing factor in creating the climate that made the Holocaust possible. Gibson may or may not agree with his father on the Holocaust, but he did trivialize it in an interview with the *Wall Street Journal* columnist Peggy Noonan: "some Jews" did die during World War II, but so did millions of non-Jews; hence, the Holocaust is of little account.

Before the film opened, Gibson reportedly said that *The Passion* could be a career killer for him. He had invested $25 million of his own money, and, even after production was under way, it was by no means certain that he would recover his investment or that the film would even open. Contrary to initial expectations, the film has been a huge money maker. Nevertheless, it is highly unlikely that Gibson's primary motive was profit. Moreover, as stated above, I do not believe that Gibson deliberately set out to produce a film overtly hostile to Jews, although hostility to Judaism was a by-product of his fundamental objective.

In my opinion, Gibson wanted to tell the story of the Passion out of genuine religious conviction, but religion as understood by traditionalists such as his father, that is, as if Vatican II had never happened and as if there had been no responsible New Testament scholarship in the twentieth century to show that the Gospels cannot be read as undiluted "history." By so doing, he was using the primary narrative of Christian civilization to correct what in his mind and that of his father had been the disastrous wrong turn taken by the church at Vatican II and thereafter. Such a film was, of necessity, hostile to Judaism and to those Jews who were faithful to their own traditions. Let us recall that Hutton Gibson had told his son that Jesus had brought an end to Judaism as a valid religion. As we shall see, implicit in this radical supersessionism is the conviction that Jews who reject Jesus, both in ancient times and today, are not only spiritually blind but satanic.

Gibson's film also demonstrates that the church of Pio Nono, that is, Pius IX (1792–1878), and his Syllabus of Errors (December 8, 1864) still retain a powerful attraction for many Catholics. Strongly disapproving of Vatican II, traditionalists such as Hutton and Mel Gibson find the spirit of the Syllabus of Errors very congenial, for, in truth, it is *their* spirit. The syllabus lists eighty of the "principal errors of our times." The concluding eightieth article effectively summarizes the entire list by characterizing as error the view that "the Roman Pontiff can and should reconcile himself to and agree with progress, liberalism, and modern civilization." The Syllabus of Errors was a call to undo the political and social results of the French Revolution and the Enlightenment. Implicitly, it was also a rejection of the application of the historical method to the study of religious texts and institutions. Such studies introduce into religious scholarship the idea of the context in which a text was composed or a tradition took root. Once introduced, historical narratives tend to become nuanced, and it becomes difficult, if not impossible, to regard historical events as expressing a cosmic struggle between that which is totally good and that which is utterly evil. In addition, questions arise such as whether the infant church might have had a strong political interest in ascribing guilt for the Crucifixion to the "Jews" and exculpating the Romans.

This may indeed have been the case. Jesus was crucified for the offense of sedition, always a serious transgression in the eyes of the Romans and perceived to be especially grave after the unsuccessful Jewish rebellion of 66–70 C.E. In the aftermath of that war, it would have been impolitic for Christians to have proclaimed that their deepest loyalty belonged to a Jew condemned by an important Roman official for sedition. This does not mean that there were no Jews among those who sought Jesus's death. Nevertheless, in view of what we know about Pilate from other contemporary sources, it stretches the limits of credibility to regard him as guiltless, as do, for example, both the fourth Gospel and Gibson's film. According to Philo Judaeus, a contemporary of Pilate, as governor

of Judea Pilate was of an "inflexible, stubborn, and cruel disposition."
His administration was characterized by "greed, violence, robbery, assault, abusive behavior, frequent executions without trial, and endless
savage ferocity." Other ancient sources depict him as harshly violent
and contemptuous of Jewish religious sensibilities.

The writers of the Gospels had not only a political motive for stress-
ing Jewish culpability, but also a theological motive. The gospel narratives depict Jesus as fulfilling God's plan for human salvation as he
confronts the dark forces that oppose that plan. By opposing Jesus, the
Jews become, ipso facto, the embodiment of those dark forces. In the
film, as in the fourth Gospel, Jesus declares, "I am the way, and the truth,
and the life; no one comes to the Father, save by me" (John 14:6). The
implication is unmistakable: those who oppose Jesus hinder God's plan
of salvation and are of Satan. Elsewhere the fourth Gospel depicts Jesus
as saying to the Pharisees: "If God were your Father you would love me,
for I proceeded and came forth from God. . . . Why do not understand
what I say? It is because you cannot bear to hear the truth. You are of
your father the devil, and your will is to do your father's desires. He was
a murderer from the beginning, and has nothing to do with the truth,
because there is no truth in him" (John 8: 44).

By filming *The Passion,* Gibson has focused with powerful emotional
impact on that which separates Judaism and Christianity. I believe that
he has done so not out of malevolence but out of very strong religious
feeling, given his distinctive religious commitment. I also suspect that
while he apparently has little hesitation about challenging the authority of the church, especially with regard to Vatican II, there is one authority he will not challenge: Hutton Gibson. Nor is it surprising that
both Christians committed to ecumenical dialogue and thoughtful Jewish leaders and thinkers have objected to Gibson's focus. Unlike Gibson,
who is indifferent to historical biblical scholarship, they know all too
well the dangers that lurk when the differences between Judaism and
Christianity are not moderated.

Vatican II represented the church's well-intentioned effort to main-
tain its claims while finding a way for Jews to live in freedom and relative security in predominantly Christian lands. The results could not
have been entirely satisfactory to either side, but they represented an
honest and largely successful attempt to place Jewish-Christian relations on a more harmonious footing than ever before. As noted, the
transformation could not satisfy those Catholics who felt that Vatican
II had undermined Christian faith, opened the floodgates of moral relativism, and misrepresented some of the most crucial Christian beliefs

about the Savior and his enemies. Nor would the passing of time result in greater acceptance of Vatican II among conservatives. Unlike
Hutton Gibson, many powerful and influential conservative Catholics
have worked within the church to undermine the reforms of Vatican II.
They have an enormous advantage. Their uncompromising version of
the church as an immutable institution and as the sole divinely ordained
institution for human redemption offers far greater religious, moral,
and emotional security than a version of Christianity that is historically
knowledgeable and emphasizes a greater measure of individual responsibility in matters religious and moral. The consecration of an avowed
homosexual as a bishop in the Anglican communion and the willingness
of the clergy of some Protestant denominations to perform same-sex
marriages are not taken by conservatives as examples of the flowering
of individual responsibility but as object lessons in moral decline and
decay.

Nor can most conservatives look with favor on the post–Vatican II
church's attempt to mitigate the deicide accusation, even for contemporary Jews. For them, nothing has changed. The separation between
Judaism and Christianity must remain unbridgeable, save for those Jews
who cross over the line by converting. Gibson has succeeded in producing an important film that gives great comfort to hard-line conservatives as well as conventional believers and great discomfort to those who
work for a softening of religious conflict, at least between Judaism and
Christianity.

12 The Passion for Social Justice and *The Passion of the Christ*

Margaret R. Miles

Popular movies, measured by their box-office success, should be examined not only for their narrative content and cinematography, but also for historical antecedents and for their relation to the cultural "moment" of their production and first-run circulation. After considering the history of instructions on meditating on the passion, I will explore the messages sent, or "effects," of *The Passion of the Christ* in the context of a dramatically growing gap between haves and have-nots in American society. Within the culture of fear created by this gap, *The Passion* can be seen as "misdirection"—a magicians' term for gestures that attract attention away from what is actually occurring. In this context I suggest that attention to what the Gospels report Jesus as saying and doing would be more fruitful than attention to what was done to him.

Let us begin with the obvious: *The Passion of the Christ* is a movie. It is neither a window on nor a mirror of reality. And we, watching it, are spectators. As spectators, we do not see a movie as if for the first time. We are *trained* by our many viewing experiences to expect and respond to a number of film conventions. A series of learned responses is activated as soon as the lights go down in the theater. The first of these is detachment. You are *not* there; you are in the comfortable anonymity of a darkened theater, perhaps eating popcorn. In other words, movies are entertainment, and entertainment places the viewer in a position of distance and passivity.

Some spectators report that *The Passion of the Christ* provided a vivid stimulus for increased Christian commitment. In what follows I consider this claim in relation to film conventions in contemporary American entertainment culture. On the one hand, viewers' reports of their own experience are to be respected. On the other hand, there are reasons to doubt that the movie ultimately enhances understanding of, and empathy with, Christianity's founder.

Two contexts help to focus *The Passion of the Christ*. The first is a long history of Western devotion to Jesus's Passion (from the Latin *patior*, to suffer). The second is the historical moment and social context in which the movie was produced and had its first run. Both contexts reveal a gap between the director's much-publicized intentions in making the film and the film's effects.

Until the fifth century of the Common Era, Christians did not use the cross as a symbol of their commitment. Not a single cross can be found in the large number of extant catacomb paintings of the second and third centuries. As depicted in *The Passion,* crucifixion was a Roman form of painful and ignominious execution used for slaves and noncitizens. Constantine, (r. 313–37 C.E.), the emperor under whom Christianity was legitimized, discontinued its use. Its association with criminal punishment had faded from living memory by the fifth century, when the first cross in Christian art appeared on the carved wooden door of Santa Sabina, Rome. In short, the earliest Christians did not consider the cross an acceptable emblem of their faith.

After this, however, the history of Western devotion to the Passion reveals increasingly realistic Crucifixion scenes in the form of paintings and tableaux. The popular devotion to the cross first arose in Western Europe in the fourteenth century. Franciscan preachers urged their listeners to place themselves imaginatively in the emotions of spectators at the foot of the cross, empathetically sharing their devotion and grief. Frescoes in churches facilitated viewers' imagination, and devotional manuals provided detailed instructions on how to place oneself emotionally within the sacred scene. In northern Italy several *sacri monti*, or sacred hills, presented tableaux from the life and Passion of Jesus, featuring lifelike figures with real clothing and hair. Pilgrims paused at each scene to meditate on the narratives and to experience the emotions represented. Some tableaux are still in use today: for example, the one

at Ste. Anne de Beaupré, outside Quebec City in Canada, attracts tens
of thousands of visitors annually.

The devotional instructions that accompany exercises in contemplation of the Passion encourage devotees to imitate its first viewers'
love and grief, prompted them to detailed imaginative reconstruction of
the smells, sounds, temperature, physical fatigue, and spiritual anguish
around the Crucifixion. Viewers were instructed to imagine themselves
in the body and emotions of one of the spectators, so as not to presume
identification with Christ's suffering. In Renaissance paintings, Saint
John, the Virgin, and the hysterically weeping Mary Magdalene are the
figures whose postures and gestures communicate their emotions and
invite the viewer's identification. In *The Passion of the Christ,* however,
there was little inducement to identify with those who watched the Crucifixion. Both Marys weep helplessly, while John is an incidental character with little substance. Rather, spectators are asked to identify with
the suffering Christ, and little or nothing of this suffering is left to the
viewer's imagination. There is a contradiction between entertainment
(passivity)—the condition in which movies are viewed—and religious
engagement that requires viewers' imaginative participation (activity).

Early Christians' rejection of the cross as a symbol of their faith
prompts further examination of the value of this symbol. Every religion must, if it is to be effective in orienting people's lives, "explain"
suffering, and the message of the cross is that, contrary to most human experience, suffering can be productive. Christians believe that the
salvation of the world was achieved through Christ's death and Resurrection. Moreover, suffering people can identify with Christ's suffering,
believing that Christ shares their suffering.

In its contemporary context, *The Passion of the Christ* might find
its visual precedents in the grotesquely suffering Crucifixion images of
the Spanish-influenced southwestern United States. Contorted bodies,
blood, and anguished expressions are featured in this art, for which
the suffering of oppressed and marginalized people provides the context. Similarly, Matthias Grünewald's early-sixteenth-century Isenheim
Altarpiece, one of the most gruesome Crucifixions ever painted, was
commissioned by a monastery hospital that served patients with the
"burning sickness," which ate into their skin and eventually caused them
to lose limbs. Patients were regularly brought to contemplate the grisly
Crucifixion scene that matched so accurately their own disease in order to identify with Christ's suffering and pray for either healing or the
grace to bear their torment. The context is different for a Hollywood
movie marketed primarily to comfortably middle-class Americans who

are shielded in every possible way from seeing and/or experiencing extreme physical suffering.

Was the real achievement of Christ's Crucifixion a physical event in which a human being suffered and died? Or was it, as Eastern Orthodox Christians believe, a spiritual event? In Orthodox icons Christ is shown reigning triumphantly from the cross, his eyes open, his body erect. The answer must be that the Crucifixion entailed both physical suffering and spiritual triumph. Jesus's real suffering was the point of the earliest theological debate in the Christian church: Gnostic Christians claimed that his suffering was only in appearance, not in reality. Other Christians said that the doctrine of the Incarnation depends on the fact that Jesus shared the human condition in every respect—birth, vulnerability to suffering, and death. By the end of the second century, "orthodoxy" (literally, "right belief") was defined by belief in the Incarnation of Jesus in a real human body. By the mid-fourth century, Jesus's full divinity was acknowledged at the Council of Nicaea, along with his full humanity. To deny one or the other became heretical. The only brief reference to Christ's divinity in *The Passion* was the moment in which Christ healed the soldier's ear, struck off by Peter in anger. Despite the director's stated intention of making a movie faithful to the Gospels and Christian belief, Jesus's physical nature dominates the film to the near-exclusion of his divine nature.

The second context important to interpretation of *The Passion of the Christ* is the culture and society in which it was produced and shown in first-run theaters. Even when a director contributes his own money toward financing a film, it will not be made unless there is a reasonable expectation that it will be successful at the box office. Box-office success is at least partly predicated on attracting the largest social group that determines box-office success, namely, male teenagers. Rated R, *The Passion* was the top moneymaker at the box office for three weeks after its release on February 25, 2004. A week after it opened it had grossed almost $214 million, a figure that climbed past the $370 million mark in the nineteen weeks it remained on the top-ten list. During Holy Week of 2004 alone, *The Passion* earned an estimated $17 million, passing the top-grossing movie of the weekend before, *Hellboy*. While *The Passion* was in the top ten of VHS rentals, it was rented 3,220,000 times. A reedited version, *The Passion Recut*, which eliminated some of the most violent footage, was released in March 2005.

Although the audience for *The Passion* was increased by intensive marketing to conservative churches, many spectators were attracted by the movie's violence. Can violence effectively convey a religious message in the context of a society in which violence is no longer shocking, but entertainment? Desensitized by screen violence, the American public takes a high level of street violence for granted. Considering it deplorable but inevitable, we are unwilling to take measures that could significantly reduce it.

Multiple film conventions besides violence ensured the popularity of *The Passion*. Traditional Hollywood gender roles and expectations were reiterated. For example, though some reviewers claimed to see an androgynous devil, the devil, played by a female actor, is a woman. The familiar bad woman/good woman dichotomy was evident: while the bad woman instigates and enjoys Jesus's torture and Crucifixion, the good women weep passively. Moreover, Hollywood movies often use beautiful music to accompany and romanticize violence. The soundtrack of *The Passion* has, at the time of this writing, gone gold (selling 500,000 CDs) and is expected hit platinum soon. The director, Mel Gibson, commented that the musical score "propels the brutal image to a higher, almost lyrical, plane." In short, recognition of the film conventions that contributed to the box-office success of *The Passion* makes it necessary to question whether these are conducive to religious inspiration.

The broader context of American society must also be considered when we seek to understand the possible cultural effects of a movie. The United States does not lack suffering people who might identify with Christ's suffering, but these people probably lack the price of admission to the movie. It is striking that the wealthiest society in the world does not adequately feed its needy young, care for the old and the sick, and assist the poor to earn a living wage. In their 1999 book, *The Social Health of the Nation: How America Is Really Doing,* Marc and Marque-Luisa Miringoff argue that while Americans receive constant reports on the nation's economic health, reports on the nation's social health are few and episodic. Reports on such factors as "the well-being of America's children and youth, the accessibility of health care, the quality of education, the adequacy of housing, the security and satisfaction of work, and the nation's sense of community, citizenship, and diversity" are not publicly and regularly available as part of "how we're doing." If social data were regularly reported, the Miringoffs say,

> Americans would have to acknowledge that despite a booming economy, several key social factors have worsened significantly over time and are currently performing at levels far below what was achieved in previous decades. Suicide rates among the young are 36% higher than they were in 1970. . . . Income inequality is

at its worst level in fifty years. . . . More than 41 million Americans are without health insurance, the worst performance since records have been kept. Violent crime remains almost double what it was in 1970. . . . Average wages for American workers have fallen sharply since the 1970s, despite the strong economy. Child abuse has increased dramatically. . . . Approximately one in five children in America lives in poverty, a 33% increase since 1970.

In a cultural context in which American society is slipping dramatically from levels of support achieved more than thirty years ago, becoming meaner and meaner, often in the name of Christian values, *The Passion* implies that contemplation of the sufferings of Christ is the sole duty of a (still dominantly) Christian society. When Christians' attention is exclusively on Jesus's suffering and death, they are not likely to understand their religious duty to be the alleviation of present suffering. Whether or not the director intended it, the movie supports the short-sighted cruelty of our society.

Focus on the last hours of Jesus's life effectively erases most of his life and teachings. Isn't Christ's life normative for Christians? Yet his ministry is given brief attention, and that only in a few flashbacks. A very different picture of the mission of the Christ would emerge if attention were focused away from what was done to him and onto his own words and actions. For, according to the Gospels, Jesus spent his adult life ministering to bodies as well as souls. He fed and healed those who were hungry and sick. But Jesus's message of loving concern for the people he encountered is not a message that American society wants to hear. The very name "Christian" has been usurped by those who advocate fewer provisions for the indigent, the sick, the young, and the old. Tax cuts that ensure the riches of the rich and the poverty of the poor are supported by leaders who identify themselves as Christian. Yet Jesus's life and work stood for the kind of compassion that would include a more equitable distribution of resources, both within the United States and across the globe. In this context, *The Passion*'s tacit encouragement to neglect the pressing needs that surround us in favor of passive engagement with a visual representation of Christ's suffering is, to many, a welcome cultural message.

Because movies are distributed internationally, they must be discussed not only in the context of American society, but also in a global context. In a world in which ethnic conflicts create wars, *The Passion* depicts caricatured and stereotypical Jews as responsible for Jesus's death.

Pontius Pilate, described by historians of his time (Philo and Josephus) as a bloodthirsty thug who liked to crucify Jews without trials, was portrayed as sensitive and reluctant to kill Jesus. In Western history, every period of increased attention to Christ's Passion has been accompanied by increased persecution of Jews. The First Crusade (1096), preached as vindication for Jesus's Crucifixion, included the first pogroms against European Jews. Persecution of Jews also accompanied renewed devotion to the Passion in the fourteenth century. The domestic screening of *The Passion* has created an uncomfortable public ambience for Jews. We can predict that its international distribution will encourage further harassment and persecution. Indeed, during Holy Week of 2004, Palestinians sold thousands of copies of the video of *The Passion* in order to spread the negative image of Jews it contains. One American reviewer wrote, "Hitler would have loved this movie."

I suggest that Christians could become better Christians, not by viewing a Hollywood director's interpretation of Christ's sufferings, but by participating in Christ's teachings and ministry. A present-day imitation of Christ might take the form of supporting social programs that feed the hungry and provide people with health care. And the Christ who drove the moneychangers from the temple would be likely to protest corporate greed. The active, compassionate Christ of the ministry years has much to teach American society. But it is not likely that a movie about that Christ would be successful at the box office.

13

The Passions of the Reviewers; Or, Why Liberals Are Right for the Wrong Reasons and Conservatives Are Wrong for the Right Ones

Mark Douglas

Few cultural events have stirred up more interest or dispute among Christians of all stripes than the release of *The Passion of the Christ*. Even before its Ash Wednesday release, people had already formed (or were supposed to have formed) strong opinions about this movie. It probably says something about both the power of the arts in our lives and the relative comforts in which we live such that we could become so utterly preoccupied by a mass-distributed movie and its success.

I am not a film critic. Although I can usually provide a decent account of my reasons for liking and disliking movies, when it comes to evaluating such matters as cinematography, lighting, editing, musical score, and all the rest of the things for which the Academy of Motion Picture Arts and Sciences awards Oscars, I am a rank amateur. So I do not know that I have anything especially incisive to say about *The Passion* on the grounds of its excellence as a movie.

As a theologian and social critic, however, I am by both training and inclination someone who attempts to examine society—its mores, its presumptions, and their implications—from a theological perspective not only in order to say something about society, but in the hope of effecting some small change in it. Thus, I want to explore responses to the movie as much as the movie itself. Social reaction to this movie has taken on a dichotomous character: people tend either to really like or to really dislike this movie—and often, at least by my observations, for pretty bad reasons. Members of the former group (who are mostly liberals) say they are disturbed by this movie for two reasons: it is extremely violent, and it is at least implicitly anti-Semitic. I will suggest that these are the right reasons to be concerned about this movie but that this group mislocates the nature of its problems with violence and anti-Semitism. That is, they are right, but for the wrong reasons. Those in the latter group (who are mostly conservatives) applaud the movie's claims about Jesus's deep love for humanity and the pain that he was willing to undergo in order to redeem human beings from sin. These points, I suggest, are the ones Gibson intended us to take from the movie. However, we ought not to take them at face value, for the movie misrepresents both Jesus's atoning work and the human beings on whose behalf he worked. That is, this group is wrong, but for the right reasons. For convenience' sake—while keeping my "mostlys" in mind as a qualifier—I'll call these two groups "liberal critics" and "conservative supporters," respectively.

Liberal Critics

I'll begin with the liberal critics and the matter of violence. Most have been appalled at the amount of violence in this movie, which seems to them to go far beyond what is necessary, appropriate, and/or helpful. The violence is so explicit, unending, and extreme that it effectively undermines any moral point Gibson wanted to make. Gibson's willingness to show this violence, they say, reveals just how attracted society is to violence, and attraction to violence is rather straightforwardly bad. To bolster their claims, they connect *The Passion* to some of Gibson's other movies, such as the *Mad Max* series or *Braveheart*. In this movie as in those earlier ones, say these critics, violence takes on its own meaning—or, rather, substitutes for meaning. It is "pornographic," a "sacred snuff film" that turns the audience into voyeurs.

I certainly agree that the violence is explicit, unending, and extreme. I don't think, however, that this violence is like the type of romanticized and abstracted violence of those other movies or of so many more movies like them. This is no *Kill Bill, Vol. 1*, and the violence, at least to judge from the seemingly universal response given to the movie by its audiences, is decidedly not pornographic. Yes, it is ugly, bloody, and horrific—as I imagine we would expect, given the various tortures Jesus of Nazareth underwent. But there is nothing attractive about this violence, romantic in its use, or abstracted from life in its portrayal. Violence in this movie doesn't cause joy or excitement or a rush of adrenaline the way *Pulp Fiction* or some video games do. It causes pain, and we, as an audience, feel what it causes in us as pain.

Indeed, intentionally or not, Gibson has helped us recover our proper human response to violence and the pain it causes: we try to turn away from it. As Elaine Scarry reminds us in her remarkable book *The Body in Pain,* pain is more or less indefinable and unshareable, but its closest definition is probably "that which we seek to get away from."

Think, for a moment, about the responses moviegoers have to this movie. Even the ones who love it are appalled. They cry. They talk of how hard it was to watch. They say that this movie made them suffer. They feel pity or anger or—especially—revulsion. Indeed, critics who are revolted by the film feel the right thing, but direct it at the wrong event: they say the problem is that the movie masochistically intends to provoke excitement by inflicting suffering. I say that the movie asks its audience to feel revulsion—not excitement or its pathological corollary, masochism.

That's not voyeuristic. It's anti-voyeuristic; it's anti-pornographic. Pornography abstracts our natural and proper responses to things such as sex and violence and treats them instead as sources of amusement or fascination. Rather than connecting sex with embodied human intimacy and love, pornography connects it with a kind of objectified and abstracted self-absorption. Rather than connecting violence with suffering and moral failure, pornography connects it with pleasure and victory. Pornography, in short, entices us to think or feel the opposite of what we should about what we are watching. Given this definition, whatever else the violence in *The Passion* is, it isn't pornographic.

Gibson has been explicit on this point. He wants us to see this violence as violence, to see suffering as its result, and to feel something other than pleasure upon seeing it. Indeed, ignored in the furor over the violence is the degree to which a strong anti-violence streak runs through the movie in the person of Jesus, who time and again refuses to respond to violence with violence and time and again calls on others to do the same. When they notice this streak, liberals say it is just a cover for promoting violence. I say that the movie is consistent in both its treatment of violence and its rejection of violence: in this movie, the violence perpetrated by the people around Jesus is clearly meant to be understood as sin, not righteousness.

So when liberals criticize the movie's violence, what they are implicitly saying is that they simply do not like violence (or at least violence portrayed as violence) and would prefer that it didn't exist. Take, for example, Leon Wieseltier's claim in the *New Republic Online* (Feb. 28, 2004) that the movie's "lurid style" shows "contempt for the moral sensitivities of ordinary people." What Wieseltier suggests as a central problem of the movie is precisely what Christians have long thought the cross was: something that ought to upset our moral sensitivities. It was torture. It was horror. It was, to use Paul's words from 1 Corinthians 1:23, a "stumbling block" at the heart of the faith—something that "ordinary people" could only address while knowing that their moral sensitivities wouldn't like it.

Of course it would be nice not to face such violence. But that isn't a position people can hold and still be attentive to the world around them. Violence does exist; it cannot finally be ignored or denied. And if art is to make comment meaningfully on the world, it needs to be given the freedom to portray violence. Art's moral responsibility (if I may use that phrase), then, is to help us look at the suffering caused by violence as just that: suffering. It seeks to evoke in us feelings of revulsion or pity or even despair—to make us aware of horrors as horrors. And the violence of *The Passion* attempts to get us to do just that.

The denial of violence, on the other hand, becomes its own peculiar form of moral pornography: it allows us to abstract ourselves from the world around us so that we can better enjoy our fabricated and insular lives. Violence denial entices us to deny its real impact—suffering—any place in our lives and instead feeds our own desire for a life apart from pain. But to live a life apart from pain is only possible by not letting the world around us touch us when we observe it. And that, quite literally, is voyeuristic.

Which is not to say that the movie gets violence or our response right. The problem with the violence in this movie is multifaceted and profound. However, the problem is not simply that it exists or that it is protracted and explicit. I will return to this criticism momentarily. Presently, however, I want to address the other chief criticism aimed at *The Passion:* its anti-Semitism.

There is no doubt that Caiaphas, the Sanhedrin, and the temple guard come off badly in this film. Nor is there any doubt that the Jewish mobs in Pilate's courtyard appear far more interested in slaking some type of

FIGURE 5 Gibson's left hand grasping the nail. Still from *The Passion of the Christ* (2004).

bloodlust than doing justice or loving mercy. There is also no doubt that in the long history of the Christian faith, Jews have been persecuted, tortured, and murdered as "those who killed Christ." Christians have much to atone for in this matter. And the very fragility of Jewish-Christian relations might make this an ill-advised time for the film.

Yet lost in all the criticisms about the film's anti-Semitism is the fact that almost all the sympathetic characters in the film are also Jewish. Beyond Jesus himself and his disciples (or at least John, Jesus's mother, and Mary Magdalene), the film not only emphasizes the figures of Simon of Cyrene (one of the few characters who is explicitly named as a Jew) and the extracanonical woman, Veronica; it beatifies them. There are even a few somewhat sympathetic members of the Sanhedrin—members who are themselves rejected for not rejecting Jesus. Noting this, some Jewish critics, such as Michael Medved and Joel Siegel, as well as the conservative rabbi Daniel Lapin, have been far kinder in their evaluations. Also lost is the sheer preponderance of unsympathetic non-Jewish characters. Indeed, most of the Roman soldiers come off as far more sadistic than Caiaphas, the Sanhedrin, and the temple guards. Moreover, Gibson—the director who filmed his own hand holding the hammer used to nail Jesus's hand to the cross—certainly appears to be authentic in his protest that he is implicating himself, and maybe everyone else, in crucifying Jesus, not simply Jews.

Again, this isn't to say that the film isn't anti-Semitic. There is a form of anti-Semitism at work here. It is not the form that critics have been most attentive to, however, and so I need to return to it shortly. First, however, let me say a word or two about conservative supporters of the movie who, I have claimed, are wrong, but for the right reasons.

Conservative Supporters

Unsurprisingly, some liberal critics and conservative supporters of the movie have been more interested in the chance the movie gives them to condemn each other than in the movie itself. Yet while conservative supporters seem to have closed ranks around this movie, they haven't done so just as a way of criticizing liberals. Instead, some have taken upon themselves the task of defending not only its accuracy as history (a task almost mind-bogglingly hard to take up, given that Gibson is working from a nineteenth-century Christian mystic's vision of events described differently in the four Gospels and from contentious church traditions— all of which are, themselves, open to historical questions) or its political and artistic importance, but also its theological understanding of the events. These theological defenses have taken two forms.

The first and maybe most important of these defenses has been to suggest that *The Passion* represents a theologically accurate conception of atonement, or the theory about how Jesus's death reconciles us to God. The movie, after all, begins with a quote from Isaiah 53: "He was wounded for our transgressions, he was bruised for our inequities; upon him was the chastisement that made us whole, and with his stripes we are healed." In this, conservative supporters have defended a particular way of thinking about how Jesus redeems human beings from sin: he who is without sin takes their sin upon himself and thereby pays the penalty they owe but cannot pay. Jesus substitutes himself for human beings.

I doubt that Mel Gibson has anything like a developed theory of atonement, and beyond this substitutionary claim (a claim, by the way, that is present in all the classic theories of atonement), I think both Gibson and his audience would be hard pressed to discern or describe how atonement happens. Of course, part of the difficulty in seeking out a theory of atonement in the movie is that the books upon which it is ultimately based—those of the New Testament—don't have a theory either. Instead, they reveal many different images of and metaphors for atonement—though the dominant ones are substitutionary as well. So it is difficult to be too hard on Gibson for lacking a theory.

Clearly, though, Gibson means to advocate substitutionary atonement of some type. And given its centrality in two thousand years of history in Christian theology, condemning Gibson for making this point only turns him into the very figure he's portrayed himself as: someone martyred for being an apologist for the faith. So by focusing on atonement, conservative critics get something importantly right about the movie's intent: they call us to think about the relationship between Jesus's suffering and death and our own lives.

However, conservatives also get some things significantly and even fundamentally wrong. The most important of these has to do with the way violence relates to atonement. For while the movie is ambiguous in describing how atonement happens, one of the themes running though the movie seems to be that the more violent acts are inflicted upon Jesus, the more efficacious our atonement will be: the greater the suffering, the more powerful the redemption.

Yet atonement, however it works, isn't quantifiable like that. There is no reason to think that Jesus's suffering pays out on our sin at a quid pro quo exchange rate. Part of the very nature of atonement and of sin is that they are unquantifiable. If Jesus had been tortured a bit more or a bit less, that wouldn't have changed the amount of atonement. Indeed, the writers of the New Testament seem far more interested in Jesus's death than in his suffering: it is his death, not the magnitude of his suffering, that atones for our sin.

But if Jesus's death atones for sin, then Gibson's emphasis on Jesus's suffering—which is to say, Gibson's attention to acts of violence—can only be seen as a misrepresentation of atonement and an expression of a dangerous and damaging preoccupation with the suffering that comes with violence. Thus, the problem with the violence in the movie is neither its quantity nor its graphic nature, nor even its artistic demonstration or historical accuracy, for that matter. The problem is with the violence's purpose. And that, to my way of thinking, is a far more significant problem with the violence in this movie than most criticisms have registered: Jesus, not violence, saves us.

But saves us from what? Let me turn to the other place where conservative critics get the reasoning right but the answer wrong. The other emphatic claim that conservative critics have made about the film is that it says something about what human beings are like such that they might need saving in the first place. That is, *The Passion* reveals just how thoroughly implicated we all are in Jesus's suffering: we make Jesus suffer. It isn't just a Roman hand or Gibson's hand holding the hammer that drives the nail through Jesus's hand; it's our hand. It isn't just Peter who denies Jesus and then disappears from the screen in shame; it's us. It isn't just Judas who betrays him; we do. This vision of human beings as sinners is no easier for most people to buy than the one that says Jesus can or must die for someone else—perhaps even harder, since most of us don't like to think of ourselves in such an ugly way. Yet conservative

Christians have always been acutely aware of human sin and human complicity in Jesus's Crucifixion, and they expect us to be as well.

So the other point that conservatives make is that Gibson's movie not only helps us viscerally understand something about what Jesus did, it also helps us understand something about ourselves and our sinfulness. In an era of "I'm OK, you're OK" social relations and self-help and self-actualizing personal ones, that point, at least for Christians, is one we need to keep ever before us. Those who don't recognize sin in their lives can find no need for grace in them and no cause for God to transform them, either.

Here again, however, *The Passion* makes an important theological point and then gets it wrong. Gibson turns human beings into caricatures. None of the characters in the movie shows any real range of emotion or attitude. The disciples are always in mourning. Most of the Sanhedrin are always bent on crucifying him. Noble characters such as Veronica and Simon of Cyrene are always noble. Roman soldiers are always either slavering animals bent on sadistic torture or persons of tortured conscience who feel they must do their job no matter how wrong it feels. Children are either confused and helpless or—in the most horrific example of what Gibson must think about when he considers original sin—demons. Pilate, whose sympathetic portrayal has been a divisive issue in itself, is still a one-dimensional character: he's always struggling with the political implications of his no-win choice. Even Jesus has an extremely limited range of emotions: bleeding, crying out, and looking heavenward are hardly the same as acting, and Jim Caviezel, who has shown himself in other films to be a capable actor, does little else. The characters are, in short, either victims or evil. The film isn't just anti-Semitic; it's anti-human.

Neither "victim" nor "evil" is the same as "sinful." Human beings are complex; they are capable of great atrocity and powerful good. They swing back and forth between their possibilities and their limitations. They are, to use biblical language, both created in the image of God and also fallen. And it is this complexity that sets the stage upon which we might think about sin, for the claim that we sin isn't so much about how evil we are as about how terminally conflicted, impossibly complicated, and finally captive we are to both the powers beyond our control and the vagaries of those within it. As Paul writes in Romans 7, "I do not understand my own actions. . . . For I do not do the good I want, but the evil I do not want is what I do. Now if I do what I do not want, it is no longer I that do it, but sin that dwells within me."

Why is it important to distinguish "being evil" from "being sinful"? Precisely because God's redeeming work is just that: *redeeming* work. Were we simply evil like Caiaphas or the Roman guards in *The Passion,* Jesus wouldn't be atoning for our sins; he would be annihilating us. Were we simply noble like Veronica or Simon, Jesus wouldn't need to worry about our sins. And were we simply suffering victims like Mary the mother of Jesus, Mary Magdalene, and John, Jesus would need to do something other than suffer and die to change our condition. It is because we are complex that we are sinful, and it is because we are sinful that we need redemption—and can be redeemed—by God. If conservatives are going to call us to attend to the human condition, they have the obligation of recognizing us as human.

Do I think this is a good movie? No. But I think it's a bad movie because it's full of bad theology. Then again, I am not especially satisfied with the various implicit and explicit theological claims being made by its various critics and supporters, either. And since the movie and viewers' responses to it not only are shaped by theological claims but are shaping them among the broader public, perhaps we ought to pay more attention to such claims.

14 The Offense of Flesh

Mark C. Taylor

Here as elsewhere the formula for essential Christianity is: the essentially Christian is always the positive which is recognizable by the negative—the highest blessedness, to relate oneself to it, is recognizable by the fact that one comes to suffer in this world.

Here are the roots of the possibility of offense.   **Søren Kierkegaard**

Christianity is inescapably offensive. No one has understood this better than Søren Kierkegaard. What makes Christianity so offensive, he argues, is its relation to suffering: "Christianity clearly considers suffering to be the mark of the God relationship: if you do not suffer, you do not have anything to do with God." The waning of offense is a sign of the disappearance of Christianity in modern Christendom. "In our age," Kierkegaard regretfully observes, "Christianity has become so naturalized and so accommodated to the world that nobody dreams of the offense." To be a Christian it is not merely necessary to suffer but, more important, to accept—indeed embrace—suffering as an unavoidable condition of life. This is the lesson the Incarnation and Crucifixion teach, and when this lesson is forgotten, Christianity vanishes even when it seems to be flourishing.

Over a century and a half after Kierkegaard penned his prophetic words, Mel Gibson's *The Passion of the Christ* has brought back offense with a vengeance. Rarely has a film been met with greater box-office success and more vitriolic criticism. While it is easy to dismiss this controversy as yet another example of media hype, the intensity of the debate in popular culture, the media, and the press, all of which Kierkegaard would have abhorred, is symptomatic of complex and troubling currents circulating in today's fragile world.

The controversy began even before Gibson released the film on Ash Wednesday, 2004. Writing in the *International Herald Tribune* on August 1, 2003, the *New York Times* cultural commentator Frank Rich fired an opening salvo in a dispute that quickly turned ugly. Citing what he regarded as disturbing anti-Semitic statements by Gibson's father and underscoring Gibson's well-known commitment to ultraconservative traditionalist Catholicism, Rich expressed concern about the exclusion of Jews from selected previews of the film. "We can only hope," Rich writes, "that the finished product will not resemble the screenplay that circulated this spring. That script—which the Gibson camp has said was stolen but which others say was leaked by a concerned member of the star's own company—received two thumbs down from a panel of nine Jewish and Roman Catholic scholars who read it. They found that the Jews were presented as 'bloodthirsty, vengeful and money-hungry.' " Rich's fears were somewhat allayed by his wishful belief that the film would be a failure: "it's hard to imagine the movie being anything other than a flop in America, given that it has no major Hollywood stars and that its dialogue is in Aramaic and Latin."

Not only was Rich wrong about the reception of the film, but what he thought would make the film a failure has contributed to its extraordinary success. Few could have predicted the astonishing response to *The Passion*. What is all the more remarkable is that this film, which, as Jack Miles insists, is "visually and theologically . . . flamboyantly counter-Reformationally Roman," has been received enthusiastically by both Catholics and Protestants—especially increasingly powerful evangelicals. (As we will see, the tradition of *theologia crucis,* or theology of the cross, which dates back to Martin Luther, makes the resonance of the film among certain Protestant groups less surprising than Miles suggests.) The louder the chorus of praise, the more vociferous the voices of criticism.

Critics make three points again and again. First, following Rich, they argue that by placing primary blame for the death of Jesus on the Jews, the film fuels the flames of anti-Semitism. The critic David Denby, writing for the *New Yorker,* expressed the view of many: "*The Passion,* in its confused way, confirms the old justifications for persecuting the Jews, and one somehow doubts that Gibson will make a sequel in which he reminds the audience that in later centuries the Church itself used torture and execution to punish not only Jews but heretics, non-believers, and dissidents." While the question raised by this criticism is important, others have considered it at length, and I will not discuss it further here. Second, and closely related to the charge of anti-Semitism, is the claim that Gibson is ignorant of or insensitive to the conclusions of historical scholarship on the Bible. By conflating the four Gospels and insisting that the authors of the biblical texts were eyewitnesses to the events they narrate, Gibson betrays the limits of his knowledge and partiality of his vision. This criticism is obviously correct, but it remains largely irrelevant to the most interesting issues the film raises, since the points of reference for the film are not works of historical scholarship but works of the imagination. While to many, the association of a kitschy popular film with artistic masterpieces from the past might seem blasphemous, it is hard to watch *The Passion* without recalling Caravaggio's *Flagellation of Christ* (1607) and Matthias Grünewald's magnificent Isenheim Altarpiece (1515). Precisely such a conflation of high and low is what the Incarnation is all about.

Finally, and most important, Gibson's film has been condemned for its excessive violence. Here the litany of criticism is relentless. A. O. Scott of the *New York Times* declared that this "version of the Gospels is harrowingly violent." Either guilelessly or ingenuously, Scott continued, Gibson "has exploited the popular appetite for terror and gore." For the intellectual gadfly Garry Wills, *The Passion* goes "beyond sadism into the comic surreal, like an apocalyptic version of Swinburne's *The Whipping Papers.*" In an article entitled "The Worship of Blood: Mel Gibson's Lethal Weapon," Leon Wieseltier wrote: "The bloodthirstiness of Gibson's film is startling, and quickly sickening. The fluid is everywhere. It drips, it runs, it spatters, it jumps. It trickles down the post at which Jesus is flagellated and down the cross upon which he is crucified, and the camera only reluctantly tears itself away from the scarlet scenery. The flagellation scene and the crucifixion scene are frenzies of blood." Denby described the film as "a sickening death trip, a grimly unilluminating procession of treachery, beatings, blood, and agony."

What is most striking about such criticisms is their theological naiveté, or perhaps ignorance. Commentators show virtually no understanding of the nature of theology and give little evidence of knowing anything

about the theological controversies that have shaped the Christian doctrine of the Incarnation. Never merely reflection about God, theology is
also discourse about self and world; theology, anthropology, and cos-
mology are inseparable. By articulating that which one takes to be real,
theology expresses the values informing one's life and relation to the
world. For Christians, the divine and the human meet in the historical
figure of Jesus of Nazareth, whom believers deem divine. The distin-
guishing feature of Christianity is the doctrine of the Incarnation, according to which God is not elsewhere but is embodied in space and
time. The culmination of the Incarnation is the Crucifixion, in which
God's flesh and blood are radically confirmed. If flesh does not bleed, it
is not real, and if flesh is not real, there is no Incarnation.

Eighteen years before *The Passion* opened, William Edwards, Wesley
Gabel, and Floyd Hosmer published an unusual article entitled "On the
Physical Death of Jesus Christ" in the *Journal of the American Medical
Association* (March 21, 1986). Its reception anticipated the furor un-
leashed by the film. (There is some evidence that Gibson consulted this
article while working on the film.) The authors' main contribution is a
careful and vivid description of the method and physiology of crucifixion as the Romans practiced it around the time Jesus is supposed to have
died. Edwards and his colleagues felt compelled to frame their analysis
with a defense of the historical reliability of the biblical sources, even
though this point is not essential to their thesis. In the months following
the appearance of the article, the editors were deluged with critical letters. The journal was attacked for publishing a study that critics claimed
was theological rather than scientific. A group of ten medical doctors, for
example, complained that "by any measure, this is a purely theological
article whose sources, far from being subject to an objective scientific editorial analysis, are the product of faith alone, and not of verifiable fact,
certainly not within the domain of referees of a medical journal." The
problem, it seems, is not theology but particularly *Christian* theology.
Many of the critics repeatedly charged the authors with anti-Semitism,
which, they suggested, is virtually inherent in the gospel narratives that
they dismissed as historically inaccurate.

As I have suggested, theological issues notwithstanding, the most important point of the article is the description of the method and physiology of crucifixion. The analysis is made all the more vivid by a series of
remarkable images illustrating the details of the process of crucifixion
in graphic detail. Flogging, Edwards and his colleagues point out, was
the legally sanctioned preliminary to executions in the Roman Empire
(fig. 6). The instrument used was "a short whip (flagrum or flagellum)

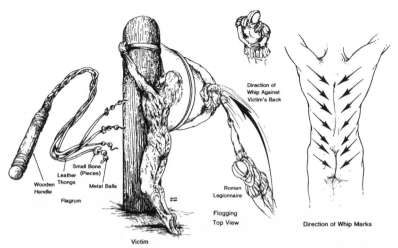

FIGURE 6 Scourging. Left, a short whip (flagrum or flagellum) with lead balls and sheep bones tied into leather thongs. Center, the naked victim tied to a flogging post, with deep stripelike lacerations usually associated with considerable blood loss. Right, view from above showing the position of the lictors. Detail of figure 2 from William Edwards, Wesley Gabel, and Floyd Hosmer, "On the Physical Death of Jesus Christ," *Journal of the American Medical Association* (March 21, 1986).

with leather thongs of variable lengths, in which small iron balls or sharp pieces of sheep bones were tied at intervals." The purpose of the beating was to weaken the victim before nailing him to the cross. "As the flogging continued," they explain, "the lacerations would tear into the underlying skeletal muscles and produce quivering ribbons of bleeding flesh. Pain and blood loss may well have determined how long the victim would survive on the cross." The actual crucifixion itself was relatively bloodless. Tapered iron spikes five to seven inches long with a shaft of three-eighths of an inch were used to nail the wrists and feet to the cross (figs. 7 and 8). The placement of the spikes was calculated to maximize the weight the punctured limbs could hold and to minimize the flow of blood. According to the authors, "The length of survival generally ranged from three or four hours to three or four days and appears to have been inversely related to the severity of the scourging." Though the pain from hanging on the cross was agonizing, the cause of death in most cases was either hypovolemic shock (organ failure due to blood loss) caused by the flogging or asphyxiation, which resulted when the weight of the body eventually made it impossible to exercise the muscles needed to exhale (fig. 9). In order to exhale, the victim would have to lift his body by pushing up on the feet, flexing the elbows, and adducting the shoulders. However, this maneuver would place the entire weight of the body on the tarsals and produce searing pain. Furthermore, flexion of

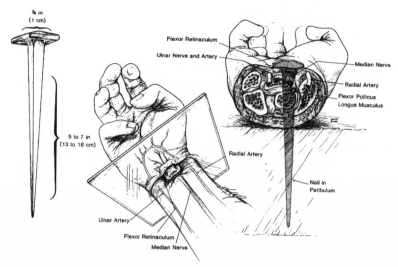

FIGURE 7 Nailing of the wrists. Left, the size of an iron nail. Center, the location of the nail in the wrist, between the carpals and the radius. Right, cross-section of the wrist, at the level of the plane indicated at left, showing the path of the nail, with probable transaction of the median nerve and impalement of the flexor pollicis longus, but without injury to the major arterial trunks and without fracture of bones. Figure 4 from William Edwards, Wesley Gabel, and Floyd Hosmer, "On the Physical Death of Jesus Christ," *Journal of the American Medical Association* (March 21, 1986).

the elbows would force the wrists to rotate about the iron nails, causing fiery pain along the damaged median nerves. In addition, as the body was lifted, the scourged back would scrape painfully against the rough wood of the cross. Muscle cramps and paresthesia of the outstretched and uplifted arms would add to the discomfort. The effort required to breathe was agonizing, and the victim would become exhausted, a condition that would eventually lead to asphyxia. It is difficult to imagine a more excruciating (*ex,* completely, + *cruciare,* to torment, crucify, from *crux,* cross) death.

Whether or not the gospel narratives are accurate, what makes Christianity such a fascinating religion is the belief that God is revealed in a person who suffered this terrifying death. The passage of the centuries and the repetition of the narrative have taken the edge off the *horror religiosus* that lies at the heart of this religion. The Incarnation is thoroughly paradoxical: high is low, activity is passivity, love is suffering, negation is affirmation, and vice versa. As Kierkegaard claims, this paradox traces the limit of reason: "It is specifically the task of human knowing to understand that there is something it cannot understand and to understand what it is. Human knowing usually has been occupied with understanding, but if it will also take the trouble to understand itself, it

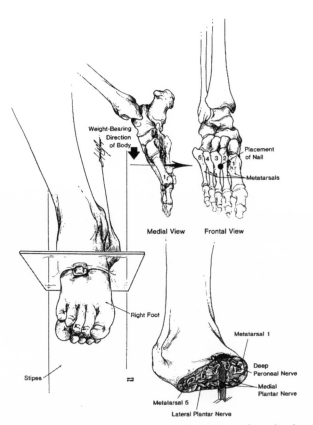

FIGURE 8 Nailing of the feet. Left, the position of the feet atop one another and against the stipes. Upper right, the location of the nail in the second intermetatarsal space. Lower right, a cross-section of the foot at the plane indicated at left, showing the path of the nail. Figure 5 from William Edwards, Wesley Gabel, and Floyd Hosmer, "On the Physical Death of Jesus Christ," *Journal of the American Medical Association* (March 21, 1986).

must straightway posit the paradox." The terms Kierkegaard uses are modern, but the wisdom he probes is ancient. The classical doctrine of the Incarnation was formulated at the councils of Nicaea in 325 and Chalcedon in 451. Though Gibson gives no indication of familiarity with this historical background, his film is obsessed with problems and questions that preoccupied Christians throughout the fourth and fifth centuries.

In the fourth century, as in the twenty-first, religion and politics were inseparable. While Constantine hoped to have found in Christianity the glue that would hold the Roman Empire together, stability in the East was threatened by a theological dispute that reached a turning point in Alexandria in 321. The issue that triggered the controversy was the

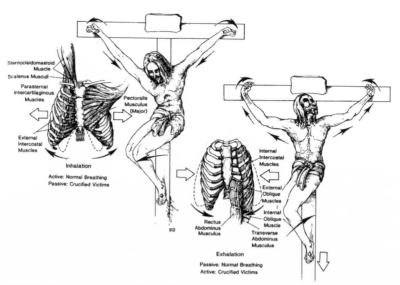

FIGURE 9 Exhalation during crucifixion. With elbows flexed and shoulders adducted, and with weight of body on nailed feet, exhalation is accomplished as active rather than passive process. Breaking legs below knees would place burden of exhalation on shoulder and arm muscles alone and soon would result in exhausting asphyxia. Detail of figure 6 from William Edwards, Wesley Gabel, and Floyd Hosmer, "On the Physical Death of Jesus Christ," *Journal of the American Medical Association* (March 21, 1986).

status of Jesus: how could an historical individual be the Son of God? Alexander, bishop of Alexandria, and Arius, who was a member of the church, represented the two sides in the debate. Alexander was preoccupied with salvation and believed that sinful human beings could not be redeemed unless Jesus were divine. Arius, by contrast, was a radical monotheist who was concerned to preserve the absolute transcendence and perfect immutability of God. If Jesus were God, the immutable would be mutable, which, according to Arius, was both a logical and a theological contradiction.

The pivot on which the argument hinged was the question of suffering: Is it possible for God to suffer? The Arians argued for the subordination of the Son (the historical Jesus) to the Father (the transcendent immutable God). Alexander, by contrast, insisted on the complete identity of the Son and the Father, and in order to preserve monotheism while at the same time affirming the divinity of Jesus, he argued that the Father, Son, and Holy Spirit are not ontologically different but are different modalities of the same substance. Thus, if Jesus the Son suffers, then God the Father suffers as well, but for Arius and his followers, the claim that God suffers was blasphemous. To avoid "contaminating" the eternal God with the vicissitudes of temporality, they argued, there can be no substantial identity between the Father and the Son. Though he resists the conclusion, Arius in effect denies the Incarnation. If God were to become flesh and suffer, he would no longer be God; but if the Son were subordinate to the Father, there would have been no Incarnation.

For Alexander and his followers, to deny the Incarnation is to deny the possibility of salvation. It was, therefore, urgent in their view to establish the full divinity of Jesus. Athanasius, who became a primary spokesperson for the Alexandrian position, explains his differences with the Arians: "If the Son were a creature, man had remained mortal as before, not being joined to God; for a creature had not joined creatures to God; nor would a portion of the creation have been the creation's salvation, as needing salvation itself. To provide against this also, He sends His own Son, and He becomes Son of Man, by taking created flesh." Unless God becomes flesh, salvation is impossible. To counter what he regarded as the pernicious subordinationism of the Arians, Athanasius insisted on the substantial identity of the Father and the Son. In technical terms, the Father and Son are *homoousios*—of the same substance.

When, amid a highly charged political atmosphere, the Council of Nicaea finally convened in 325 at the behest of Constantine, representatives sided with Alexander and Athanasius and explicitly rejected the Arian position. The Trinitarian structure of the Nicene Creed asserts without explaining that the divinity of the Son does not compromise the unity and eternity of God:

> We believe in one God, Father, Almighty, maker of all things, visible and invisible,
>
> And in one Lord Jesus Christ, begotten of the Father uniquely, that is, of the substance of the Father, God of God, Light of Light, true God of true God, begotten, not made, consubstantial with the Father, through whom all things were made, both things in heaven and those on earth, who for us men and for our salvation came down and was incarnate, [and] became man; he suffered and rose on the third day, ascended into heaven, and is coming to judge living and dead,
>
> And in the Holy Spirit.

The debates surrounding the Council of Nicaea were so preoccupied with establishing or denying the divinity of the Son that the status of Jesus's humanity remained unclear. In the years immediately following the Council of Nicaea, bitter theological disputes again erupted and were not resolved until the Council of Chalcedon in 451. This time Alexandria and Antioch became the centers of the controversy. According to Apollinaris, one of the staunchest supporters of the Alexandrian position, human nature, which is temporal, transient, and corruptible, is opposed to the divine nature, which is eternal, unchanging, and incorruptible. The question, then, is how the divine and the human can be united. Apollinaris argued that it is philosophically impossible for the divine and the human to be fully present in a single undivided being, and that the only way to give a reasonable account of the Incarnation is to insist that while one nature is completely present, the other nature is only partially present. Since the divine nature cannot be imperfect, human nature must be incompletely present in Jesus Christ. Apollinaris concluded that the divine is present as Jesus's mind, but his body remains completely human: "For God incarnate in human flesh keeps His own active energy, Mind being untouched by animal and bodily passions, and guiding the body and its movements divinely and sinlessly; not only unconquered by death but destroying death. And he is true God, the incorporeal appearing in flesh, perfect in true and divine perfections, not two persons, not two natures." In subsequent debates, it became clear that Apollinaris's denial that Jesus Christ is two natures—both divine and human—was also tantamount to the rejection of the Incarnation.

Antiochean Christology takes a position that is the polar opposite of the Alexandrians'. Antiocheans tended to be more literal, interested the historical figure of Jesus and devoted to Jesus as an ethical model for life in the world. Whereas Apollinaris tended to deny Christ's humanity in order to affirm his divinity, the Antiochean Nestorius tended to deny Christ's divinity in order to affirm his humanity. What neither could imagine was that Jesus Christ could be *fully divine* and *fully human*. Yet this is precisely what is required for salvation, according to what eventually became Christian orthodoxy. Gregory of Nazianzus makes the point most concisely: "For that which he has not assumed he has not healed." Gregory condemns both Apollinaris's denial of the full embodiment of divinity in humanity and Nestorius's rejection of the full divinity of the human person named Jesus. Though it took many years, the church eventually accepted the position Gregory articulated at the Council of Chalcedon, that Jesus Christ was "truly God and truly man":

> acknowledged in two natures without confusion, without
> change, without division, without separation, different natures
> being by no means taken away because of the union, but rather

the distinctive character of each nature being preserved, and [each] combining in one Person and hypostasis.

Here at last is the formulation of the hypostatic union, which still remains orthodox Christology: *one person, two natures—fully God and fully man.* To proclaim, however, is not to explain. Throughout the centuries, Christian believers and theologians have tended to ignore the puzzles posed by orthodox Christology and, therefore, have failed to fathom the depth of the Incarnation.

No one has a more profound understanding of the paradox of the incarnation than Søren Kierkegaard. As we have seen, Kierkegaard maintains that "the supreme paradox of all thought is the attempt to discover something that thought cannot think." What thought cannot think is that the infinitely and qualitatively different God has become incarnate in the particular historical figure of Jesus. Not merely paradoxical, the Incarnation is the Absolute Paradox. "The paradox," Kierkegaard argues, "unites the contradictories, and is the historical made eternal, and the Eternal made historical." Although the Incarnation can obviously be interpreted in many ways, Kierkegaard's insistence on the paradox involved with this *coincidentia oppositorium* is an important reminder of just how peculiar the central claim of Christianity is.

When opposites collide, passion and, correlatively, suffering result. Kierkegaard goes so far as to insist that "in suffering, religiosity begins to breathe," or, in more philosophical terms, "the negative is the mark by which the God-relationship is recognized." Kierkegaard rediscovers the *theologia crucis* that lies at the heart of Lutheran Protestantism. From this point of view, both the incarnate God and the individual believer *must* suffer. Far from being incidental to religious life, "suffering as the essential expression for existential pathos means that suffering is real, or that the reality of the suffering constitutes the existential pathos." Unless God or the real is embodied in the frailty and vulnerability of human flesh as it is manifested in the suffering and death of Jesus, there is no Incarnation, and Christianity is a fraud. The pathos of the believer reflects the Passion of the Christ. Christendom's glib doctrines and easy faith repress the offense of faith.

For Kierkegaard, then, passion is created by the conjunction of the absolute opposites of eternity and time. "The essentially Christian," he insists, "is always the positive, which is recognizable by the negative— the highest blessedness . . . is recognizable by the fact that one comes to suffer in this world." Insofar as life becomes an *imitatio Christi,* suffering is not necessarily mental or psychic but can be physical. What is most offensive about Christianity is the claim that the ultimately real is found in the flayed flesh of a crucified human being. Contrary to all expectation, broken, bleeding flesh is the embodiment of God's love of the world. In contrast to every form of spirituality that attempts to deny, escape, or transcend the world, the doctrine of the Incarnation, which comes to completion in the Crucifixion, entails the belief that the real is nowhere else than in the turbulent and often treacherous fluxes and flows of the world.

Theological doctrines, I have stressed, always express beliefs about the world and our place in it. The claim that Jesus is fully God and fully man, therefore, harbors important implications for human existence. While Nietzsche's declaration of the death of God, which was first articulated by Luther, is usually regarded as a nihilistic aberration of Christianity proper, it is actually a necessary correlate of orthodox Christology. If the Son is divine, then the death of Jesus is the death of God. Rather than the negation of the world, the death of God figured in the Incarnation is its radical affirmation. The real, the doctrine of Incarnation-Crucifixion declares, is *within* rather than *beyond* the passion, suffering, and travail of earthly life. If, as Nietszche has put it, "all things are entwined, enmeshed, enamored," then to accept anything is to accept everything. It is impossible to embrace moments of bliss without saying "yes" to all pain; and by affirming pain, one discovers a bliss that surpasses understanding.

Some of his most vociferous critics have charged that Gibson's message is thoroughly negative; they go so far as to argue that he has made a "war movie" that threatens to ignite a "Jesus war." While this interpretation is seriously misguided, it does suggest one of the reasons the film continues to generate such heated responses among both critics and admirers. What is most surprising at the beginning of the twenty-first century is that religion has never been a greater global force in society, politics, and culture. This is not the way it was supposed to be. During the 1960s and 1970s, the widely accepted wisdom was that modernization and secularization were inseparable; as societies modernized, the argument went, they secularized. This process was believed to be both inevitable and irreversible. While religion never disappeared, its social and political impact declined during the years following the end of the Second World War. With the social and cultural turbulence of the 1960s, mainline religion retreated as secularism and alternative forms of spirituality advanced.

By the end of the 1970s, however, things began to change in unexpected ways. Faced with a world that was increasingly complex and often incomprehensible, many people sought the reassurance that simple answers bring by turning to conservative forms of religiosity—most important among them in the United States, Christian fundamentalism and evangelical Protestantism. This religious revival was not limited to the United States but was a global phenomenon. Throughout the world, ancient religious traditions began to attract masses of followers in ways that few had anticipated. It is a mistake to understand this development as a return to premodern sensibilities; to the contrary, what is occurring is a calculated response to modernism and as such is a distinctly postmodern phenomenon.

While the visions informing various versions of neo-fundamentalism differ significantly within and among traditions, they tend to share two important characteristics: literalism and a Manichaean view of the world. In contrast to the sense of complexity, multiplicity, and irony that pervaded society during the 1990s, the new millennium is marked by a longing for the simplicity that literalism seems to bring. In a world where everything is caught in endlessly tangled webs, there is a strong desire for things to be what they appear to be and nothing more: what you see is what you see and what you get. One name for this desire is *realism*. Politics, economics, and religion are all experiencing a call to return to basic values and fundamental principles. *The Passion*'s purported realism is part of the draw. Gibson has repeatedly claimed that he wanted to make a "realistic film" about what he takes to be the literal truth of the Gospels. For many of his admirers, it seems, he has succeeded beyond his expectations. Luz Fontanez, a repeat viewer, spoke for many when responding to a reporter's question about the film: "It's very violent, but then it's very realistic. It wasn't less than when it happened. What I learned, usually when you learn stuff from the Bible about the Crucifixion, you don't see it so visually, like the movie, and it has changed my way of thinking." What some find attractive, others find repulsive. For many critics, the blood and violence are too realistic and in fact excessive and gratuitous. Neither admirers nor critics pause to consider is that what passes for realism in today's culture is a non-Hollywood Hollywood film about the Greatest Story Ever Told. When reality becomes image, there is a longing for blood, even if it is on celluloid.

It is much easier to divide the world between good guys and bad guys when you think you know the literal truth. Literalism and some form of Manichaeism, in other words, are inseparable. A. O. Scott titled his article, published the day the film was released, "Good and Evil Locked in Violent Showdown." As several of Gibson's earlier films suggest, there is considerable evidence that he actually views the world as a battleground where invisible forces struggle. His signature role as a "holy" warrior in these films makes it clear which side he thinks he is on. With religious wars all too real today, some people question the wisdom and timeliness of Gibson's vision. Denby concluded his review, entitled "Nailed," by reflecting: "The despair of the movie is hard to shrug off, and Gibson's timing couldn't be more unfortunate: another dose of death-haunted religious fanaticism is the last thing we need." But matters are considerably more complex than this. If *The Passion* is a war movie, the tactics of the main character are, to say the least, unusual. Jack Miles is closer to the mark when he observes: "What is astonishing is that political conservatives should embrace—during wartime—a film whose message is that when under murderous attack, one should not fight back but instead forgive one's attackers and accept one's death humbly as the will of God." Many of today's so-called Christians do not understand the figure in whose name they speak.

Like most forms of religion, Christianity as it is usually interpreted speaks to the pervasive human desire for happy endings. What makes Christianity distinctive, however, is the notion of the Incarnation, which, when fully elaborated, entails the claim that redemption, however it is understood, is possible only in and through crucifixion. Far from being limited to claims about an historical figure or interpretations about the central character in the gospel narratives, the doctrine of Incarnation-Crucifixion poses an existential challenge: live in such a way that you accept, affirm, even embrace life in all of its glory and horror. To live this life is to confront rather than evade the offense of the flesh:

> Take, eat, this is my body broken for you . . .
> Take, drink, this is my blood.

Part Three: Passion, Media, Audience

15 The Passion and the Death of God

Thomas J. J. Altizer

Mel Gibson's *The Passion of the Christ* is surely unique as
a film in terms of its immediate and ecstatic impact upon
such a vast audience, and yet it is quite ordinary if not
mediocre in its cinematography and direction, and truly
distinctive only in the sheer brutality and comprehensive-
ness of its violence, a violence that is purely gratuitous
and that goes wholly beyond its textual sources. All too
significant are its flashbacks to pre-Passion primal events;
these are not only extraordinarily brief but banal as well,
as though they were wholly without fundamental significance. Nothing is real in this film except the total horror
and violence of the Passion, and that extends throughout
the film as a whole, a film that is manifestly grounded
in a purely orthodox Christianity and that enacts itself
as a contemporary sacred event, an event embodying a
uniquely Christian redemption. Or so it has seemingly
been received by the largest immediate audience in film
history, one that has already become a major if not a primal event in American church history, and one that is a
decisive way into a uniquely contemporary Christianity.

This is a Christianity that at bottom is a reflection of
the Passion of God, a Passion so horrible that it must
be greatly diluted and wholly disguised. The result is the

most banal and shallow expression of Christianity ever released in history, one that realizes a seemingly new vitality, but a vitality that is
a new and all too comprehensive passivity. Yet that passivity is not a
simple passivity; it is made possible only by the repression of a total
passion, and it ever threatens to relapse into its source, a source that is
a pure and total violence, and one openly evoked only in the uniquely
Christian symbol of the cross. Now the cross is not only the symbol of
the sacrifice of Christ, but ultimately the symbol of the sacrifice of God,
which is just why the cross is an absolute offense, but an offense hidden
and suppressed in orthodox Christian dogma, which can only know this
sacrificial death as the sacrifice of the humanity and not the divinity of
Christ. Is that deep suppression now being loosened and unveiled as the
repression that it is, an unveiling at the center of a uniquely modern
world, a world comprehensively embodying the death of God?

It would be difficult to deny that *The Passion of the Christ* evokes the
Passion of God, which is why this horror is so total and so comprehensive. But this horror has an immediacy that is undeniable, an immediacy
that clearly has had an overwhelming impact upon its audience. Why?
Is this at bottom a return of the repressed, and a return of that which
has most deeply been repressed, or most deeply been repressed by our
world, a world seemingly innocent both of absolute evil and of absolute
passion, but only so innocent because of just such a repression? And is
this a uniquely Christian repression, one only made possible by the Crucifixion, a crucifixion that is ultimately the Crucifixion of God, which is
just why it demands such a total repression? Already Paul could know
the Christianity that he encountered as a suppression of the Crucifixion,
just as Luther could know Catholicism itself as just such a suppression,
a suppression Gibson reverses in this film, thereby evoking an ecstatic
response, but does that very response demonstrate the power of the repression that is here at hand?

Does a history lie behind this film that is ultimately a history of
the repression of the Crucifixion, and a repression of the Crucifixion
of God, a crucifixion of God that is certainly the death of God, which
is just why this is an absolutely sacrificial death, and the sole source of
what the Christian uniquely knows as redemption? We can sense the
depth of this repression by noting that the Crucifixion does not enter Christian iconography until the end of patristic Christianity, does
not actually enter Christian thinking until Luther or Christian poetry
until Milton, and can be understood theologically only by truly radical forms of Christian theology. Hence the Crucifixion has been virtually suppressed or disguised or diluted in the dominant expressions of

Christendom, a suppression that is a repression, and a repression of the depths of Christianity itself, depths that can always return, and with an explosive power. But it is just the most repressed forms of Christianity that can explode with the greatest power, or the greatest immediate power, a power that is overwhelming, and when loosening its disguise or veil, such an explosion can occur as a pure horror, and a pure horror that is all consuming.

Christians are commonly baffled by the horror that Christianity can now inspire in Islam, but such horror has been present in the Christian world itself since the advent of modernity, and the purest horror has been seen in the greatest expressions of modern Christian art. Of course, such art has increasingly been banished from our churches, churches that are havens from modernity itself, and if these are havens of a new innocence, such innocence can disappear. Perhaps a paradigmatic occurrence of that disappearance occurs *in The Passion of the Christ*. Are we here given an enactment of the return of the repressed in Christianity itself? Is this a future that awaits us, a future even now at hand, even now seething about us, arising from a loosening of our new passivity, a loosening occurring in a new and comprehensive violence? Of course, such violence need not be an overt violence, need not be so brutally literal as in this film, but that all-too-literal violence could be a symbolic enactment of a new interior violence that could consume us, and consume us with a true return of the repressed.

What this film can teach us is that if Christianity truly has repressed the Crucifixion, truly has repressed its deepest ground, that repression as repression is profoundly pathological, profoundly self-destructive, and the return of the repressed can only be a genuine horror. Such horror is surely evoked in this film, and comprehensively evoked, so much so that nothing else stands forth or is manifest. Shocking as it is, does it nevertheless evoke a deep and immediate and ecstatic desire, or do so among those who are victims of this repression, victims comprehending far more than we can imagine, and victims who at this moment in history may well undergo an actual awakening to their condition? Do we now stand in an apocalyptic condition in which our deepest, even if our most unconscious, desire is a desire for pure horror itself, one openly unveiled in this film, and one seemingly leading innumerable contemporary Christians to an ecstatic state?

For the deepest horror is finally inseparable from the most ecstatic joy, and if Christianity knows the Crucifixion as the only source of redemption, it thereby knows an ultimate horror as the source of ultimate joy. So it is that Paul knows the Crucifixion as apocalypse itself, just as the fourth Gospel enacts the Crucifixion and the Resurrection as one event, and if these primal Christian motifs are reversed in orthodox Christian dogma, that is the consequence of a profound repression, a repression that is a uniquely Christian pathology. Is such a pathology now being openly unveiled among us, and unveiled in truly brutal terms, a brutality reflecting this pathology, even reflecting it as an ecstatic brutality? That ecstasy could only be the consequence of an ultimate repression, and an ultimate repression inseparable from a uniquely Christian repression, which could be nothing less than the repression of the death of God, or the repression of the absolute sacrifice of God in the Crucifixion, a sacrifice that is a uniquely Christian apocalypse.

Is an opening to that sacrifice as the sacrifice of God a way to a transcendence of our repression, and a transcendence of our deepest repression? Such a transcendence would be the very opposite of the return of the repressed, for it would be an unveiling of our repression itself, and an unveiling that could only be a disenactment of that repression, a disenactment that is its very reversal. Hence it would be not a return of the repressed, but rather a reversal of this repression, and a reversal by its actual affirmation of the death of God, an affirmation that is an absolute affirmation of the Crucifixion, and precisely thereby an affirmation of Crucifixion as Resurrection, or of absolute death as absolute life. Clearly such an affirmation is wholly absent from *The Passion of the Christ,* and wholly absent if only because all joy is wholly absent here, an absence that is the absence of a uniquely Christian Crucifixion, and the full and actual presence of a total repression of that Crucifixion.

16 Kill Jesus

Amy Hollywood

To those who complain about the violence of my film I have two words: *Kill Bill.*
Mel Gibson

Crucify him!   **Mark 15:13; see also Mark 15:14; Matthew 27:22–23; and Luke 23:21**

During the Roman Catholic Good Friday liturgy, the congregation repeats the words of "the crowd," which, "stirred up" by the Jewish high priests, demands that Pontius Pilate release to them the murderer, Barabbas, and crucify Jesus of Nazareth. The theological grounds for the identification are clear—Christ died for the sins of all human beings, hence all human beings participate in nailing Christ to the cross. Mel Gibson, writer, director, and producer of *The Passion of the Christ,* underlines the theological claim and its implications for him as a Christian when he films his own hand grasping a thick iron nail just before it is pounded into Jesus's flesh. (Perhaps more to the point, Gibson publicizes the fact.)

Beginning in the Middle Ages, manuals of prayer and meditation, devotional images, and visionary texts have called on Christians to reenact Christ's sacrifice in similarly dramatic ways. A central goal of the religious life of the Middle Ages was the imaginative re-creation of

Christ's extraordinary suffering and gruesome death. Narrative accounts of Christ's life and death, often accompanied by visual illustrations of key moments in the drama, provided guidebooks for this meditative practice. The texts and images are often excruciating, elaborating in seeming endless detail on the cruelties Christ sustained. Authors speculate on the manner in which Christ was flogged, mocked, and crucified, often adding moments of torture and degradation not found in the Gospels. The widely read thirteenth-century *Meditations on the Passion of Christ* gives two different accounts of how Jesus was nailed to the cross, thereby exploring a wide range of the bodily indignities to which he might have been subjected. One particularly adept practitioner of the art of Passion meditation, the Italian laywoman Angela of Foligno (d. 1310), devotes herself to a long meditation on the piece of flesh pushed out of Christ's hand by the nail that pierced it.

Meditation is a kind of memory work, and meditation on Christ's life and death inscribes the central moments of salvation history in the heart and mind of the Christian. There are many reasons for the extreme violence of Christian meditative practice. In the medieval West, Christ's death was his central redemptive act. Meditation on Christ's Passion demands that believers recognize their role in Christ's death in order to understand the ramifications of their sinfulness and feel true sorrow for it. Through compassion for Christ's suffering, sinners feel contrition, share in Christ's pain through their compassion and remorse, and thereby participate in their own redemption.

In addition, violence plays a crucial role in eliciting memory and emotion. According to the medieval theories of memory studied by the historian Mary Carruthers in *The Craft of Thought: Meditation, Rhetoric, and the Making of Images, 400–1200,* Passion narratives heighten the violence of Christ's final hours and death because (1) violent images are more memorable than nonviolent ones, (2) violent images carry with them emotions of grief and fear that render the images even more memorable, and (3) through these emotion-laden images the believer scares, saddens, and shames himself or herself. The theological centrality of Christ's death and the requirements of memory, then, fit together seamlessly.

Although some Passion narratives focus solely on the material provided by the four Gospels, the desire for detailed apprehension of Christ's suffering leads to ever more intense embellishment over the course of the later Middle Ages. In the *Meditations on the Life of Christ,* the unknown author explains to his audience:

> you must not believe that all things said and done by Him on
> which we may meditate are known to us in writing. For the sake
> of greater impressiveness I shall tell them to you as they occurred
> or as they might have occurred according to the devout belief of
> the imagination and the varying interpretation of the mind.

The author justifies his additions and imaginative recreations on the basis of an understanding of scriptural interpretation derived from Augustine (d. 430).

Augustine's handbook on biblical interpretation and preaching, *On
Christian Doctrine,* argues that any interpretation of the Bible that leads
to the love of God and of one's neighbor is warranted. Similarly, the
author of the *Meditations* insists that

> it is possible to contemplate, explain, and understand the Holy
> Scriptures in as many ways as we consider necessary, in such a
> manner as not to contradict the truth of life and justice and not
> to oppose faith and morality. Thus when you find it said here,
> "This was said and done by the Lord Jesus," and by others of
> whom we read, if it cannot be demonstrated by the Scriptures,
> you must consider it only as a requirement of devout contempla-
> tion. Take it as if I had said, "Suppose that this is what the Lord
> Jesus said and did," and also for similar things. And if you wish
> to profit you must be present at the same things that it is related
> that Jesus did and said, joyfully and rightly, leaving behind all
> other cares and anxieties.

Detailed additions to the Gospels' brief account of Jesus's Crucifixion,
then, are justified as forms of interpretation through which "what might
have been" fills in gaps in the sparse biblical text. The goal of meditative
practice is to make Christ's Passion so vivid to believers that they cannot
not see it enacted before their mind's eye. Only a very few adepts ever
attain the goal, but for some women and men, meditation on Christ's
suffering and death not only becomes involuntary but also engenders
supernatural visions that provide further details about that suffering on
which the visionary (and often others) can then meditate. The Carthu-
sian prioress Marguerite of Oingt (d. 1310), for example, justifies her
additions to the Passion narrative by proclaiming that although she does
not know whether the account she gives (of Jesus being hit on the head
with a bowl) is in the Bible, she does know that

she who put [it] into writing [Marguerite herself] was one night
so enraptured by our Lord that it seemed to her that she saw all
these things. And when she came back to her senses, she had all
these things written in her heart in such a way that she could
think of nothing else, and her heart was so full that she could
not eat, drink, or sleep until she was so weak that the doctors
thought she was on the point of death.

The only remedy for her illness was to "put these things into writing in
the same way that our Lord had put them into her heart. . . . And when
she had written everything down, she was cured."

The medieval Christian tradition of meditation on, contemplation of,
and visionary experience about Christ's death continues well into the
modern era, as witnessed by the visions of Anne Catherine Emmerich
(1774–1824), a German Augustinian nun whose visions were recorded
by Clemens Brentano and serve as one of the many sources for Gibson's film. Although Gibson acknowledges the influence of Emmerich's
visions and hence self-consciously places the film within the context of
medieval and modern devotion to Christ's Passion, he simultaneously
insists on the film's biblical basis. This conflation of meditative traditions with scriptural texts also occurs in Emmerich. In a preface to the
Passion visions, the author, presumably Brentano, notes that "whoever
compares the following meditations with the short history . . . given in
the Gospel will discover some slight differences between them." Yet the
author goes on to insist that "the following pages will appear to the
attentive reader rather a simple and natural concordance of the Gospels
than a history differing in any point of the slightest importance from
that of Scripture."

Some of the episodes in Gibson's movie that bear no relationship
to anything in the four Gospels have their origin in Emmerich's visions
(e.g., Satan's appearance in the garden of Gethsemane and Pilate's wife
providing Mary the mother of Jesus with an armful of white cloth with
which Mary then wipes up the blood of her flayed son). Others (e.g.,
the woman wiping Jesus's face with her mantle as he walks, or crawls,
the road to Calvary) are rooted in much more ancient albeit similarly
nonbiblical traditions. Others Gibson appears simply to have invented.
The *Meditations on the Life of Christ* and other medieval texts insist
that elaborations of the Gospels are justified if they do not contradict
the spirit of scripture. In the context of modern debates about the absolute authority of the Bible, on the other hand, Brentano equates Emmerich's visionary elaborations of the Gospels with the Gospels them-

selves. Gibson, perhaps not surprisingly given his desire to appeal to both Protestant and Catholic viewers, follows Brentano. Similarly, many who find the film powerful argue that it depicts "what really happened" and, adopting Gibson's rhetoric, claim that the film's rendition of Jesus's final hours and death is rooted in a literal reading of the Bible. These appeals, however, crucially distort how the film itself and the traditions on which it is based operate.

The powerful effect these scenes have on many viewers depends not on their claimed biblical origins, but on their extraordinary violence and the constant pressure placed on the viewer toward empathy for the victim of that violence. The film seems real or literal, not because it follows the letter of the Bible, but because of the extreme violence it depicts. (Stories of the injuries Jim Caviezel sustained during filming reinforced the illusion that the violence depicted in the movie was real.)

The double emphasis—on violence and compassionate identification with its victim—again has its origins in the meditative and visionary traditions from which Gibson draws. The Passion narratives in the Gospels do not directly enjoin the reader to share in Christ's suffering, to identify with Mary the mother of Jesus and Mary Magdalene at the foot of the cross as they suffer with Christ in his agony, or to take on Christ's suffering as his or her own. Narratives such as the *Meditations on the Life of Christ,* however, continually remind the reader that his or her salvation depends on compassionate meditation.

> He who wishes to glory in the Cross and the Passion must dwell with continued meditation on the mysteries and events that occurred. If they were considered with complete regard of mind, they would, I think, lead the meditator to a (new) state. To him who searches for it from the bottom of the heart and with the marrow of his being, many unhoped-for steps would take place by which he would receive new compassion, new love, new solace, and then a new condition of sweetness that would seem to him a promise of glory.

The truth of "the mysteries and events that occurred" depends less on their biblical or authoritative origins, although these are assumed, than on the violence of the images that heighten imagination and emotion, enabling the meditator momentarily to bring Christ, his mother, and his followers back to life.

The tradition of meditation on Christ's Passion, then, continuously writes the onlooker into the story. The *Meditations on the Life of Christ* not only directly addresses its readers, calling on them (and, by extension, us) to "behold, the Lord Jesus . . . crucified and extended on the cross so that each of His bones can be numbered, as He complained by the prophet (Psalm xxi, 18)," but also pays close attention to those who were present and looking on as Christ suffered and died. The reader is asked not only to see Christ, but also to "see how desolate [Mary the mother of Jesus] is, consumed with sadness all the day." In meditating on Christ's Passion one identifies not only with Christ, but also—and in some cases more immediately—with Mary as she identifies with Christ. Moreover, the emphasis on the onlookers escalates as Christ nears the cross.

Film is, of course, a radically different genre from the stories, prayers, and relatively static devotional images produced during the Middle Ages. Through film, Gibson allows his audience to see and hear a richly imagined, intensely corporeal meditative reenactment of the Passion. As a result, the film and the extremity of its violence do much of the work for the viewer, almost inevitably arousing strong emotions. (I know of only a very few viewers, mostly disaffected Roman Catholics, who simply found the film boring.) Unlike Passion narratives (medieval or modern), however, the film does not—and perhaps, as film, cannot—tell the viewer how to interpret the violence. Medieval Passion narratives, like the Roman Catholic Good Friday liturgy, insistently remind the reader that compassion and horror are the proper responses to Christ's suffering. They also insist on positioning readers, in their sinfulness, as participants in Christ's death. Their compassion, then, leads to guilt and remorse, which contribute to their salvation. Film viewers, on the other hand, receive few explicit directives for how to position themselves in relation to that which they see and hear. Their position is more passive and more voyeuristic than that of those actively engaged in the process of meditation and so, at least potentially, more sadistic than compassionate. (However, sadism and masochism come together in the medieval Passion tradition as they do in Gibson's film. This, together with the related movement between homosociality, homoeroticism, and homophobia in medieval and modern devotion to the Passion, will require another essay.) Without directives for how to understand one's emotions, viewers' fear, disgust, repugnance, guilt, or compassion is often unreflectively shaped by how they situate themselves in relationship to the Christian drama.

One way in which Gibson implicates the viewer in the film, again following the meditative Passion tradition, is through visual elaboration of the varying roles of the onlookers. Each provides a guide to how a person differently situated with regard to the Christian story of suffering and redemption will respond to the violence depicted. Although I cannot elaborate the point here, many of the positions viewers voice about the film are found in the film itself, in the differing reactions to Jesus's suffering. (Here is one key to the anti-Semitism of the medieval meditative tradition and of Gibson's film—both of which far surpass the anti-Judaism of their scriptural sources. Jewish characters demonstrate the disgust and occasionally the pleasure elicited in unbelieving onlookers by Christ's suffering. Simon of Cyrene [played by Jarreth J. Merz] then enacts the possibility that Jewish repugnance and indifference can be transformed into compassion and hence into faith.)

As in the Passion narratives, representations of the onlookers to Jesus's suffering proliferate as events unfold. The depiction of Christ's Crucifixion occurs in a flurry of jump cuts—from the brutal tying down of Jesus's arm on the cross, to the face of John (Hristo Jivkov), to a flashback of the Last Supper, to a nail clutched by an unseen Roman soldier's hand, to the faces of Mary the mother of Jesus (Maia Morgenstern), Mary Magdalene (Monica Belluci), and John, to yet another flashback of the Last Supper. The constant movement from brutality to the onlookers' horrified responses to that brutality continues unabated. Jesus's arm is stretched and broken so that it will fit the hole in the cross through which the nail must pass. Mary the mother of Jesus and the other women lament. Jesus cries out, "Father, forgive them." John's anguished face appears. Nails are pounded into Christ's hand. We see Mary the mother of Jesus, then Mary Magdalene. Blood drips through a hole on the back of the cross. Later, as the Roman soldiers flip the cross and pound down the nails jutting out from it, we see Mary Magdalene, first prostrate on the ground looking under the cross at Jesus's face, then rising up over it, her face wrenched in anguish.

More violence, more depictions of Jesus's broken body, and more distraught faces follow, interspersed with flashbacks to the Last Supper and Jesus's words to his disciples. The film, like the Passion narratives from which it derives, renders concrete the identification of the privileged onlookers' suffering with the suffering of Christ most prominently in the figure of Mary the mother of Jesus. When the Roman soldiers allow Mary and John to approach the foot of the cross, Mary kisses Jesus's feet, and for the remainder of the film her face is smeared with blood. (After Jesus's death, a Roman soldier pierces Jesus's side, and blood and water pour over those standing at the foot of the cross. Bloody identification with Christ's suffering then moves from Mary to include John and the newly converted Roman soldier.)

FIGURE 10 Mary holding Jesus's dead body. Still from *The Passion of the Christ* (2004).

Throughout these final moments of the film, the images become more and more static, increasingly resembling medieval and early modern religious paintings, sculptures, woodcuts, and manuscript illuminations derived from and often used as pictorial aides to the meditation on Christ's Passion. The two Marys, John, two Roman soldiers, and an old Jew (presumably Joseph of Arimathea) take Jesus down from the cross—the deposition. Mary holds her dead son in her arms—the pietà. The film then cuts to a pile of objects: Jesus's garment, the ropes and nails with which he was hung on the cross, and the crown of thorns. These are the *arma Christi*—the "weapons of Christ"—with which Christ conquered sin and the devil. Another pietà follows. Here, as in many medieval and early modern images, we see Jesus's entire body. Mary holds his head and upper body, John kneels by his side, and Mary Magdalene weeps over his feet. Another shot of the "weapons of Christ" appears. Most tellingly, perhaps, the Passion ends not with an image of Christ, but with a long shot of Mary's bloodstained face.

The film, of course, does not end here. Instead, the screen fades to black, and light slowly returns as if from behind a stone rolled from the front of a cave. Yet Gibson's depiction of the resurrected Christ lacks the imaginative force of his crucified Jesus. There is no joy in this Christ's face, no peace in his departure from the tomb. Instead, the martial music, especially when coupled with the extremity of the violence Christ has just undergone and the reminder of that violence in a shot of his scarred hand, suggests vengeance rather than salvation. The film foreshadows the coming vengeance in two key scenes: when the bad thief mocks Jesus on the cross, a crow pecks out his eye; and later, when Jesus dies, we see the destruction of the temple and the accompanying distress of the high priest who had sat in judgment over Jesus. (Revenge is a familiar motif in the Passion traditions—most often at the expense of the Jews. The risen Christ's apparent vengefulness, however, brings the film much closer to *Kill Bill* than Gibson seems ready, consciously at least, to acknowledge.)

For many viewers, *The Passion*'s extreme violence reinforces and perhaps even elicits belief in Christ through detailed attention to the extremity and viscerality of his suffering. By juxtaposing Jesus's almost continual torture and seemingly inexhaustible bodily anguish with the relatively bloodless crucifixions of the two thieves, Gibson's film seems premised on the theological claim that no human being has ever suffered as Jesus suffered. (Moreover, devotion and faith—evidenced, for example, in the conversions of Simon of Cyrene and of the Roman centurion—are elicited by Christ's sheer physical endurance rather than by the power of his words or his deeds.)

In the face of the atrocities committed daily throughout the world and throughout history, claims to the exceptional nature of Christ's suffering are historically, theologically, and ethically untenable. Yet that one human being would willingly undergo suffering in solidarity with the suffering of others—for the Christian believer, that *God* would become human and take on the suffering of human flesh and blood—can and does offer comfort and hope to many, including many who are themselves the victims of violence and injustice. The seeming inevitability of extreme physical suffering during the European Middle Ages renders this a likely contributory cause of medieval fascination with the Passion. In the end, I do not think this is Gibson's vision. Yet the position of the onlooker inevitably shapes what he or she sees, rendering it a vision available to those who watch Gibson's film with different eyes.

17 Jesus's Extreme Makeover

William G. Little

In Mel Gibson's *The Passion of the Christ,* Jesus is made out to be a figure that, on his way to death, undergoes an extreme physical makeover. The images marking this transformation—the body flung, flayed, beaten, and nailed —are disturbing, but so is the fact that commentators have had trouble attending carefully to their significance, in some cases merely dismissing the violent images as, well, extreme.

The trouble is particularly noteworthy given that contemporary American culture appears otherwise obsessed with physical makeover. A *New York Times* article (May 2, 2004) cites telling statistics in this regard: "At the hands of cosmetic surgeons, Americans underwent a total of 8.3 million procedures last year [2003]. The number of surgeries rose 12 percent, to 1.8 million, and the number of non-surgical procedures, like Botox, rose 22 percent, to 6.4 million." In addition to the popularity of new technologies for suctioning, injecting, and implanting, the proliferation of reality television shows devoted to chronicling these procedures and their effects (e.g., *Extreme Makeover, The Swan,* and *I Want a Famous Face*) illustrates how preoccupied the national imagination is with radical physical alteration.

Given the intense cultural investment in nipping and tucking the flesh, it seems important to inquire patiently into Gibson's graphic depiction of Christ's flesh being repeatedly sliced, punctured, and pinned. By making over the Passion story as, among other things, a story about extreme physical makeover, *The Passion of the Christ* begs certain questions. To what extent does the film challenge assumptions built into contemporary culture's idealization of the makeover? And to what extent is the film attentive to the problem of what it means to try to imitate a model life?

In the media-hyped, medically assisted version of the makeover, an individual willingly submits to body alteration in an effort to achieve a substantially different appearance. Examined closely, the aim of such transformation is something more than just a flat stomach, a strong jaw, straight teeth, or higher cheekbones. The virtues of the makeover may not be marketed using explicitly religious discourse, but the promise of a radically new appearance is nevertheless inextricably bound up with the idea that the individual's re-formation will be spiritually profitable. More specifically, while the makeover's emphasis on the achievement of physical beauty harks back to ancient Greek ideals of self-creation, its aggressive, invasive, sometimes painful techniques betray a suspicion of the body that has more in common with the practices of early Christian ascetics. As Geoffrey Galt Harpham points out in his book *The Ascetic Imperative in Culture and Criticism,* the ascetics' exercise of extreme self-denial was designed to make the self approximate a certain standard of beauty. Whereas the contemporary makeover relies on celebrity features as a model, the early monastic makeover relied on Christ as a model:

> In the fourth century Gregory of Nyssa wrote of asceticism as a repetition of Christ's original "taking-form," the act by which he fashioned "a beauty in accord with the character of the Archetype" and made of himself an "image of the invisible God." . . . Remarkably, the ascetic "image" reflected a strict attention to certain canons of beauty. . . . The body wasted away, grew pallid and insubstantial as the soul gained in ascendance, and so the horrifying emaciation of the ascetic body could testify to such traditional artistic virtues as "a mastery of one's materials," or "technical control of the medium."

What the contemporary cosmetic surgery patient shares with the early Christian monastic is a desire to master the body, to subdue its unruliness. Though ostensibly a means of giving the body a "lift" (of skin, of energy, of years, etc.), the modern makeover is really an effort to transcend the body altogether: its history, its shifts, its slants, its letdowns, its betrayals.

Thus, despite its apparent materialism, the extreme makeover turns out to be infused with idealism. It constitutes a secularized attempt to manipulate an impure substance (the flesh) so as to redeem, in this world, a pure essence (the spirit). For all the attention the body receives in this scheme, it is ultimately treated as something extrinsic that when properly molded will reveal something intrinsic, namely an unchanging, authentic selfhood. By eliminating from the body whatever is deemed ragged or unfit, the makeover promises to display the subject's life as a neat, coherent narrative of self-understanding. The seamless face yields a seamless autobiography. Participants on the show *Extreme Makeover* voluntarily retreat from friends and family into the wilderness of a city in the desert (Los Angeles) not just to achieve a more presentable appearance, but also to secure a representable life. Through submission to procedures, such as rhinoplasty, that straighten up loose ends, the unknown figure is transformed from a disorderly "profile" into a "somebody" now clearly legible both to family (the staged reunion at the end of the show supports this idea) and to members of the viewing audience, for whom the participant may, in turn, become a model. In this context, an *Extreme Makeover* participant could be considered the postmodern version of an eremite—a type of Christian ascetic whose solitary, heroic renunciations in the desert might, if his deprivations proved exemplary in their extremism, be made into a hagiography, a biography of a model life.

In addition to promoting suspicion of the body's materiality, the concept of the extreme makeover relies on certain assumptions about imitation. The makeover subject expects that by imitating a particular type of model he or she will transform a mean life (a dull, shabby, scattered life) into what might be called *an extreme life* (a life lived at the highest, most intensely self-realized pitch). The imitation itself is extreme in that the model to be imitated is admired solely on the basis of superficiality (the word "extreme" comes from the Latin *exter,* meaning "on the outside"). One does not imitate a remarkable biography or distinguished pattern of conduct. Indeed, while makeover culture certainly worships individual Personalities, what qualifies someone to be a model worth imitating (in addition to the standard physical features) is his or her ability to fashion a personality that is comforting, homogenized, and easy to consume. The Personality that inspires fantasies of an extreme life does so, paradoxically, by coming off as somewhat anonymous.

Like the anonymity of the androgynous, airbrushed fashion model, the anonymity of the Personality provokes no extreme reaction, generates no intense passion.

The lure of this brand of anonymity is reflected in the faces of makeover participants, many of whom display what Alex Kuczynski, writing in the *New York Times,* called "an eerie Stepford-spouse similarity." A prime-time example of the anonymous Personality as model is Ryan Seacrest, the *American Idol* host who made *People* magazine's 2003 list of the most beautiful people. According to a 2004 *Times* profile titled, appropriately enough, "Bland Ambition," Seacrest successfully made himself over from overweight child to "perhaps one of the most ubiquitous Personalities pop culture has ever produced" by fashioning himself as "likable, nonthreatening and, most important, reachable— never too handsome or too happening or too sharp." Designed never to be at cross-purposes with the contemporary consumer, the Personality promises that, through imitation, the extreme life is altogether attainable or "reachable." To purchase model skin—to consume the model's smooth, unbroken flesh—is to be guaranteed measurable savings. Language used to describe the makeover process reinforces the idea that imitation is a profitable investment. On *The Swan,* for instance, post-makeover individuals are described as "graduates." More generally, all forms of cosmetic surgery are referred to colloquially as "work," so that an individual who submits to an extreme makeover is said to have had "a lot of work done." Of course, the work doesn't involve much effort on the individual's part other than working through the passing discomfort when flesh is cut. Nevertheless, the belief is that imitation's shortcut work involves a build-up (of labor as well as lips) from which the makeover subject can expect a reasonable payoff.

The extreme physical makeover that Jesus undergoes in *The Passion of the Christ* challenges the values informing the makeover culture's investments in the flesh and in Christ. The makeover is extreme in the extent of the disfigurement and in the extent to which it departs from previous cinematic depictions of the suffering. These extremities, in turn, raise an important question about the spiritual business of imitation: if what Christ offers as a model is a body that disfigured, what profit can be made from him by those seeking to make themselves over in his image?

The film's violence creates a crucial hang-up about imitation that was already in evidence in an extended *New Yorker* piece by Peter J. Boyer, published before the film's release: "Gibson has been told by friendly audiences that 'The Passion' is several measures too violent, that seeing Jesus subjected to such protracted scenes of brutality will have a numbing effect upon audiences, detaching them from Christ's pain. Gibson acknowledges that possibility, but then adds that the event in question 'was pretty nasty.' " While the question of a "numbing" effect may merit consideration, the very language of detachment raises an even more compelling concern in light of the pervasiveness of makeover culture: how exactly does one attach to a model that looks so broken and bloodied, so difficult to swallow, so "nasty"?

Significantly, this crucial hang-up with respect to imitation is played out in the Crucifixion itself. According to long-standing Christological formulations, Christ is the Incarnation, a figure embodying the extreme step God took of making himself over as human without losing godliness. The central feature of the Incarnation is not the personal history of Jesus's life. It is that Jesus, as the Christ, embodies in one figure the earthly and the divine, the temporal and the eternal. Moreover, since the Incarnation culminates in the Crucifixion, it primarily models the suffering and death of God. Throughout Christian history, the Incarnation has proved extraordinarily difficult to imitate, for although it is bound up with the flesh, it simultaneously thwarts expectation that investment in the flesh will yield an extreme life of undifferentiated bliss. The bloody truth of the Crucifixion is that it reveals God's improbable investment in the world's fractures and tears. For those who embrace a form of Christian spirituality according to which imitation of a model enables one to transcend the suffering that marks material existence, God's death on a cross is bound to be a real hang-up. The culminating event of the Incarnation, the Crucifixion creates a "real" or considerable hang-up because it drives home the point that God's real face is revealed (while buried) in the folds of the flesh: its passions, its wounds, its hang-ups. To face up to the Crucifixion is to approach the death of God as something other than the first segment of a theological makeover show that ends with the resurrection of a real life that is out of this world.

To get around the Crucifixion, many forms of Christian spirituality have made Jesus over into a heroic Personality of sorts, casting him as a model of formless perfection or ethical conduct ("What Would Jesus Do?"). A popular contemporary example of a Jesus makeover that seeks to leave behind the hang-up of the flesh and the hang-up of imitation is the Left Behind series of evangelical novels, which in America now outsell any other novels marketed to adults. The series co-authors, Tim LaHaye and Jerry B. Jenkins, lend Jesus the personality of a virile warrior who, at a cataclysmic end-time called the Rapture, returns to earth, wreaking apocalyptic destruction on spiritual offenders and transporting the faithful to heaven, leaving the world behind.

Instead of trying to leave the hang-up of the Crucifixion behind, *The Passion of the Christ* foregrounds it. The film's theological concerns are dramatized through its technical attention to the physical makeover, attention that excludes emphasis on the history of Jesus's life. Though a few moments from the life—the Sermon on the Mount, the Last Supper—are inserted into the text, they appear as brief, decontextualized flashbacks that fail to amount to a biographical portrait. In the absence of personal narrative, the viewer's attention is drawn to the presence of the flesh, the matter of Incarnation.

The film intensifies this draw by repeatedly placing Jesus in postures that call attention to the sheer weight of the body. Not coincidentally, some of the most dramatic postures are ones in which Christ is literally hung up: suspended by a rope from a bridge after his initial capture, pulled limp from the whipping post, and staked to the cross as it is flipped over to hammer down nails. While these postures might seem to make the suffering figure a model of heroic endurance, the violence done to the body transforms it so radically as to make the person difficult to identify, let alone identify with or look up to.

Gibson emphasizes this depersonalization in the title of the film, where he refers to the figure not by a personal name (Jesus), but by an official designation (the Christ). It turns out that in the film the only aspects of the person with which the viewer is permitted familiarity are the body's surfaces and extremities: a swollen eye, matted tips of hair, gouged-out chunks of flesh, crucified hands and feet. In other words, the physical makeover renders Christ virtually anonymous, an effect heightened by the fact that it was achieved by making over an already relatively obscure actor using layers of make-up and prosthetic application.

This anonymity is altogether different from the anonymity of the Personality. Christ's anonymity subverts the idea of a model that offers a shortcut to an extreme life, and it bears traces of a profoundly unavailable other that never shows its full face. The Personality's smooth-faced anonymity is a golden calf. Christ's crossed-up anonymity is the forever hidden face of God. As Gibson's "nasty" depiction of the Crucifixion suggests, God does not show up to host an (American) idol.

Not coincidentally, the film opens with Jesus coming face to face with an anonymous figure in the garden of Gethsemane. On the one hand, this figure, whose anonymity is featured in its androgyny, tempts Jesus with just the kind of shortcut the Crucifixion challenges. It tries to seduce with the promise of an extreme life free from burdens of the flesh: "Do you really believe that one man can bear the burden of sin?" Tempting Jesus to shed human sin, it peddles a makeover, one that Jesus resists by crushing the symbol of the temptation—the skin-shedding snake. In this context, the pale, slinky figure that many critics have identified as Satan resembles a demonized version of a hollow-cheeked fashion model. On the other hand, it is not exactly an easily consumable Personality. Its face cowled and its gender uncertain, it is a figure whose identity remains scandalously rather than smoothly veiled. For instance, is the figure clearly other than Christ, or is it an otherness within Christ? This question is a legitimate one, since its whisperings in the garden could be read as expressions of Jesus's own doubts. In the same scene, when the figure asks Jesus, "Who are you? Who is your father?," the questions might, read one way, suggest Satan's teasing promise of extreme self-knowledge (if one consumes what the serpent has to offer). Read another way, however, they might serve to highlight the degree to which so many questions about Jesus's identity are fueled by a demonic passion to make him conform to conventional expectations about models.

Jesus's face-off with this figure suggests that the model of Christ is meaningful only insofar as, paradoxically, it *lives through* the hang-up of crucifixion. In this case, to live through does not mean to live beyond or to live after. To live through means to abide within. The film dramatizes living through crucifixion in the way it painstakingly stages the cross-bearing procession to Golgotha. Gibson's slow-motion shots and briefly interruptive flashbacks stretch out the time the passage seems to take. More important, throughout the extended scene the soldiers and by-standers hold up the procession's progress. Under the blows and the weight of the cross, Jesus stumbles and falls numerous times. At the same time, the agents of the humiliation repeatedly mock the resulting hold-up: "We haven't got all day"; "Get up, your Highness." The mockery is telling in that it reveals the hang-up Christ as model presents. Alongside a sadistic desire to see this figure brought low while holding up the cross, there appears a desire, screened with sarcasm, to be done with this figure quickly because it so confounds expectations about what constitutes low and high, or down and up. This cross-up of expectation about models is heard throughout the earlier questioning directed at Jesus, including Pilate's impatient line: "Tell us, are you the Messiah?"

In closing, it should be said that while *The Passion* uses an extreme physical makeover to dramatize how Christ crosses up expectations about models, in other places the film is insensitive to important hang-ups. As the controversy surrounding the film's release indicated, the question of how to represent the specific history of the Passion creates an interpretive hang-up. Gibson takes a dangerous shortcut through this hang-up by interpreting the past through a conservative Catholic perspective that has triggered accusations of anti-Semitism and by asserting that his interpretation is the literal truth. The extremism of the perspective and the slickness of the assertion about literalism show Gibson to be engaged in what might be termed an extreme makeover of the past. Furthermore, the film ends with a brief image of Jesus in profile emerging from the tomb, looking virile and heroic. This image seems tacked on and unearned, a narrative shortcut designed, in true Hollywood fashion, to redeem Jesus as a seductively anonymous Personality by making him over into a consumable model. Perhaps such a concession to makeover culture was inevitable. After all, the previously less-than-superstar actor who played Jesus, James Caviezel, has now, by virtue of the film, moved closer to assuming the status of anonymous Personality. In 2004, *People* selected him as one of the fifty most beautiful people in the world.

18 Lights! Camera! Action!

José Márquez

It was like they were more or less saying I have no right to interpret the Gospels myself, because I don't have a bunch of letters after my name. But they are for children, these Gospels. They're for children, they're for old people, they're for everybody in between. They're not necessarily for academics. Just get an academic on board if you want to pervert something! **Mel Gibson, quoted in Peter J. Boyer, "The Jesus War," New Yorker, September 15, 2003**

If what you want is to make an action movie with Jesus Christ as the protagonist, you'd best turn to an action movie star and director. So it is that Mel Gibson's interpretation of the Via Dolorosa, a modern-day Passion play for a society that regularly baby-sits its infants and elderly by parking them in front of television sets, is as true to form as the realistic sculptures of Donatello were in fifteenth-century Florence. For it is form, not content, that makes or breaks a Hollywood movie, and Gibson's tightly crafted if folkloric movie *The Passion of the Christ* is as much a testament to its makers and their moment in time as it is testimony to the Son of God.

As a lapsed Catholic with a Jesuit education and an unabashed fan of *Mad Max*, the 1979 Australian action film that launched Gibson's Hollywood career, I might very well be an ideal audience member for *The Passion*.

For starters, I'm already familiar with the plot, which is essential when you consider that Gibson's contribution to the Greatest Story Ever Told has scant dialogue, almost no exposition, and cardboard characters. Of these various choices, the lack of exposition has a clearly ideological intent: this director, like any other cult filmmaker, is preaching to the choir.

The rules of mass-audience moviemaking, even though they continue to evolve into ever more self-referential conventions, as in the recent *Charlie's Angels* or *Kill Bill* series, require the use of exposition to create a sympathetic bond between the viewer and the film's protagonists. Tellingly, no such effort is made in *The Passion*, where the scarce moments of character development are presented almost as an afterthought. In fact, with the exception of some likely apocryphal moments such as those involving Pontius Pilate and his wife or Judas Iscariot and his demons, almost all of the requisite backstory, which typically provides viewers with a reason to care about the fate of the movie's principal characters, is delivered in a few fleeting flashbacks. For the uninitiated viewer, the resulting story is as slippery as it is bloody. Which is just as well, since the movie is not for them but for those who are already— or were once—believers. Rather than convert filmgoers to Christianity, Gibson has apparently set out to convert Christians to his particular sect of Catholicism.

As is the case with the so-called prequels to the *Star Wars* trilogy, or, more recently, the movie *Hellboy,* which was adapted to the big screen from an underground comic book series (and, incidentally, bounced *The Passion* from first place at the U.S. box office in April of 2004), Gibson's hectic screenplay requires the audience to fill in the story's considerable gaps while acknowledging their familiarity with knowing, esoteric nods. A case in point is the flashback in which we witness Mary Magdalene's first encounter with Jesus. We see the stone throwers, we see the stones, we see Mary Magdalene on the floor, and we see Jesus standing next to her, confronting the now reluctant and retreating stone throwers. That's it.

If you don't "get it," then this movie is not for you.

But if you do "get it," then you'll love the scene where we get to see the possible origins of the Shroud of Turin, as a woman bystander wipes the face of Jesus while he stumbles in his agony. For fans of Christ, such seemingly banal sequences are a rare treat—Hollywood seldom deigns to lavish its moviemaking magic on such scriptural details as the sound made by a Roman soldier's whip as it sails through the air before tearing open human flesh.

Or is it human flesh? While there can be no doubt that Gibson has made a sincere movie, it is nonetheless a work of art—and artifice. In particular, as an action movie, it adheres to a tradition within the canon of filmmaking that is more phenomenal than symbolic. Thus, rather than a journey, *The Passion* is an event. Instead of offering its viewers a story, it gives them an experience: a slow, gut-wrenching mechanical ride through an old-fashioned house of horrors tucked away for centuries within the church.

Just as we understand the paintings of Michelangelo and Caravaggio, however inspired, to bear the imprint of the artists' cultural values (what demure critics might call their "taste"), we would be foolish to overlook the artistic career of this movie's director as well as the broader culture in which he earned the $30 million required to make this picture without tapping a single additional investor. That career is inextricably tied to the action film and its most obvious component: the unstoppable and seemingly immortal action hero.

In many ways, *The Passion* could not have been made prior to such action films as the Bruce Willis vehicle *Die Hard* (1988) or its aptly titled sequels *Die Harder* (1990) and *Die Hard: With a Vengeance* (1995). Gibson, whose previous movie *Braveheart* was such a successful contribution to this genre that it won the Best Picture Oscar in 1995, is a demonstrable master of this form in which seeing is believing and feeling is knowing.

Although the action film has been described as an unpretentious and immediate genre, ostensibly popular with moviegoers of all ages, nationalities, and educational backgrounds, its conventions are, nonetheless, as artificial as any of the pretentious devices used by "art house" films. But where the artsy protagonists are ideas, action heroes are designed to exalt the viewer's emotions. Any action movie that doesn't make your pulse quicken is a failure. *The Passion,* to be sure, is a successful action film.

However, action movies are not bereft of ideas—even powerful ones. Action movies transform their maker's ideas into physical gestures as well as the appearances of their protagonists. One of the cornerstones of this genre, the 1966 spaghetti western *The Good, the Bad and the Ugly,* not only delivers on the promise of its title by depicting incarnations of all three qualities, but also manages to redefine each of these terms by asserting a new kind of brutal beauty. It is no small detail that the protagonist of this highly influential movie is called the Man with No Name.

Of course, like any genre, the action film has various and competing tendencies. One way to describe these internal rifts is to distinguish between action movies that present an ambiguous or ambivalent hero—such as Clint Eastwood in *The Good, the Bad and the Ugly,* Mel Gibson in *Mad Max* and *Lethal Weapon,* or Sylvester Stallone in *First Blood*—and those that offer a less equivocal, morally righteous protagonist, such as John Wayne in *The Alamo,* Mel Gibson in *Braveheart,* or Sylvester Stallone in *Rambo: First Blood Part II.* In recent years, as special effects have extended the range of the action genre, the tension between neat and messy protagonists has sometimes been depicted as a battle between human and superhuman qualities.

But with its emphasis on sensational realism and its reliance on the physical to communicate the abstract, the action movie is a poor vehicle for any hero in whom both transparent and opaque impulses coincide. Propelled by the dynamic of opposing forces, the plot of most action movies simply cannot allow a paradox to enter the picture. Where other genres insinuate, action films demonstrate; where other styles rely on intimation, action films typically resort to exclamation. It is within this tradition that Gibson has crafted *The Passion of the Christ,* choosing a portion of the New Testament that is best told in the manner most familiar to him: the action film.

Yet, in choosing such a path, Gibson also has to overcome—or, at least, recognize—many of the formal rules of this genre, if he also wishes to convey the fundamental paradox at the heart of Christianity, the belief that Jesus is the both the Son of Man *and* the Son of God. Unfortunately, this director is either unable or unwilling to preserve this mystery, choosing instead to attempt to realistically portray something that defies reason and requires faith in the unseen. For those believers who make pilgrimages to shrines and honor relics, the eventual DVD release of *The Passion* should provide a take-home version of a related experience. But for those filmgoers who, like me, wish to explore rather than experience their faith, *The Passion* is a sideshow, an earnest curio ill suited to the curious.

What is most disheartening about Gibson's final product is that it comes so close to success. The very act of enjoying a movie is akin to ecstatic rapture—the bread and butter of the mystics the director sought to imitate. As moviegoers we file into a dark theater and quietly wait to be transported. We are nervous with raw hope and unbridled expectation—our hearts and minds given over to the director, to the cinematographer, to the editor, cast, and crew. We go to movies because we want to see the light. It's not called "suspension of disbelief" for nothing. But, sadly, the credibility problems that weaken *The Passion* start early on and are only compounded as the movie, determined to highlight "facts" with special effects, undermines its own premise of theological accuracy with heavy-handed literalness.

When, in the opening scenes, a fight sequence between the Pharisees and Jesus's disciples makes generous use of a newfangled cinematic device—that of seamlessly slowing down and then speeding up the action—I take it in stride. After all, why can't Jesus, a subject of the Roman Empire, be the star of an action movie like *Gladiator,* which first made use of this particular time-stretching special effect? But whereas that movie's director, Ridley Scott, was judicious in his use of such illusions—for example, to illustrate the split-second difference between life and death in combat—the application of special effects in Gibson's allegedly literal accounting of the death of Jesus is, instead, used to drive home a fantastical claim about his life.

As Jim Caviezel, playing the role of Jesus, takes thirty-nine carefully enumerated lashes for the home team, my hopes for cinematic delivery are dashed. For when his body is torn open by sundry and historically accurate Roman instruments of torture, his flesh is, in fact, replaced by prostheses. Gibson, attempting to depict with scientific accuracy the suffering of Christ, resorts to make-up rather than make-believe to depict our hero's agony. Instead of being shown pain—a psychological response to physical stimuli—we are presented with the character's literal insides; rubber and red paint take the place of personality and charisma.

Which is not to say that Caviezel is a poor actor or Gibson a heartless director. It may very well be that both are working harmoniously to deliver a credible performance in front of the cameras. I just can't tell, because our protagonist is wearing both full-body and facial prostheses of flayed and swollen skin.

One would have to revisit such horror classics as *Darkman* or *A Nightmare on Elm Street* for instances of drama enabled—rather than hindered—by that much evidence of mutilation. Moreover, it's worth noting that both of these films are also, underneath their thin veneer of terror, dark comedies that tease the folly of the living with the obvious evidence of our mortality.

Sadly, there is no such self-consciousness in *The Passion,* where every assault on the body of Christ is intended to prove the director's earnestness rather than prompt the audience to question their skin-deep civility. Movies like *Halloween* and *Friday the 13th* have a light touch that allows them to be transformed by their teenage viewers from spectacles of occult horror into cult comedies (a cultural phenomenon both recognized and exploited by the *Scary Movie* series and the later *Freddy vs. Jason*). Where the risible gore in these pulp horrors is a gift to the audience, the similarly flamboyant carnage in *The Passion* is intended as a debt.

Perhaps because I have come to understand Jesus as someone who forgives rather than collects debts, I respond to the most delirious depiction of gore in *The Passion*—a geyser of slow-motion blood seen and heard spurting from Caviezel's hand—not with shame but with laughter. While Gibson may want viewers to follow in his path to redemption through such shame (or pity), I want no part in the staged humiliation. Not because I believe Jesus did not suffer, but because I believe he suffered as a man; indeed, as many men and women did, before and after his Crucifixion. Thus, according to my beliefs, it was not the death of Jesus that was extraordinary, but, rather, his life and Resurrection.

The Passion, however, likely intends to portray a different set of beliefs. The movie, which begins with the threat of violence and ends with the risen Jesus exiting his grave to the sound of martial drums, gives this hero very little to say and a great deal (of suffering) to do. Of the dozen or so brief lines delivered by Gibson's protagonist, two uttered toward the end make striking references to persecution. Only time will tell whether *The Passion* is meant to preface forthcoming films devoted to the slaughter of Christians in Roman coliseums or is the first in a series that culminates with the Crusades. The arc of the movie's truncated storyline, however, clearly communicates the director's vision of Jesus Christ as a warrior whose mission is to absorb rather than dole out punishment—at least in this installment.

Gibson's protagonist expresses few words and fewer emotions while repressing more than any man could bear. What emerges from this intense action film is a theology of repression—a spirit of resistance rather than transcendence. In order to follow in the footsteps of the Jesus depicted by *The Passion,* we would need to seek out persecution at the hands of our enemies. Moreover, while the movie left me wondering who these enemies might be, it was clear they would not be won over by persuasion, but only by their own remorse and shame.

Throughout *The Passion,* we are shown bystanders who quietly intuit that they are in the presence of God, despite not having heard Jesus utter a single word. They already know that Jesus, caked in blood and gore, is just wearing a human disguise. Nor is the true identity of Jesus lost upon the movie's villain, the high priest Caiaphas. Whereas the character of Satan is more ugly than evil—a fey version of the Machiavellian emperor in *Star Wars*—Caiaphas is responsible for the mutilation and

murder of Christ. Because *The Passion* provides no historical context—
and, thus, no rational political or theological motivation—for the high
priest's desire to see Jesus terminated with extreme prejudice, we are
left to conclude that, like the wife of Pilate or the African slave in
King Herod's court, Caiaphas knows who he's dealing with but rejects the truth for reasons that are never presented to the believer—er,
viewer.

Of course, as in any such Hollywood contest between good and
evil—rather than, say, between knowledge and ignorance—an ironic
and spectacular ending settles the score. Thus, when Gibson allows
Caviezel to succumb finally to his hours-long execution, putting an
end to the suffering of both the hero and the audience, a tremendous
earthquake confirms what we should have known all along: this Jesus
was no mere mortal. Freed from the limitations of his frail alter ego, a
now-invisible God quickly destroys the villain's lair (the Temple), and
Caiaphas, in a close-up, delivers a classic B movie look of horrified remorse. It was Caiaphas, after all, who freed Jesus, lash by lash, from his
cumbersome carnal disguise.

In this telling, Caiaphas does not fail to recognize the writing on the
wall; but he refuses to read it out loud. As the movie imparts its final
lesson to the bad guys, the audience is also instructed on its own choices
for judging the success of Gibson's artwork: either you are "with me,"
the director, or you are against him, the Savior. For this reason, there is
no need for Jesus to deliver his achingly beautiful sermons to a public
audience. Instead, in the very few scenes where Jesus is allowed to speak,
he is usually conversing privately with his disciples—or, as he says, his
"friends." How, then, does this motion picture bring out the single most
significant detail of its protagonist's truly *mysterious* identity?

Truth by torture.

It begins when an already-bloody Jesus is brought to the Roman
procurator Pontius Pilate, a likely stand-in for the audience given both
his reluctance to harm Jesus and the fact that he is one of the few characters with multiple lines of dialogue. I suspect that when Pilate bemoans
the dreary responsibility of empire, so, too, might the American movie-
goer of March 2004. Likewise, when Pilate laments the relativism of his
age—asking Jesus "What is truth?" in a tone both pained and hopeful—
so does the audience.

Jesus, of course, does not answer. But Gibson does. For the remainder of the movie, save for a few carefully chosen words, we are shown
little more than sadism and an increasingly unrecognizable Jesus who
takes a licking and keeps on ticking. In essence, Gibson is turning the

mortal body of Jesus into a bloody cocoon, out of which the immortal Jesus will eventually emerge.

Unfortunately, this aesthetic decision has serious theological repercussions. As a filmgoer, I can forgive and forget the computer-generated demons that—rather than guilt—drive Judas Iscariot to hang himself at the start of the movie. What I can't fathom is how I am to believe in the most significant mystery of Jesus Christ—that he was an ordinary man—when he is made to perform superhuman feats of endurance while enveloped in a superhero's rubber flesh. Gibson's decision to thoroughly and continuously ravage Jesus's body onscreen while keeping his personality (his teachings, his relationships, his birth and childhood) almost entirely offscreen results in a protagonist largely devoid of humanity. Although believers are expected to fill in these gaps with their own prior knowledge of Jesus, they are given a very shallow vessel into which to pour their faith.

Throughout *The Passion,* Caviezel is instructed to endure in almost perfect silence torture that would kill an ordinary human being. No doubt this silence is intended as a sign of the patience and boundless love of the Son of Man for his sinful fellow man. Yet, in the context of a movie without symbolism, in which all that *is* must be seen (from Satan to the weight of the cross), the action hero's silence takes on another, far more prosaic significance. In the physical logic of the action film, the body is the only portrait of the soul.

Any audience of seasoned moviegoers in the year 2004 will understand, implicitly, how our protagonist is able to survive the onslaught of blows that would kill a mere mortal: Gibson's cinematic Jesus is a not just a hero but a superhero. Of course, the theological implications of this mistaken identity are hardly in keeping with the director's avowed faith. (If Jesus's suffering is superhuman, is his ability to forgive his enemies a special power?) While Gibson may not have intended to break with tradition, his insistence on literalism leads him to blur the line between Hollywood magic and, well, magic. While Jesus's tremendous suffering is a matter of record, exaggerating such suffering to superhuman proportions is a matter of theology.

The mystery of Jesus's miracles, from walking on water to resurrecting the dead, is a complex matter and, I must admit, beyond the scope of my understanding. Yet, if one takes the stance that these miracles are signs of grace, bestowed by the Heavenly Father, rather than powers that emanate from within the body of Jesus, it is not hard to reconcile their appearance with a nonetheless mortal Son of Man. Surely it is not by chance that while most of *The Passion* is filmed outdoors, there are only a few shots of the sky, and even these are mostly devoted to a cloudy, inscrutable heaven.

By attempting to sidestep mystery and present fact instead, using gore for emphasis, Gibson intends to control the audience's relationship to Jesus in a way that smothers their imagination. In its cluttered minutiae of wounds and moaning, *The Passion* leaves no room for viewers to make a leap of faith.

One can, of course, imagine an alternative course for this polished presentation of the Via Dolorosa. For a director clearly willing to play with time, via both special effects and the screenplay, it must be asked: what if the scenes of torture, rather than the scenes of teaching, had been delivered via brief and intermittent flashbacks? Likewise, what if the character of Jesus had been, well, a bit more human?

In fact, Gibson, the action movie star, need not have looked much further than his own body of work to find the inspiration for this kind of figure. A quarter of a century before the release of *The Passion,* Gibson starred in the titular role of "Mad" Max Rockatansky, a cop in a post-apocalyptic world ravaged by terrorism and oil shortages. Written, produced, and directed by George Miller, who would later direct the movie's two sequels, the original *Mad Max* achieves a formal clarity and moral complexity not unlike that of *The Good, the Bad and the Ugly*. It is a violent, brutal movie that appears to delight in a rather dim view of human nature. Granted, with its psychotic, sadistic villains, heroic automobiles, and expressionistic use of the Australian outback, *Mad Max* is certainly not Shakespeare. But it's not supposed to be Shakespeare—or the Bible, for that matter. Rather, *Mad Max* clearly aims to be just a good movie. What it ultimately means is for the audience to decide.

Consider, for example, the dialogue in the following much-quoted scene, where Max's commanding officer, the charmingly avuncular Fifi (played by Roger Ward), attempts to reenlist the hero after the latter quits his post in a fit of frustration and self-doubt:

> FIFI: They say people don't believe in heroes anymore. Well, damn them! You and me, Max, we're gonna give 'em back their heroes!
>
> MAX: Ah, Fif. Do you really expect me to go for that crap?
>
> [*Pause*]
>
> FIFI: You gotta admit I sounded good there for a minute, huh?

A more confident director might have given *The Passion* enough room to grow into its own ambitions. After all, the Holy Roman Empire wasn't built in a day. Even in our age of global telecommunications and cinematic propaganda, there's no substitute for a believable hero—not even the heroism of a director's beliefs.

19 Seeing Is Not Believing

Jody Enders

They are grotesque men, toothless, brutal. They skip, dance, and giggle as they inflict unspeakable violence upon the body of Christ. One of the torturers is volunteering to hold Christ's feet so that his buddy can strike better blows. Another whistles a happy tune, while yet another, as if from the palette of Hieronymus Bosch, gleefully chants, "Look at the blood gushing down his mug! Hey! I've got flesh now coming out with the blood!" Their blows have rhythm, their beatings an almost musical beat as they spin him around and "make him dance." Blood seems to ooze from every pore. It spatters upon the earth, such that the entire set "glistens with blood." Special-effects experts have seen to it, thanks to all manner of technological miracles: hidden capsules full of vibrant vermilion dye, flesh-suits with pre-imprinted gash marks, unpeeled layer by layer and with great sleight of hand as the scourging progresses. The brutality is so overwhelming that viewers feel they must turn away, yet they are compelled to watch this piece of instructional entertainment that has been provided by their culture, by their community, and by their church.

They are not seated at a cinematic spectacle in any one of thousands of darkened movie theaters worldwide.

Rather, they inhabit public spaces all over fifteenth- and sixteenth-century Europe. They are watching a Passion play, an epic work that might span upward of fifty thousand verses and whose four or five "acts" or "days" in the life of Christ typically mobilized entire cities for weeks on end as ecclesiastical and civic officials poured money and artistry into a vast participatory drama that constantly touted its noble mission of instructing and edifying the Christian people (if not the Jews or the Muslims). They were watching a *mystère de la passion,* that morally slippery genre about which the distinguished French theater historian Gustave Cohen (1879–1958) once mused, "Instead of showering the people with faith, hope, charity, and the love of sacrifice, the Passion plays nourished their cruelty. In fact, charity is confounded on every page." Today, the proverbial Dark Ages shine a spotlight on the heart of darkness of that modern mystery play known as Mel Gibson's *The Passion of the Christ* as critic after critic, from the local news to the *New York Times* to *Entertainment Weekly* to *Time* magazine, have wondered what this latter-day mystery play can possibly be teaching and to whom.

When earlier generations of theater scholars faced the medieval mysteries of the Passion, Cohen, along with his eminent predecessor, Louis Petit de Julleville (1841–1900), denounced the "fuzzy and dormant sensibilities of the medieval public," surmising that "if the people hadn't liked torture, they could not have tolerated the sight of it." They were mystified as to why "the ordeal at the theater lasted as long as it did in real life," a remark with which any cinematic spectator of the Gibson *Passion* might identify when likewise faced with scourging scenes that feel endless. And they worried that sadism cloaked in ecstatic religious fervor might have had something to do with it. In his classic work of 1926, *The History of Performance in the Medieval French Religious Theater,* Cohen even went so far as to offer an insight that sounds all too familiar today from virtually any conversation about violence in the media: "It is a question here of a universal tendency toward cruelty: something like those perversions of the sexual instinct that make men murder women and turn them into slashers." During the weeks following the release of *The Passion of the Christ,* many have resurrected those questions about the unholy alliance of cruelty, faith, and the unspeakable pleasures—and politics—of pain.

Long before medieval props masters devised their extensive repertoires of fake blood, soft clubs, dummies, dolls, and mannequins in order to render violence, torture, and death as realistically as possible; long before modern commentators, public and private, pondered almost daily the social and moral effects of watching violence, medieval law, theology, and drama had drawn on classical traditions to answer such nagging questions. There could be no doubt about it: graphic violence made creed believable. The problem, of course, was that the very truths that violence holds to be self-evident by dint of its so-called realism are *not* evident simply because they are seen. Notwithstanding the adage that "seeing is believing," seeing is *not*, in fact, believing, no matter how repeatedly or brutally a play or a film promotes its pretensions to accuracy by bringing horror before our eyes. And yet, in the quintessential cultural move that is theater, a personal fear, pathos, and pity—to say nothing of piety—are precisely what make a viewer's authentically powerful emotions feel like historical fact.

The Roman orator Quintilian (35–95 C.E.) once instructed lawyers pleading their cases in court that the best way to sway a jury about the guilt of murderers was to "make our audience feel as if they were actual eyewitnesses of the scene"—to reenact the crime, bringing "such a vivid image of that crime before their minds that the victim seems not to have been murdered, but *to be being murdered before their very eyes.*" So it was that the great Passion plays of medieval Europe took a forceful collective stab at proving through gory spectacle that the Jews had "put an innocent to death." In France, which boasts the most extensive repertoire of extant Passion plays, spectators are called *témoins oculaires,* or eyewitnesses, and are even exhorted to "put to death the entire nation of the Jews." Meanwhile, across the channel in England, narrators of the cycle of mystery plays from Chester invited audiences to "see soberly Christ's doleful death, his scourging, his whipping, his bloodshed, and passion, and all the pains he suffered till his last breath." With a violence inflamed by dramatic spectacle, these pieces reenacted the alleged truth of the greatest crime that the medieval Christian public could imagine: the Crucifixion of their Savior. And they did so before new generations of witnesses and believers: indeed, before people whose belief was fortified when drama placed them at the scene of a crime that they already believed to be historically true. "Have you a mind for blood?" asked the church father Tertullian (150–222 C.E.). "You have the blood of Christ!" There is every reason to conclude that that principle was taken literally not only on the late medieval stage, but in the early medieval church, and at Easter itself.

For example, when the twelfth-century faithful attended vespers on Easter Monday in the French city of Beauvais, they heard anew that the Lamb of God would be beaten and silenced when "the Jews condemned him and killed him on the cross." This particular moment of the Mass, one of many of the musical and gestural interpolations into the Easter liturgy called tropes, has long been celebrated by literary historians as one of the very origins of medieval drama. Part of that celebration, however, involves calling upon "all the prophets" as witnesses (*testes*) not only to the faithlessness of the original doubting Thomas but also to the efficacy with which tangible violence stimulates belief in the Resurrection. Unwilling to accept what he has not seen, Thomas demands physical proof that Christ has risen from the sepulcher. In so doing, he rejects the very essence of faith, which is belief in what *cannot* be seen: "Except I shall see the print of the nails, / And shall *touch the wound with my finger,* / And thrust my hand into his side, / Know this: I will never believe." At that point Christ appears and (in a translation by David Bevington) invites Thomas to do just that: "*Put your finger in the place of the wound,* and now be not faithless in me."

Mel Gibson has put the collective finger of the faithful into that wound, opening it up again and launching fear and controversy about just what other wounds might be thus opened. In the contemporary legal arena, we would deem such proof inflammatory; but, again, long before contemporary jurists caught on to what they now term "the legal storytelling movement," narratives of crime and punishment had always resurrected before witnesses violent, contested events, the better to shape and reshape belief and to motivate either forgiveness or punishment. Bloodshed and belief went hand in hand (or hand in fist) with graphic, spectacular violence. So one scarcely needed a Friedrich Nietzsche to come along to teach us in his *Genealogy of Morals* that "a thing is branded on the memory to make it stay there; only what goes on hurting will stick." A latter-day Tertullian, Gibson has anointed himself a new father of the church, seeking to deploy all the time-dishonored theatrical devices of violent realism in order to create, through something that "hurts good," the illusion of authenticity.

In a way, many of us remember this from elementary school as one of the oldest pedagogical techniques in the book: the deliberately melodramatic "you are there" mode of placing impressionable students at the unfolding scene of history, usually at some of its most notorious dénouements. Sometimes the dénouements had a different message, as in one of my favorite stories from my mother's childhood. As a young Jewish girl, she walked to and from school every day with her Catholic best friend, Dorothy. One day, under Dorothy's escort, she took a path through a different neighborhood, where the taunts began: "Jew!," the boys cried out, and began to throw pebbles. "Christ Killer!" As feisty as she was full of the milk of human kindness, Dorothy reared up to

face the cruel boys: *"She wasn't even there!"* Mel Gibson has made sure
that we *are* there. Indeed, he has seen to it that the Jews are there at
every step of the way when, during moments of extreme cruelty, he cuts
repeatedly to the eager spectatorship of clerical figures in full rabbinic
regalia, smiling approvingly at the torments, looking on unmoved, and
even going so far as to taunt the suffering Christ on the cross. In contrast,
tears are shed by a blond Roman soldier who looks less like an ancient
citizen and more like a member of Hitler Youth.

Whether or not "we are there" courtesy of a director's zealous imagination, *The Passion of the Christ* is not a documentary. The dramatic
illusion of our presence at the scene does not render a historical subject
true, no matter how proudly Gibson suggests that it does and no matter how convincing that suggestion may be to audiences (as when my
students have repeatedly described the film as "accurate"). Whence one
of the great paradoxes of any theologically inspired performance, be it
cinematic or theatrical, medieval or modern. Religion never really needs
what theater always needs: what the Greek philosopher Herodotus once
called "the credible evidence of the eyes." Theology demands the absence of precisely what makes for the presence of theater. Religious faith
is based on what people *cannot* see, unless they happen to bear witness
to a miracle. A Passion play, whether for stage or screen, is based on
what they *can* see. It deploys verisimilitude where verisimilitude has no
place: in the context of faith. Such is the crux of the power of drama:
its ability to portray "being there" in such a way as to make the events
portrayed seem more real for having been performed in a verisimilar
manner. It can do what even the most trustworthy chronicler is unable
do without arousing suspicion. In real space and real time, it tenders—
sometimes anything but tenderly—the illusion that, because people have
seen something displayed "with their own eyes," then what they have
seen is true.

Nevertheless, truth is the first casualty of theater, a medium that
deals not with what is true but with what is true-seeming, its trademark verisimilitude. And not all the Latin and Aramaic in the world can
transmute verisimilitude into truth or perspective into dogma. Contemporary audiences are in no better a position to judge the alleged accuracy
of these languages than were their medieval forebears. The authors of
the great medieval Passion plays, for instance, frequently included biblical citations in Latin, which spectators might have heard in sermons
at church; and they kindly provided translations for the illiterate. For
his own part, Gibson supplies Latin and Aramaic dialogue ostensibly
authenticated by the credited work of Father William Fulco, Ph.D., and

he kindly provides, in subtitles, translations for the literate. Although the hermetic and esoteric nature of these languages might impress the public with the erudition behind the production—an erudition that is unverifiable during the spectacle itself—the theatrical display of scholarship is not the same thing as scholarship. Seeing is not the same thing as believing; reason is not the same thing as sentiment; drama is not the same thing as history.

Be that as it may, it has always been the mission of art to make these things *seem* the same, from the preachiest polemic to the countless aesthetic efforts to dispel any impression of ponderousness or pretentiousness by means of that occasional respite known as comic relief. Witness the dancing, bumbling, thieving, and brawling shepherds of late medieval drama. They seem to have set the stage for a curious Gibson farce that might be titled "Jesus, Inventor of the Dining-Room Set," when the young carpenter apparently revolutionizes upright eating habits with his tall table and chairs as his mother predicts—presumably for a charitable chuckle—that "this will never catch on." But, whether earnest and popular or, for that matter, deceptive and unpopular, a truthful appearance is just that: an appearance of truth, not truth itself.

Who, then, is more "medieval" in their take on the theatrics of theology—citizens of the 1500s, of the 1900s, or of the twenty-first century? Thanks to digitization, video, DVD, the Internet, and franchising, a modern *Passion of the Christ* reaches a global audience in ways that no medieval mind could ever have fathomed. But in these two cases, separated by over six hundred years of history, audiences turned to venues within their popular cultures that promised the dual combination of entertainment and instruction: medieval religious drama and modern religious cinema. Both media celebrate and publicize their alleged commitment to the gratifying dissemination of useful information that is presumably not fictional but documentary. And, to the glory of the faith of some and the detriment of others, both blur any semblance of the boundary between "story" and "history."

At stake here is more than the need to decipher just why it is that real and imitated violence has transfixed spectators for centuries. At stake is more than the elucidation of arguments that are positively "medieval." At stake is the way in which theatrical Passions reenact their own version of a crime against humanity as they "play" with belief.

As we have been forced to see (if from nothing else than interviews with Mel Gibson's father), revisionist history, coupled with the substitution of sentience for fact, is a dangerous thing. With its relentless focus on the universal legalistic resonance of its quintessential scene of trial and punishment, *The Passion of the Christ* leaves little room for understanding subsequent crimes against humanity. It makes much more room for what the historian R. I. Moore calls "the formation of a persecuting society."

When we watch *The Passion of the Christ*, a film so dimly lit that its scenic contours are often unrecognizable, we still see through a glass darkly and know only in part. But, should we ever see face to face, just what would we face at the end of the movie? What do we see when we find ourselves staring outward from inside a tomb, gazing through the eyes of Christ upon a sun-soaked Resurrection? Just what is being resurrected here?

The resurrection of theatrical productions past has a special name: revivalism. And one of the great revivalist efforts of the twentieth century may shed some light upon this vexed subject.

In addition to being a prolific editor of medieval play texts, a literary critic, and a theater historian, Gustave Cohen was also a teacher, a director, and the artistic force behind the revival of medieval theater in Paris. His theater troupe, the Théophiliens, modernized Old and Middle French so that they could bring religious drama back to life for modern audiences. In Cohen's self-ascribed mission to "resurrect the dead," saints, martyrs, and Christ figures returned to populate the Parisian stage. But Cohen's revivalist efforts attracted an unusual admirer who thought such worthy homages to the Christian past might suit a modern political purpose. As my colleague Helen Solterer discovered, his troupe was invited to perform before none other than Adolf Hitler himself. We know for a fact that Cohen said no. One can only wonder: what would Gibson have said?

20 *The Passion* in Black and White

Robert M. Franklin

The Passion of the Christ has been seen by millions of people around the globe. A movie about a poor, virtuous religious teacher has made its director a very rich young ruler—that is, for those who believe that "Gibson rules."

Before the film's release, erudite commentary and emotional arguments rained down upon the earth like fire and brimstone. Having seen a preview, I was certain that many people would treat the film as a religious event, with the power to transform movie theaters into houses of worship. Others condemned Gibson for portraying Jews as unrepentant Christ killers and for imposing a unified narrative on the Bible's textual pluralism, which allows for varying portraits of Jesus. Jewish and Christian leaders vigorously expressed worries about the film's potential to arouse anti-Semitism. Indeed, it would be an unfortunate irony for a film about Jesus to inspire hate and harm toward anyone.

Amidst the swirling pre-release controversy, I was intrigued by another possibility of response and advanced two predictions. First, I suspected that the movie would offend many mainstream and evangelical white religious audiences but resonate deeply with most blacks. The icons, art, and Passion plays in most white churches tend to present Jesus as the subject of a radical makeover. The rugged, sun-baked Palestinian Jew of the Bible usually gets morphed into a manicured, middle-class model citizen just like one of the neighbors. The theology that underwrites this sanitized Jesus avoids the brutal manifestations of oppression and violence he experienced. Observing sacred art in Anglo-American congregations, I noticed that when Crucifixion scenes appear at all, one may see a little blood and a wound or two, but almost never the dirty and broken body that endured torture for several hours. I was certain that *The Passion*'s lingering gaze upon the grotesque would be difficult for viewers accustomed to such art.

Boy, was I wrong. I was astounded to discover that exceedingly conservative evangelicals loved the movie. Never difficult to predict, my mainstream, liberal friends hated it or refused to see it at all. But why did the evangelical segment of the church embrace the movie, even as it offended their white-bread aesthetic tastes? Because in it they encountered the holy, or, as the theologian Paul Tillich teaches, they participated in a new, divine reality. And, perhaps more strategically, they found in this film a vehicle for doing twenty-first century, media-savvy evangelism, not something that would occur to the mainstream establishment. They loved the film because, despite Gibson's brand of medieval Catholicism (certainly not their cup of latte), it opened doors of inquiry about the person, life, and death of Jesus that no amount of televangelistic preaching could accomplish. They made peace with a divergent theological voice and embraced the film as a "Christ in culture" moment.

I did better on the second prediction. I thought that most black audiences would embrace the film's content more positively. Since the era of slavery, blacks, more than other American believers, have taken seriously images of Jesus as a "suffering servant" and a grassroots leader who was the victim of state-sponsored terror. Black theology has focused on the humanity and socially marginal status of Jesus. More than that, blacks have been attracted to the Jesus who experienced unjust victimization by the authorities and the community, but found empowering comfort in the conviction that a just God would someday even the score. This spirituality and faith generated the Negro spirituals, gospel music, prayers, sermons and, to a lesser extent, religious art that embraced the graphic reality of political death and dying.

In *Jesus and the Disinherited,* the Christian mystic and black theologian Howard Thurman said that whenever we sanitize the grotesque image of the "suffering servant," we again inflict violence upon his identity and mission. He endured each moment of that suffering; we dare not minimize it to suit our sensibilities. Not surprisingly, Martin Luther King Jr. always carried Thurman's book in his briefcase.

I heard numerous black viewers affirm that while viewing the film they found themselves revisiting painful memories of young men from our communities who were hanged from trees, their clothes drenched with blood, as the local white townspeople looked on with satisfaction. Billie Holiday captured the horror of these scenes in the heartbreaking song "Strange Fruit." Whenever African Americans revisit the Passion scene, we know what that young Jewish mother Mary felt. We know the agony of those disciples who yearned to avenge their leader but were too powerless and afraid to try. We feel this grief and indignation deep in our guts.

White and black Americans sat in the same theaters and felt many of the same emotions, but, not surprisingly, they discovered slightly different messages and attached different meanings to the images they saw. My hope is that works of art like this one will inspire conversation across the color line. This has in fact slowly begun to happen, and if it continues, it could open windows of curiosity about and insight into the varying religious perspectives and sensibilities that animate our wonderfully diverse nation.

21

They Know Not What They Watch

Timothy K. Beal

Like many other religion professors in American colleges and universities during the early spring of 2004, I was interested in how *The Passion of the Christ* would play out on campus, especially in how it would affect relations between different religious groups. Various campus ministries and religious organizations were taking groups to the film or arranging special screenings. Evangelical ministries such as the Fellowship of Christian Athletes and Intervarsity Christian Fellowship were inviting non-Christian students to join them, seeing the film as an opportunity for evangelism. National organizations such as Youth Specialties went so far as to develop whole programs of study and worship centered on the film, believing that the intense and conflicted emotions of student viewers would provide "an ideal lock-in situation."

At the same time, many other scholars and religious leaders from different traditions were hoping that the film might offer "teachable moments" and opportunities for interreligious dialogue about relations between religion and violence and about the ways some Christian theologies have contributed to anti-Judaism and anti-Semitism. Many hoped that, whether the viewer loved it or loathed it, the film would give us a "text" for conversation among various groups on our ever more religiously diverse campuses.

So how did these hopes play out? Not well. In fact, the movie has been largely divisive among religious groups.

On the one hand, Christian students, conservative and liberal alike, respond to the film positively. Those who've seen it feel as though they "get it." They are "moved" by it—even when they see its anti-Jewish implications and potentials (few do), and even when they express concern about its excessive violence (more than one pre-med student has noted that any fully human person would have died at least a few times along that Via Dolorosa). In fact, some conservative evangelical students say they don't think the violence is excessive at all. It didn't surprise them, because they "already knew about it." As a veteran Sunday School kid, I think I know what they mean: conservative preachers often give sermons around Easter that go into great gratuitous detail about Roman crucifixion practices in order to drive the point home about Jesus's extraordinary sacrifice for "your" sins—this despite the fact that the Gospels themselves don't specify much about it. In fact, in the Gospels, it seems to me, the real scandal of the Crucifixion is that it was such a base, common, ordinary way to be executed.

Whether or not they are accustomed to the violence, however, most Christian students see the film in terms of divine Incarnation and vicarious atonement. They recognize the Jesus in this movie as the Incarnation of God, and they understand that he's there, in flesh and blood, to be sacrificed as expiation for their sins. One student said she cried during the movie, not because she was overwhelmed by the violence, but because she felt that it provided a "visible reality" of what she already knew about Christ's sacrifice on her behalf. It is this sense of sacrifice that Christian students say they "get" in the film.

On the other hand, those non-Christians (religious or not) who see the film come away baffled—"at a complete loss," "clueless" as to what this movie is doing for their Christian colleagues. One of the students who saw the film with a group from the Muslim Student Association on our campus said she simply could not see what lesson such morbid suffering could have for humankind. Some recognize how the film could contribute to anti-Jewish sentiments, especially in the treatment of the Jewish mainstream as a collective mob controlled by an insecure cabal of lawyer-priests. But what repels most non-Christian students is what they see as utterly meaningless violence. Indeed, this sense of meaninglessness is what repels them most. The movie gives them no way to interpret the violence, no way into its symbolic world. As a result, they come away alienated, feeling like outsiders.

Some Christian defenders of the film will counter that it's all made clear in the opening epigraph from Isaiah 53: "He was wounded for our transgressions, crushed for our iniquities; by His wounds we are healed." But they forget how unfamiliar such a theology of substitutionary atonement, read back into this prophetic text, is for those outside the evangelical fold.

I suspect that the feeling of being outsiders that most non-Christians experience while watching the film is entirely intentional. But it is less an effect of the film's excessive violence and anti-Jewish tendencies, and more an effect of its biblical basis: the Gospel of John.

As is well known, *The Passion* draws many of its narrative elements from extrabiblical sources, including the mysteries of the rosary, the Stations of the Cross, and the collection of visions of the nineteenth-century Augustinian nun Anne Catherine Emmerich (not to mention the flamboyant Herod in *Jesus Christ Superstar* and the shock rocker Marilyn Manson, who had to be in someone's mind, consciously or not, as the model for Satan). With regard to biblical sources, it draws from all four Gospels, but it is based primarily on John. Elements from the other Gospels, such as Matthew's description of Judas's hanging himself and the Jewish pronouncement that "his blood be upon us and our children" (spoken by the high priest Caiaphas in Aramaic, but not captioned in the final cut), are woven into the Johannine Gospel, which provides *The Passion* with its basic narrative structure.

John stands out among the New Testament Gospels for its emphasis on the Christological chasm between insiders and outsiders. It is an insider text, full of ironies that outsiders just don't get. Its Jesus repeatedly baffles those not part of his inner circle of "friends"—above all, the Jews—with his teachings, which focus predominantly on his own identity as the Incarnation of God, the Way, the Truth, and the Life. His explanations bewilder and alienate others but are eminently clear to his disciples and the Gospel's readers, who have the necessary insider gnosis. As Jesus expounds on the need to be "born again," the Jewish lawyer Nicodemus's rising frustration parallels the readers' growing clarity. And as Jesus explains to Pilate that those who know the truth will hear it, Pilate's confounded "What is truth?" is set against the reader's awareness of exactly what's going on. Pilate doesn't get it, but "we" do.

Likewise *The Passion*. Indeed, in this respect it is something of a filmic version of John's Gospel. It works the same way on its viewers as the Gospel of John does on its readers, bringing insiders together and affirming their special knowledge while snubbing the rest. It makes little effort to help them "get it." Those who know the truth see it, it seems to be saying, and those who don't, can't.

How does the film work this Johannine effect on its viewers? Most obviously, it does so by drawing material from the text of John itself. As we see, John provides the basic narrative content and structure into which other gospel elements are integrated. Those insider viewers who know their gospel texts immediately recognize that fact. As in John, the film's Jesus speaks about himself according to a well-formed Christology, with the firm knowledge that his suffering and death are necessary so that others may have everlasting life. As in John, outsider groups, especially "the Jews," are treated as collective types—thoughtless mobs, power-hungry priests, Roman brutes. And as in John, the story is driven by a sense of irony, which only the audience of believers and a handful of characters share with Jesus. The priests misunderstand Jesus's claim to be king of the Jews as a political claim to rule over Judea. When Caiaphas asks Jesus why he doesn't come down from the cross if he's the Messiah, believers understand that his messianic work can be done only on the cross. When Mary sees Jesus under arrest, she knowingly says, "It is begun. So be it," and when she comes to his aid while he's carrying the cross, he tells her, "See, mother, I make all things new." None of this makes sense to an outsider unequipped with a theology of sacrificial atonement. But insiders are able to identify both with Mary's anguish and with her otherwise confounding resignation. And when Jesus cries out from the cross, "Father, forgive them, they know not what they do," the outsider may be impressed with his refusal of vengeance, but the insider understands that the Roman executioners and Jewish crowds are only pawns in a divine game of cosmic redemption.

Beyond its use of narrative strategies drawn from the literary text of the fourth Gospel, *The Passion* also deploys several cinematic strategies to create this Johannine insider-outsider experience. First is its use of captions to translate the Aramaic and Latin dialogue. Given that so much of the dialogue is drawn from gospel texts, these captions are relatively easy to follow for the biblically literate, for whom a few words can call whole lines to mind. For others, however, it is difficult to keep up with the captions, especially when there's so much going on visually. Indeed, many of the lines themselves read like fragments taken from larger passages, making little sense to those unfamiliar with the larger narrative contexts from which they're taken.

Second is the film's use of shot-reverse shots to create identification between insider viewers and certain characters in the film. Shot-reverse shots involve an initial shot facing a character looking at someone or something, immediately followed by a shot turned 180 degrees around, so that viewers see what that character sees (often followed by a third shot that returns to the original point of view). The effect of such sequences is to make the film's viewers identify with the point of view of the character in the first shot. There are several shot-reverse shots in *The Passion* that focus on relationships between the main insider characters and Jesus. Most of them start with his mother, Mary, then turn to Jesus, and then turn back to Mary. There is also one involving Peter, one involving the man who helps Jesus carry the cross, and one involving the thief who begs from the cross for forgiveness. Each of those sequences leads insider viewers to identify with a character who clearly knows what's going on—that is, someone who recognizes who Jesus is and understands what he's doing. These shot-reverse shots are "knowing exchanges" between Jesus and insiders. But they have that effect only on those who already know the theology. Without coming to the film with that insider knowledge, viewers are left with a sense that some recognition has taken place in these sequences, but they have no way into that point of view.

Third is the use of brief flashbacks to earlier points in Jesus's life and ministry. Most run less than a minute and present tightly edited close-up scenes from larger episodes in the gospel story—teaching and preaching, saving Mary Magdalene, washing the feet, the Last Supper. For insiders, those flashbacks function much like the captions, providing meaningful theological commentary. In the final Crucifixion scene, the flashbacks come more frequently, focusing on the Last Supper and other freighted words about Jesus's divine identity (for example, "I am the way, the truth, and the life. No one comes to the father but by me").

For those in the know, those quick back-and-forth cuts between the Crucifixion and the Last Supper during the last few minutes confirm what's happening on the theological plane, making clear that Jesus knew it was coming and was necessary (fig. 11), and culminate in his final words, "It is accomplished. Father, into your hands I commit my spirit." For outsiders, it's just too many cuts too quickly, with little context for the flashbacks. They're nothing more than reprieves from the violence. Such a perception is certainly forgivable, for they know not what they watch. And the film doesn't do anything to help them.

FIGURE 11 Flashback to the Last Supper while Jesus's hands are being nailed to the cross (subtitle: "This is my blood of the new covenant . . . which is given for you and for many, for the forgiveness of sins"). Still from *The Passion of the Christ* (2004).

So much for interreligious dialogue. Except, perhaps, dialogue between conservative evangelicals and Catholics. Indeed, the film seems to have been the perfect mediator between these two groups, which have often been greatly at odds, each one the other's theological outsider. I think that the film accomplishes this ecumenical mediation on the Passion by combining elements from the rosary and the Stations of the Cross, familiar to Catholics, with the Gospel of John, which has primacy among the Gospels for evangelicals. (New converts are invariably instructed to start reading there once they are among the insiders.) In both respects, moreover, the film zeroes in on the theological common ground between the two groups, namely an understanding of the Crucifixion as a divinely ordained act of sacrificial or vicarious atonement.

A Muslim colleague made a particularly perceptive comment about the film, born of a thought that came to him as a result of a conversation about the film with members of the Muslim Student Association. He wondered whether the film speaks to a certain subconscious desire shared by many Christians these days, a desire for a common ground. They have no Mecca, no Jerusalem, he said. At the same time, he felt that many Christians have been worn down by priestly scandals and humiliations. Perhaps this film provides a common ground on which to stand. What I found most striking about this suggestion was not the hypothesis itself, true as it may be. Rather, it was the genuinely pastoral gesture of sympathy, offered by someone who was in fact repelled by the film as an outsider. Here, then, it seems to me, is an opening to dialogue as disarming as any in the Gospels.

Contributors

THOMAS J. J. ALTIZER is professor emeritus of religious studies at the State University of New York at Stony Brook. He is the author of fourteen books, including *The Genesis of God: A Theological Genealogy* (1993). His memoirs, "Living the Death of God," are forthcoming.

TIMOTHY K. BEAL is the Florence Harkness Professor of Religion and director of the Baker-Nord Center for the Humanities at Case Western Reserve University. His books include *Theory for Religious Studies* (2004) and *Roadside Religion: In Search of the Sacred, the Strange, and the Substance of Faith* (2005). He has written essays for the *Washington Post* and the *Chronicle of Higher Education* and is co-editor of the series Afterlives of the Bible, published by the University of Chicago Press.

KENT L. BRINTNALL is a doctoral student in the Graduate Division of Religion at Emory University. He holds an M.A. from the Graduate Theological Union in Berkeley and a J.D. from Northeastern University School of Law in Boston. His dissertation research focuses on contemporary visual culture and Christian theological discourses, specifically on representations of the male body in pain and their relation to theologies of the cross.

BRUCE CHILTON is the Bernard Iddings Bell Professor of Religion, Chaplain of the College, and Director of the Institute of Advanced Theology at Bard College. His books include *Rabbi Jesus: An Intimate Biography* (2000), *Rabbi Paul: An Intellectual Biography* (2004), and *Mary Magdalene: A Biography*

(2005). He founded both the *Bulletin for Biblical Research* and the *Journal for the Study of the New Testament.*

JOHN DOMINIC CROSSAN is professor emeritus of religious studies at De-Paul University. He has written more than twenty books on the historical Jesus in the last thirty years, including *The Historical Jesus* (1991), *Jesus: A Revolutionary Biography* (1994), *Who Killed Jesus?* (1995), *The Birth of Christianity* (1998), and (with Jonathan L. Reed) *Excavating Jesus* (2002). His most recent book (also with Jonathan L. Reed) is *In Search of Paul* (2004). He is a former co-chair of the Jesus Seminar and a former chair of the Historical Jesus Section of the Society of Biblical Literature.

MARK DOUGLAS is assistant professor of Christian ethics at Columbia Theological Seminary. His article on Reinhold Niebuhr appeared in the *American Journal of Theology and Philosophy* (2001), and another on just-war theory was published in *Theology Today* (2003).

JODY ENDERS is professor of French and dramatic art at the University of California, Santa Barbara. She is the author of *Rhetoric and the Origins of Medieval Drama* (1992) and *Medieval Theater of Cruelty* (1998). Her most recent book, *Death by Drama and Other Medieval Urban Legends* (2002), was the winner of the 2003 Barnard Hewitt Award for Outstanding Research in Theater History and Cognate Studies.

ROBERT M. FRANKLIN is Presidential Distinguished Professor of Social Ethics at the Candler School of Theology, Emory University. His publications include *Liberating Visions: Human Fulfillment and Social Justice in African American Thought* (1990), *Another Day's Journey: Black Churches Confronting the American Crisis* (1997), and (with Don S. Browning et al.) *From Culture Wars to Common Ground: Religion and the American Family Debate* (2000).

PAULA FREDRIKSEN is the William Goodwin Aurelio Professor of the Appreciation of Scripture at Boston University. In addition to her books on Augustine (*Augustine on Romans,* 1982) and on Jesus and Christian tradition (*From Jesus to Christ: The Origins of the New Testament Images of Jesus,* 1988), she has written extensively on conversion, apocalypticism, Paul and his interpreters, and Jewish-Gentile relations in late antiquity. In 1999 she received a National Jewish Book Award for her most recent publication, *Jesus of Nazareth, King of the Jews: A Jewish Life and the Emergence of Christianity.*

SUSANNAH HESCHEL holds the Eli Black Chair in Jewish Studies at Dartmouth College, where she is also associate professor of religion. She is the author of numerous studies on modern Jewish thought, including *Abraham Geiger and the Jewish Jesus* (1998). She is the co-editor (with David Biale and Michael Galchinsky) of *Insider/Outsider: American Jews and Multiculturalism* (1998). She is the editor of *On Being a Jewish Feminist,* which first appeared in 1983, and has recently completed a book about a group of Protestant theologians in

Nazi Germany who sought to create a synthesis of Christianity and National Socialism by declaring Jesus an Aryan, eliminating the Old Testament from the Christian Bible, and running an anti-Semitic propaganda institute.

AMY HOLLYWOOD is the Elizabeth H. Monrad Professor of Christian Studies at Harvard Divinity School. Her first book, *The Soul as Virgin Wife: Mechthild of Magdeburg, Marguerite Porete, and Meister Eckhart* (1995), received the International Congress of Medieval Studies' Otto Grundler Prize for the best book in medieval studies. She is also the author of *Sensible Ecstasy: Mysticism, Sexual Difference, and the Demands of History* (2001) and is currently writing about memory, mourning, and Christian mysticism.

MARK D. JORDAN is Asa Griggs Candler Professor of Religion at Emory University. His academic interests center on the performance of religious identities, Christian teachings on sex, and the varieties of theological rhetoric. His books include *The Invention of Sodomy in Christian Theology* (1997), *The Silence of Sodom: Homosexuality in Modern Catholicism* (2000), *The Ethics of Sex* (2001), *Telling Truths in Church* (2002), *Blessing Same-Sex Unions* (2005), and *Rewritten Theology: Aquinas after His Readers* (2005).

WILLIAM G. LITTLE is associate professor of English at DePauw University. He is the author of *The Waste Fix: Seizures of the Sacred from Upton Sinclair to* The Sopranos (2002). He writes on modern American literature, film, and popular culture, and is currently writing a book about the dynamics of self-reinvention in American culture.

TOD LINAFELT is associate professor of biblical literature at Georgetown University. He is the author of *Surviving Lamentations: Catastrophe, Lament, and Protest in the Afterlife of a Biblical Book* (2000) and of a commentary on the book of Ruth in the *Berit 'Olam* series. He has edited or co-edited three other books, including *A Shadow of Glory: Reading the New Testament after the Holocaust* (2002), and is co-editor of the series Afterlives of the Bible, published by the University of Chicago Press.

JOSÉ MÁRQUEZ is an artist. He has written fictional "news reports" for the *San Francisco Bay Guardian* and the *San Francisco Weekly* and is working on a fairy tale about instant travel, the human family, and high finance. With Mark C. Taylor, he produced *The Réal, Las Vegas, NV* (1997), an interactive scrapbook about Las Vegas and America's future. Under the moniker of Pepito, he has recorded three albums of electronic pop music.

JACK MILES is currently senior advisor to the president of the J. Paul Getty Trust, a foundation supporting art and scholarship. He has been the literary editor at the *Los Angeles Times* and a member of the *Times* editorial board. His first book, *God: A Biography* (1996), won the Pulitzer Prize for biography, and his second book, *Christ: A Crisis in the Life of God* (2002), was named a *New York Times* Notable Book.

MARGARET R. MILES is professor emerita of historical theology, The Graduate Theological Union, Berkeley. Her books include *Image as Insight* (1985), *Carnal Knowing: Female Nakedness and Religious Meaning in the Christian West* (1988), *Seeing and Believing: Religion and Values in the Movies* (1996), *Plotinus on Body and Beauty* (1999), and *The Word Made Flesh: A History of Christian Thought* (2005).

VINCENT J. MILLER is associate professor of theology at Georgetown University. His research bridges Catholic systematic theology and the study of religion and culture. He is the author of *Consuming Religion: Christian Faith and Practice in a Consumer Culture* (2004).

RICHARD L. RUBENSTEIN is president emeritus and Distinguished Professor of Religion at the University of Bridgeport, as well as Lawton Distinguished Professor of Religion Emeritus at Florida State University. Rubenstein is the author of *After Auschwitz*, first published in 1966 (rev. expanded ed., 1992). Among his other books are *The Religious Imagination* (1968), *The Cunning of History* (1975), *The Age of Triage* (1983), and (with John K. Roth) *Approaches to Auschwitz* (1986; 2nd edition, 2003).

JANE SCHABERG is professor of religious studies and women's studies at the University of Detroit Mercy. Her books include *The Illegitimacy of Jesus: A Feminist Theological Interpretation of the Infancy Narratives* (1987; 2nd edition, 1995) and *The Resurrection of Mary Magdalene: Legends, Apocrypha, and the Christian Testament* (2002).

GEORGE M. SMIGA is a priest of the Catholic Diocese of Cleveland and serves on the faculty of St. Mary Seminary and Graduate School of Theology in Wickliffe, Ohio. He is author of *Pain and Polemic: Anti-Judaism in the Gospels* (1992) and a commentary on the Gospel of John (2006; part of the Word Set Free series). He has recently contributed to *Pondering the Passion: What's at Stake for Christians and Jews* (2004). Since 1991, he has served as pastor of St. Noel Catholic Church in Willoughby Hills, Ohio.

MARK C. TAYLOR is the Cluett Professor of Humanities at Williams College and visiting professor of religion and architecture at Columbia University. Among his many books are *Hiding* (1997), *About Religion* (1999), *The Moment of Complexity* (2002), *Grave Matters* (2002), *Confidence Games* (2004), and *Mystic Bones* (forthcoming).